Leadership ar  ..ng

Education at SAGE

SAGE is a leading international publisher of journals, books, and electronic media for academic, educational, and professional markets.

Our education publishing includes:

* accessible and comprehensive texts for aspiring education professionals and practitioners looking to further their careers through continuing professional development

* inspirational advice and guidance for the classroom

* authoritative state of the art reference from the leading authors in the field

Find out more at: **www.sagepub.co.uk/education**

Leadership and Learning

Edited by Jan Robertson and
Helen Timperley

Los Angeles | London | New Delhi
Singapore | Washington DC

Editorial arrangement © Jan Robertson and Helen Timperley 2011

First published 2011

Chapter 1 © Helen Timperley and
   Jan Robertson
Chapter 2 © Christopher Day
Chapter 3© Russell Bishop
Chapter 4 © Kenneth Leithwood
Chapter 5 © Philip Hallinger and
   Ronald H. Heck
Chapter 6 © Geoff Southworth
Chapter 7 © David Hopkins
Chapter 8 © Louise Stoll
Chapter 9 © Helen Timperley
Chapter 10 © Viviane M.J.
   Robinson, Linda Bendikson and

   John Hattie
Chapter 11 © Helen Wildy and
   Simon Clarke
Chapter 12 © James P. Spillane,
   Kaleen Healey, Leigh Mesler
   Parise and Allison Kenney
Chapter 13 © Marianne Coleman
Chapter 14 © Lorna Earl and Lynne
   Hannay
Chapter 15 © Megan Crawford
Chapter 16 © Jan Robertson
Chapter 17 © Andrew Hargreaves

SAGE Publications Ltd
1 Oliver's Yard
55 City Road
London EC1Y 1SP

SAGE Publications Inc.
2455 Teller Road
Thousand Oaks, California 91320

SAGE Publications India Pvt Ltd
B 1/I 1 Mohan Cooperative Industrial Area
Mathura Road
New Delhi 110 044

SAGE Publications Asia-Pacific Pte Ltd
33 Pekin Street #02-01
Far East Square
Singapore 048763

Library of Congress Control Number: 2010932774

British Library Cataloguing in Publication data

A catalogue record for this book is available from the British Library

ISBN 978-1-84920-173-5
ISBN 978-1-84920-174-2 (pbk)

Typeset by C&M Digitals (P) Ltd, Chennai, India
Printed in Great Britain by MPG Books Group, Bodmin, Cornwall
Printed on paper from sustainable resources

Contents

Acknowledgements

The Editors and Publisher would like to thank the following for permission:

The Australian Council for Educational Leaders (ACEL), 2007. SAGE acknowledges that *Leadership and Learning* draws upon work and carried out within and funded by the New Zealand Ministry of Education's Iterative Best Evidence Synthesis (BES) Programme. http://www.educationcounts.gvt.nz/goto/BES

Notes on Contributors

Linda Bendikson is a senior manager in the Ministry of Education in New Zealand and a PhD student in the Department of Teaching, Learning, and Development at the University of Auckland, New Zealand. The majority of her career has been spent as a primary school principal in low socio-economic communities.

Russell Bishop is foundation Professor of Māori Education in the Faculty of Education at the University of Waikato, New Zealand. He is currently the project director for Te Kotahitanga, a large New Zealand Ministry of Education funded research/professional development project that seeks to improve the educational achievement of Māori students in mainstream classrooms through the implementation of a culturally responsive pedagogy of relations.

Simon Clarke is currently the Deputy Dean of the Graduate School of Education in the University of Western Australia where he teaches and researches in the substantive area of educational leadership and management. He is widely published in international journals and the co-author of a recent book on leading learning in the Routledge Leadership for Learning series.

Megan Crawford is Reader in Education and Professional Development at Oxford Brookes University, UK. Formerly a primary school deputy headteacher, she has written extensively about emotion, principal preparation and primary schools. She is Chair of the British Educational Leadership, Management and Administration Society (BELMAS), and has won awards for her work in school governance. At Brookes, she is currently developing professional doctoral pathways.

Marianne Coleman is an Emeritus Reader in educational leadership and management at the Institute of Education, University of London. She is an experienced teacher, researcher and evaluator with major research interests in leadership, particularly focusing on gender and diversity issues in relation to leadership.

Christopher Day is Professor of Education at the University of Nottingham and Director of the Teacher and Leadership Research Centre. He is currently leading a 12-country international research project on successful school principalship and has recently led a national-government funded project on the impact of effective leadership on student outcomes.

Lorna Earl is Director, Aporia Consulting Limited and the president of the International Congress of School Effectiveness and School Improvement. She has worked for over 20 years in schools, school boards, ministries of education and universities. As a leader in the field of assessment and evaluation, she has been involved in consultation, research, evaluation and staff development with teachers' organizations, ministries of education, school boards and charitable foundations in Canada, Europe, Australasia and the USA.

Philip Hallinger is Chair Professor and Director of the Asia Pacific Centre for Leadership and Change at the Hong Kong Institute of Education. His research focuses on school leadership effects, leadership development and problem-based learning. He received his EdD in Administration and Policy Analysis from Stanford University, He can be reached at hallinger@gmail.com. His research publications can be accessed at philiphallinger.com.

Lynne Hannay is an educator who has taught and researched at school and university levels. As a teacher, a teacher educator and a researcher, she has examined and facilitated educational change for teachers, schools and school districts. Currently, she is exploring the relationship between knowledge management processes in social organizations and sustained changes to practice.

Andy Hargreaves is the Thomas More Brennan Chair in Education in the Lynch School of Education at Boston College. He has published almost 30 books in education – most recently in the fields of leadership and change. These have attracted four outstanding book awards. His most recent books are *Sustainable Leadership* (with Dean Fink) in 2006, *Change Wars* (with Michael Fullan) in 2008, *The Fourth Way* (with Dennis Shirley) in 2009, and *The Second International Handbook of Educational Change* (with three other editors) in 2009. His most recent honours include the Contribution to Professional Development Award from the US National Staff development council, and an Honorary Doctorate from Uppsala University in Sweden. His most recent research (with Alma Harris) is on organizations that perform above expectations in business, sport and education.

John Hattie is Professor and Director of the Education Research Institute at the University of Melbourne. His areas of interest are measurement models and their applications to educational problems, including item response models, structural equation modelling, measurement theory and meta-analysis. John is President of the International Test Commission, associate editor of the *British Journal of Educational Psychology* and serves on many editorial boards.

Kaleen Healey is a doctoral student in the Human Development and Social Policy programme at Northwestern University. She holds a bachelor's degree from the University of Notre Dame and a master's degree from Loyola University Chicago. Her research interests include the interactions between leadership, diversity, and organizational change in schools.

Ronald H. Heck holds the Dai Ho Chun Endowed Chair in Education at the University of Hawaii-Manoa. He received his PhD in Education from the University of California at Santa Barbara. His research focuses on the relationship between school leadership and school improvement. He has also written on research methodology. He can be reached at rheck@hawaii.edu.

David Hopkins is Professor Emeritus at the Institute of Education, University of London where, until recently, he held the inaugural HSBC iNet Chair in International Leadership. He is a Trustee of Outward Bound and is Executive Director of the new charity 'Adventure Learning Schools'. David holds visiting professorships at the Catholic University of Santiago, the Chinese University of Hong Kong and the universities of Edinburgh, Melbourne and Wales and consults internationally on school reform.

Allison Kenney is the research programme coordinator for the Distributed Leadership Studies at Northwestern University. She received her BA in Public Policy from Duke University. Her research interests include education policy, language policy, school leadership and school reform.

Kenneth Leithwood is Professor of Educational Leadership and Policy at OISE/University of Toronto. His most recent books include *Leading School Turnaround* (with Harris, Jossey Bass, in press), *Distributed Leadership According to the Evidence* (Routledge, 2008) and *Leading With Teachers' Emotions In Mind* (with Beatty, Corwin, 2008). Professor Leithwood is the recent recipient of the University of Toronto's Impact on Public Policy award and a Fellow of the Royal Society of Canada.

Leigh Mesler Parise is a doctoral student in the Human Development and Social Policy programme at Northwestern University. Her research interests include teacher quality, teacher learning and development, school leadership, policy implementation and the effects of policy on school leaders, teachers and students in urban schools.

Jan Robertson's research and development focuses on professional learning relationships and the building of relational trust. Her work in leadership coaching and boundary-breaking leadership development has highlighted the importance of co-creating new knowledge in leadership and learning through partnership and cooperative relationships. Jan is an Adjunct Professor of Griffith University, Brisbane, Australia and a Senior Associate of the New Zealand Coaching and Mentoring Centre. She works as a freelance researcher and international leadership consultant and can be contacted at info@janrobertson.co.nz.

Viviane M.J. Robinson is a Professor in the Faculty of Education at The University of Auckland and Academic Director of its Centre for Educational Leadership. Her specialities are school improvement, leadership, and interpersonal and organizational effectiveness. She is passionate about doing research and development that is both rigorous and relevant to policy and practice.

Geoff Southworth started as a teacher, and headteacher, and then directed programmes for school leaders at the University of Cambridge where he also conducted a series of research projects. He was Professor of Education at Reading University and then moved to the National College for School Leadership (NCSL), as Director of Research and then as Deputy Chief Executive Officer. He now works as a freelance consultant.

James P. Spillane is the Spencer T. and Ann W. Olin Professor in Learning and Organizational Change in the Human Development and Social Policy programme in the School of Education and Social Policy at Northwestern University. He also serves as a Professor of Management and Organizations and a Faculty Fellow at Northwestern University's Institute for Policy Research. His research interests include education policy, policy implementation, organizational change, school reform and school leadership.

Louise Stoll is Visiting Professor at the London Centre for Leadership in Learning at the Institute of Education, London, and a freelance researcher and international consultant. Author of many publications, her research and development work focus on how leaders promote change and create capacity for learning and improvement, with a particular emphasis on development of learning communities.

Helen Timperley is Professor of Education at the University of Auckland in New Zealand. Her main research area focuses on promoting leadership, organizational and professional learning in ways that improve the educational experience of students currently underachieving in our education systems. She has published widely in international academic journals and has written several books focusing on the professional practice implications of her research.

Helen Wildy is currently the Dean of the Faculty of Education in the University of Western Australia where she teaches and researches in the substantive area of educational leadership and school reform. Her research focuses on the use of assessment data for school improvement and, with Simon Clarke, on the leadership of small rural and remote schools. She is widely published in international journals.

Foreword

Geoff Whitty

As Timperley and Robertson point out in Chapter 1, there is a considerable amount of work in the area of educational leadership, but relatively little that examines the impact of leadership on student attainment. The relative scarcity of research in this area may be surprising to some readers, given that raising student attainment is one of the key purposes of educational institutions. However, in terms of research, establishing the relationship (let alone causality) between school leadership and student outcomes is highly complex.

Of course, it is not only the head teacher or school principal who is involved in leadership in a school. While some may not sign up to the label 'distributed leadership', it is undoubtedly the case that driving improvement is now beyond the scope of a single individual, particularly in a large secondary school. For example, the importance of strong heads of department, in terms of explaining variance in pupil outcomes, has been known for some time from research in the school improvement and school effectiveness paradigm.

Given the iterative and relational aspects of successful leadership, it is perhaps not surprising that collaboration and partnerships have been seen as crucial. Professional Learning Communities appear to be a promising vehicle for improvement through fostering supportive communities focused on practice (as described in Stoll's Chapter) and opening up lines of communication and dialogue. Partnership and collaboration across institutions is also key if we are to move our education systems forward and see systemic change across whole education systems, as highlighted by Hopkins. Unfortunately, though, this often seems at odds with prevailing accountability structures and with systems where competition between units is actively fostered. These are tensions increasingly faced by education leaders across the globe.

Over the last few years policy makers seem to have rediscovered the importance of teachers, as opposed to structural reform, in improving student attainment (see for example Barber and Mourshed, 2007). Given the central role of teaching and teacher quality in determining learning outcomes, this book's theme of leadership focused on improving teaching and learning – the instructional core – is welcome. The emphasis throughout on learning – by both pupils and education professionals – provides the focus necessary to raise standards, cutting through the often distracting noise found in some other leadership literatures. At the same time, however, the contributors to the volume rightly recognize and reflect on the various different routes and strategies that can foster and enable improvements in teaching and learning – for example, the importance of the emotional and how this interacts with other factors in the classroom.

The complexity of leadership in today's education institutions reflects the multifaceted aims of schooling in a learning society. This complexity means that successful leadership does not fit neatly into a 'one-size-fits-all' approach. Not surprisingly, then, this book does not claim to provide 'the answer' but rather, refreshingly presents findings and analysis from leading researchers in the field of education leadership aimed at enabling and supporting practitioners to find their own paths.

Geoff Whitty

Director of the Institute of Education, 2000–2010

References

Barber, M. and Mourshed, M. (2007) *How the World's Best-Performing School Systems Come out on Top*. McKinsey & Company: London. Available at: http://www.mckinsey.com/clientservice/SocialSector/ourpractices/Education/KnowledgeHighlights/Bestperformingschool.aspx [accessed 30th July 2010].

Section I

Exploring Models for Leadership and Improvement

CHAPTER 1

Establishing Platforms for Leadership and Learning

Helen Timperley and Jan Robertson

Traditional understandings of leadership have focused on individuals who occupied formal positions of authority within organizations; the 'leaders', their personality traits and their work. In business, the focus was on the chief executive officer (CEO). In education, the equivalent was the school principal. Studies of leadership within this framework typically examined how the leadership styles of these individuals allowed them to exercise influence and have authority over others. Of particular interest was, 'the heroic leader standing atop a hierarchy, bending the school community to his or her purposes' (Camburn et al., 2003: 348). Such a view of leadership, however, failed to realize its promise. On a practical level, there were simply insufficient numbers of heroes (Copland, 2003; Elmore, 2002; Harris, 2008) or 'want-to-be heroes' (Gronn and Rawlings-Sanaei, 2003) to run all our businesses and schools. On an empirical level, the evidence demonstrated that effective organizations were not typically run by a single leader who controls the activities of others who, in turn, play minor support roles. What happens within any organization is more complex than this. Many people are involved in both formal and informal leadership practice in influencing direction and outcomes. Thus, the vocabulary of 'leadership' replaced that of 'leaders' to reflect this complexity and the relational nature of leadership influence.

While there might be a general consensus about the importance of leadership rather than focusing on individual leaders and their dispositions, there is less agreement about how we should think about leadership. Ideas have been proposed, fallen into disuse, only to re-emerge some time later. Most of these ideas have been captured in the form of 'adjective-plus leadership'. Leadership, for example, might be transformational, shared, instructional, pedagogical or distributed. The 'adjective plus leadership' label has been deliberately avoided in the title of this book because it is not another book about a depiction of, or prescription for, leadership. Rather, it is designed to answer the question raised by Starratt (2004) that asks, 'Leadership of what, for what?' Clearly, given the title of this book, it is leadership of and for learning.

This learning focus is a relatively new area of scholarship but it draws on, and has emerged from, a tradition of research and thinking in the area. There are many possibilities for how these ideas can be broadly grouped and we have chosen three themes to include in this introductory overview because each has contributed to the foundations of what we know about leaders and learning. These themes include empowering relationships, patterns of leadership distribution, and how leadership contributes to improvements in teaching and learning. Our reason for providing this overview is to locate the central theme of this book on leadership and learning within the broader ideas and traditions of the study of leadership.

Empowering relationships

One of the early alternatives to the heroic leader involved a focus on empowering relationships between leaders and followers. Volumes have been written on these relationships and the associated micro-politics (for example, Blasé, 1991) but probably the best known adjectival label is transformational leadership. The origins of transformational leadership came from the generic literature on leadership rather than that specifically focused on education (Burns, 1978). The central question of this early work was why some leaders were able to engage with others in ways that raised each party to higher levels of motivation and morality. These leaders were able to motivate their staff to pursue the goals of the organization over their own interests.

These ideas gained currency within the education sector and shaped much of the educational leadership training through the 1980s and 1990s (Leithwood et al., 1999). Initially four categories of transformational leadership behaviours were the focus. These included idealized influence, inspirational motivation, intellectual stimulation and individualized consideration. They were seen in combination with what was referred to as transactional dimensions of contingent reward and management-by-exception. Through the research of Leithwood and colleagues (Leithood et al., 1990; 1996; 1999), these dimensions were subsequently combined into four broad categories according to the immediate intended outcome. These categories included: setting directions (vision, group goals, high-performance expectations); helping people (individualized consideration/support, intellectual stimulation, modelling key values and practices); redesigning the organization (helping to build collaborative cultures, creating structures to foster collaboration, building productive relations with parents and the community); and transactional and managerial aggregate (contingent reward, management by exception, management).

Many of these key concepts within transformational leadership have underpinned some chapters in this book, particularly with the emphasis on developing clear visions and high expectations, together with promoting collaboration and productive relations. The problem, however, has been the difficulty in linking the dimensions of transformational leadership to outcomes for students in an environment of increasing international pressure for accountability within schools for these outcomes. In a review of research on transformational leadership and student outcomes, Leithwood and Jantzi (2005) found reasonably consistent relationships to measures of school engagement but more equivocal relationships with student achievement. These authors concluded that the effects of leaders on students were largely indirect – an idea that has gained increasing currency in the leadership literature.

Some argued (for example, Robinson, 2006) that the reason for the limited impact of transformational leadership on students' learning and achievement was the focus on relationships among the adults within the system, rather than on the students they were supposed to be serving. To achieve the impact on student learning and achievement, more focus was needed on developing the kind of relationships that would develop professional knowledge about the improvement of teaching and learning more directly. Focusing on relationships alone, however empowering, was unlikely to be sufficient in bringing about this change.

Patterns of leadership distribution

Another alternative to the heroic leader came with the work of Camburn et al. (2003), Gronn (2003) and Spillane et al. (2004). Their collective empirical work confirmed that leadership involves activities and interactions that are *distributed* across multiple people and situations. This work had its origins in the ideas of shared leadership (Etzioni, 1965) and distributed cognition which shows how material and social artefacts aid in the distribution of understandings across situations (Cole and Engeström, 1993). This work shifted the focus from the 'what' of leadership concerned with people, structures, functions, routines and roles, to 'how leadership gets done through the ordinary, everyday practices involved in leadership routines and functions' (Spillane, 2006: 5). Who leads and who follows is dictated by the task, and not necessarily by the hierarchical positioning of any individual (Copland, 2003).

In line with this rather non-heroic view of leadership, Spillane defines leadership in the following way: 'Leadership refers to activities tied to the core work of the organization that are designed by organizational members to influence the motivation, affect, or practices of other organizational members or that are understood by organizational members as intended to influence their motivation, knowledge, affect or practices' (Spillane, 2006: 11–12). While the main premises of this definition (core work, influence, practices) appear to be widely accepted, inevitably differences in perspectives have arisen. Spillane and colleagues have been concerned about developing analytical and conceptual frameworks for studying this influence process through a distributed lens. Others have transformed the leadership descriptor to the adjectival form of 'distributed leadership'. This latter group have advocated that greater distribution of leadership is something to which educational organizations should aspire if they are to meet the challenges of the twenty-first century education (for example, Harris, 2008).

Something on which most researchers taking a distributed leadership perspective agree is the potential benefits of utilizing expertise across and within organizations through the co-construction of knowledge (Harris, 2008). Effective distribution of leadership creates more opportunities for professionals to learn. The increased opportunities, coupled with the focus of distributed leadership on the core work of the organization, create strong links between leadership and learning. Thus many of the chapters in this book implicitly, if not explicitly, take a distributed perspective on leadership.

While most researchers have welcomed the shift to studying the 'how' of leadership practices with its focus on learning rather than analysing styles or tasks, nagging doubts have surfaced about whether distributing leadership per se will actually be what makes the difference to some of our enduring educational problems. Harris (2008), for example, explains that it is not the distribution of leadership that determines effectiveness, but rather how it is distributed. Timperley (2005) showed that greater distribution may lead to greater distribution of incompetence. Robinson (2009) argues that to tackle the kinds of endemic achievement problems evident in many countries, more focus is needed on the educational content of the leadership process. What this educational content might look like and how leadership contributes to improvement in teaching and learning for students is the focus to which we turn next.

Leadership for the improvement of teaching and learning

While the other two themes of empowering relationships and patterns of leadership distribution have as an important goal the improvement of teaching and learning in schools, this third theme addresses this issue more explicitly and brings us closer to the central task of this book. Part of this reorientation towards leaders being more focused on teaching and learning arose from a concern with the introduction of self-managing and governing schools in many countries in the 1990s. This movement led principals to become more focused on the efficient undertaking of management tasks than on providing professional direction for the school (Southworth, 1998). This emphasis on learning-centred leadership is partly about reclaiming the professional role of school leaders, albeit in a more modern guise than that existing prior to self-managing schools.

Another impetus for more instructionally focused leadership was the research on effective schools. As those studying schools with high student achievement compiled lists of these schools' characteristics, references to strong leadership were invariably among them (for example, Reynolds et al., 2000). Similarly, in the schooling improvement literature, it became evident that unless leadership influenced what was happening in the instructional core, it was unlikely to have an impact on outcomes for students. As Elmore states:

> Improvement occurs ... by raising the capacity of key relationships in the instructional core: by increasing teachers' knowledge of content and their knowledge of how to connect the content to specific students, by increasing the prerequisite knowledge that students bring to their interactions with

teachers and by deepening their own knowledge of themselves as learners, by increasing the complexity and demand of content. (Elmore, 2002: 122)

As researchers have sought to identify the kind of leadership activities that lead to improvement in teaching and learning in the instructional core, adjective-plus forms of leadership have inevitably emerged. These forms have included instructional leadership, learning-centred leadership, pedagogical leadership and educational leadership. Each provides nuances on the central theme of learning for both the leaders and teachers within the organization and the students that educational organizations are designed to benefit. What is common among them all is the priority given to thinking about how particular leadership tasks and activities might impact on student achievement and well-being (Hallinger, 2005; Robinson et al., 2009; Southworth, 2004).

A recent meta-analysis of leadership practices that had high impact on student outcomes by Robinson et al. (2009) is one such example of this kind of pursuit. These authors found that those practices that could be construed as 'pedagogical leadership' were associated with highest effect sizes for student achievement. In a subsequent analysis, they established that the dimensions with greatest impact included: establishing goals and expectations; resourcing strategically; planning, coordinating and evaluating teaching and the curriculum; promoting and participating in teacher learning and development; and ensuring an orderly and supportive environment. Three of these dimensions are supported by Hallinger's (2005) review of the literature that described instructional leaders as those who frame and communicate the school's goals; manage the instructional programme by supervising and evaluating instruction, coordinating the curriculum and monitoring student progress; and align the school's structures and culture within the school's mission.

While these approaches to leadership have a stronger instructional focus, they also draw on the other two constructions of leadership, albeit with a different lens. Robinson et al. (2009), for example, include a relationship dimension of indirect influence called creating educationally powerful connections, which has similarities with the transformational leadership literature. Similarly, Elmore (2002) writes that cohesive schools occur when there is a high degree of alignment between individual responsibility and collective expectations complemented by a relatively explicit internal accountability system.

The contribution of the three themes

These three themes, empowering relationships, patterns of leadership distribution, and leadership for the improvement of teaching and learning, come together to provide a strong base for understanding what it takes to create the conditions for successful learning, for adults and for students – in fact, for all in the educational community. The challenge is that systematic investigation into the field of how leadership influences learning has been relatively recent. However, emerging and strengthening evidence indicates that leadership that is relational, and is an influence process focused on successful learning relationships that are reciprocal, collaborative and empowering for all parties have an impact on student engagement, achievement and well-being. This means that leaders are learners as much as their teachers and students. All have a willingness to learn from the people one works with in order to work more effectively with them and deliver an education system to which all contribute.

Leaders talking about learning, students talking about learning, communities talking about learning and through these, reciprocal, collaborative processes create new knowledge about the leadership of learning to improve systems and practices within the school.

About this book

Each of the broad traditions we have outlined above have influenced our collective thinking about leadership and learning, with different chapters in this book giving more or less emphasis to particular ideas: transformational leadership with its emphasis on inspiring shared vision and values for learning through strong relationships; distributed leadership with its focus on how the everyday interactions and activities of leaders influence the work of the organization; and instructional leadership with its focus on improving teaching and learning.

This volume brings together the work of a number of leading scholars who have been researching and thinking about this emerging and important field for many years. They are held in high regard by practitioners and research colleagues alike, and they readily agreed to contribute to a book that we have brought together in three important sections, with a central, underlying principle of developing capability of all within the organization to improve student outcomes. All chapters are about leadership focused on making a difference to students; leadership as an indirect influence; and developing leadership capacity through learning.

Section 1: Exploring models for leadership and improvement

The chapters in this section focus on models for overall change and improvement. In Chapter 2 Chris Day presents a five-part model which focuses attention not only on what leaders know and do, but who they are. He suggests successful system change is a 'layered' leadership approach. The chapter ends with some clear messages for principal educators and policy-makers.

A social justice agenda for leadership is right at the forefront of Russell Bishop's chapter as he challenges that leadership is about reducing disparities for indigenous and other minoritized peoples. He presents six key areas that leaders need to know and do to achieve school change. He acknowledges that school reform is complex, but challenges that we know the conditions that are necessary to support student learning, and that is where we should start.

In Chapter 4, Kenneth Leithwood synthesizes two lines of inquiry: '*what* leadership practices nurture improved student learning' and '*how* successful leadership practices are connected to the experiences and eventually the learning of students'. He identifies four paths along which the influence of successful leadership practices flow in order to improve student learning and puts forward that one of the major leadership challenges is the alignment of leadership influence across the paths. He presents a case study of one leadership practice on the rational path, 'Improving teachers' pedagogy' to illustrate this theory.

Philip Hallinger and Ronald H. Heck examine the ways in which the field of educational leadership and management has approached the study of leadership impact on student learning over past decades. They present a variety of conceptual models as well as empirical evidence that addresses whether and how school leadership impacts learning in practice. They challenge policy-makers that a comprehensive and valid model of leadership for learning must place leadership in a specific context.

Geoff Southworth, in Chapter 6, is unequivocal that learning has to be the number one priority for leadership. He argues that leadership should be strongly focused on learning and teaching, particularly pedagogy, and he elaborates on what this priority focus on learning means and how it can be achieved. He presents three leadership strategies and organizational conditions that need to be in place to maximize their effect. Southworth challenges that a modern, twenty-first century approach to human resource management needs concerted attention.

The potential of system leadership and the moral purpose inherent in such leadership practice is the essence of David Hopkins's, chapter. He challenges principals about their need to care for and work towards the success of other schools as well as their own as only through such systemic reform will every student be enabled to reach their potential and every school have the possibility to be great. He explores the 'policy conundrum' and offers four drivers for system reform.

Section 2: Challenges in developing learning-focused leadership

The chapters in this section have a clear focus on the key leadership for learning challenge – creating the conditions for teachers to be effective instructional professionals.

In Chapter 8, Louise Stoll not only defines and critiques the difference professional learning communities make, but also offers eight succinct processes that are involved in leading professional learning communities. She argues that 'creating and developing capacity is an imperative for anyone passionate about improvement and transforming learning' and that professional learning communities support sustainable improvements because they build such capacity.

Acknowledging the complexity of changing teachers' practice, Helen Timperley offers a way forward to an enquiry mindset, based on a synthesis of international literature, in Chapter 9. The five-dimensional cyclical model of enquiry and knowledge-building for teachers and leaders 'begins and ends with students'. Timperley provides questions and examples at each stage of the cycle, and ends the chapter with the implications for school leaders in creating the conditions that support and develop such enquiry mindsets in the school community.

Viviane Robinson, Linda Bendikson and John Hattie study and critique the empirical evidence from meta-analyses to ascertain whether there is a difference in the extent and type of instructional leadership between primary and secondary schools. They challenge researchers to more clearly differentiate between instructional leadership as direct influence on teachers' practice and instructional leadership as 'creating the social and technical infrastructure for quality teaching and learning' if there is to be a greater understanding of instructional leadership by principals in large secondary and primary schools.

In Chapter 11, Helen Wildy and Simon Clarke explore instructional leadership at the teacher level. They address three questions: What do we mean by instructional leadership? How is instructional leadership practised at the teacher level? What, if any, are its effects? They conclude that cultural change 'with investment in professional learning and collaborative communities of practice' is the key to improvement.

Section 3: Broadening ideas of learning and knowledge development

This section focuses on leaders co-constructing new knowledge and new ways of being that lead to the sharing of knowledge. Honouring diversity, acknowledging the emotionality of leadership and social interactions are explored.

Writing from a distributed perspective, and presenting empirical research evidence to support their argument, James Spillane, Kaleen Healey, Leigh Mesler Parise and Allison Kenney study relations between school leadership and formal professional learning as well as on-the-job professional learning. They call for researchers to 'cast a wider net' in their efforts to understand such relations, and focus more on the social interactions within the school, to 'estimate the investment in professional learning and its effects on valued school outcomes'. They argue that the context is not only a site for, but also an element of, professional learning, either enabling or constraining professional learning.

Marianne Coleman focuses on the implications of diversity for leadership theory and practice. She states that 'diversity is not just about difference but also the ways in which differences are perceived and valued' and challenges that the idea of diversity bringing value to leadership has not yet been embraced fully by the research community and resulting theorizing.

Knowledge work and knowledge leaders, state Lorna Earl and Lynne Hannay, in Chapter 14, are the essentials for innovation in schools within this knowledge society. They present a cycle of knowledge work and outline seven major activities of knowledge leaders, with illustrated examples from case studies. They argue that educational leaders must be knowledge leaders and that they 'are morally obligated to bring a disciplined process to the creative and divergent activities inherent in innovation, that allow it to flourish, to be shown to work and to spread through the profession'.

Arguing that emotion is a key part of the social reality in which leadership is exercised, in Chapter 15 Megan Crawford calls for more research in this important area. Because leadership is relational, she argues that workplaces, and therefore the leadership therein, are full of emotion and that leaders need an understanding of how emotion affects their work and the social context of the organization as a whole. Crawford explores the affective concepts of emotional intelligence, emotional regulation and emotional contagion in this chapter.

In Chapter 16, Jan Robertson puts forward that the concept of 'partnership' provides an avenue for thinking about leadership and learning and the development of mutuality and reciprocity within relationships. These spaces for leadership, learning and professional practice are more collaborative and less hierarchical with all participants learning from the interaction and involved in the creation of new knowledge. The meta-cognitive processes of coaching leadership, developed through learning partnerships, with enquiry-mindedness, are illustrated in a case study of such work with leaders in British Columbia.

In the final chapter, Andy Hargreaves looks at future directions for leadership and learning. He draws parallels between the evolution of fusion in cooking and in leadership. Fusion in cooking has come to mean the finding of new compatibilities; a blend that is deliberate, principled and practical; an 'inner and individual integration', an 'outer and collective integration' and a 'temporal and sequential integration'. Hargreaves picks up these threads by extending Draft and Lengel's (1998) conceptualization of leadership fusion to present a theory of fusion leadership in action which culminates in innovative and creative connections and partnerships. A case study completes the chapter that 'exemplifies the presence and the power of fusion leadership in a secondary school in the North of England'.

We hope that this book not only challenges your thinking in your pursuit of the theory and practice of leadership, but that it also affirms the many powerful examples of exemplary practice that we experience and hear about in our studies of leadership internationally. These thought leaders are continually in quest of leadership *for* learning: leadership practice that has a positive effect on learning outcomes for *all* students, everywhere. Leadership *for* learning is always focused on addressing the disparities in education and recognizes that as such these disparities are key indicators that the theory and practice of leadership remains incomplete.

References

Blasé, J. (1991) The micropolitical orientation of teachers toward closed school principals, *Education & Urban Society*, 23(4): 356–78.

Burns, J.M. (1978) *Leadership*. New York: Harper & Row.

Camburn, E., Rowan, B. and Taylor, J.E. (2003) Distributed leadership in schools: the case of elementary schools adopting comprehensive school reform models, *Educational Evaluation and Policy Analysis*, 25(4): 347–73.

Cole, M. and Engeström, Y. (1993) A cultural-historical approach to distributed cognition, in G. Salomon (ed.), *Distributed Cognitions: Psychological and Educational Considerations*. New York: Cambridge University Press. pp. 1–46.

Copland, M. (2003) Leadership of inquiry: building and sustaining capacity for school improvement, *Educational Evaluation and Policy Analysis*, 25(4): 375–95.

Daft, R.L. and Lengel, R.H. (1998) *Fusion Leadership: Unlocking the Subtle Forces that Change People and Organisations*. San Francisco, CA: Bernet-Kochler.

Elmore, R. (2002) *School Reform from the Inside Out: Policy, Practice, and Performance*. Cambridge, MA: Harvard Education Press.

Etzioni, A. (1965) Dual leadership in complex organizations, *American Sociological Review*, 30(5): 688–98.

Gronn, P. (2003) Leadership: Who needs it? *School Leadership and Management*, 23(3): 267–90.

Gronn, P. and Rawlings-Sanaei, F. (2003) Recruiting school principals in a climate of leadership disengagement, *Australian Journal of Education*, 47(2): 172–84.

Hallinger, P. (2005) Instructional leadership and the school principal, a passing fancy that refuses to fade away, *Leadership and Policy in Schools*, 4: 1–20.

Harris, A. (2008) *Distributed School Leadership: Developing Tomorrow's Leaders*. London: Routledge.

Leithwood, K. and Jantzi, D. (2005) A review of transformational school leadership research 1996–2005, *Leadership and Policy in Schools*, 4: 177–99.

Leithwood, K., Jantzi, D. and Dart, B. (1990) Transformational leadership: How principals can help reform school cultures, *School Effectiveness and School Improvement*, 1(4): 249–80.

Leithwood, K., Jantzi, D. and Steinback, R. (1999) *Changing Leadership for Changing Times*. Buckingham: Open University Press.

Leithwood, K., Tomlinson, D. and Genge, M. (1996) Transformational school leadership, in K. Leithwood, C. Chapman, D. Corson, P. Hallinger and A. Hart (eds), *International Handbook of Educational Leadership and Administration*. Dordrecht: Kluwer Academics. pp. 785–840.

Reynolds, D., Teddlie, C., Hopkins, D. and Stringfield, S. (2000) School effectiveness and school improvement, in C. Teddlie and D. Reynolds (eds), *The International Handbook of School Effectiveness Research*. London: Falmer. pp. 160–86.

Robinson, V. (2006) Putting education back into educational leadership, *Leading and Managing*, 12(1): 62–75.

Robinson, V. (2009) Fit for purpose: an educationally relevant account of distributed leadership, in A. Harris (ed.), *Distributed School Leadership*. Dordrecht: Springer.

Robinson, V., Hohepa, M. and Lloyd, C. (2009) *School Leadership and Student Outcomes: Identifying What Works and Why*. A Best Evidence Synthesis Iteration, Ministry of Education, Wellington, New Zealand.

Southworth, G. (1998) *Leading Improving Primary Schools*. London: Falmer Press.

Southworth, G. (2004) *Primary School Leadership in Context*. London: RoutledgeFalmer.

Spillane, J. (2006) *Distributed Leadership*. San Francisco, CA: Jossey-Bass.

Spillane, J.P., Halverson, R. and Diamond, J. (2004) Towards a theory of leadership practice: a distributed perspective, *Journal of Curriculum Studies*, 36(1): 3–34.

Starratt, R.J. (2004) The ethics of learning: an absent focus in the discourse on educational leadership, paper presented at the 2nd International Summit for Leadership in Education, Boston, MA, 2–6 November.

Timperley, H.S. (2005) Distributed leadership: developing theory from practice, *Journal of Curriculum Studies*, 37(6): 395–420.

CHAPTER 2

The Layering of Leadership

Christopher Day

This chapter focuses upon what it is about school principals and what they do which makes them successful in managing change for improvement. It finds that personal traits (attributes) and strategies are two sides of the successful leadership coin; and that successful school principals manage transitions through the phased application of 'layered' leadership strategies.

Recently, I was a guest speaker at a principals' conference. Before my own speech were two others. The first was provided by a former internationally renowned artistic performer from China who had found refuge in America in the 1990s. The story of his life was enthralling and the presentation, charismatic. The second lecture was equally charismatic and provided by a man who had recovered from a life-threatening illness to found a successful business.

I have referred to these experiences because, although both stories were heroic, they were about the heroism of individuals who were acting in their own interests. The work of principals is different. First, effective principals' stories centre upon serving the interests of others; and second, being a school principal is essentially a social process which focuses on working for the betterment of others. From time to time, effective principalship may demand elements of both charisma, defined as the ability to inspire great enthusiasm and devotion, and heroism – defined as 'extraordinary strength or courage' – depending upon context. Despite, or perhaps because of, the many academic voices which are critical of charismatic leadership, it is important to distinguish these from the personal traits or attributes which are essential to effective leadership.

Growing and sustaining principalship which leads to sustained school improvement demands such powerful sets of personal traits or attributes and knowledge and expertise, but it is much more than these. As Jorunn Möller and her colleagues (2007: 83) observed: 'Successful leadership was an interactive process involving many people and players, and both the context and the persons involved were key variables in understanding what counted as successful ... successful leadership should not be separated from deeper philosophical questions, because education is essentially a moral enterprise.' Because leadership of schools always takes place in the intersection between political (policy), ethical (values), educational (learning and achievement) and personal contexts which are often in tension, its success cannot be defined only by the individual qualities of the head. Rather, success in schools is defined by the kinds of direct and indirect influence of principals upon the individual and collective mindsets, emotional and intellectual lives and practices of a range of internal and external stakeholders over time through their leadership and management of change and change processes.

Knowledge of two key themes are, research suggests, fundamental to improving understandings of the management of school systems by principals and the strategic and person-centred leadership of the people within those systems.

1 Complex systems leadership: the importance of mindset
2 Building and sustaining improvement – six pillars of success

Theme 1: Complex systems leadership: the importance of mindset

There has been much writing recently, which promotes a 'systems thinking' approach to leadership as being that which is most likely to result in success. Yet while systems of, for example, behaviour management of students, monitoring of students' progress and achievement, staff appraisal/performance management are essential, they will have limited success without the cooperation, motivation, engagement and commitment of staff and students, and without the principal's ability to acknowledge and respond to changing realities in the personal, policy and social worlds outside the school which inevitably affect the worlds within. How principals think (their mindset) about systems leadership is, therefore, an important determinant of their approaches to system leadership and management. Senge's (1990) 'fifth discipline' of leadership is 'systems thinking' which he describes as: 'A discipline for seeing the 'structures' that underlie complex situations ... systems thinking offers a language that begins by restructuring how we think' (Senge, 1990: 69).

Fris and Lazaridou (2006) contrast a 'Newtonian' with what they term a 'quantum' perspective on organizational life and leadership. The Newtonian perspective is associated with ways of thinking (as in policy-related standards) which focus upon systems design and linear, causal relationships between intentions, actions and outcomes. The quantum perspective focuses upon the need for insightful identification of patterns in interactions between relationships, action, contexts and outcomes which are much less predictable. Which of these 'mindsets' is held by principals – and those with responsibility for their training and development – may be associated with the way they lead and manage their school and, thus, their capacity to be effective.

Two contrasting views of organizations (schools) as 'machines' or 'living systems' which are featured in Wheatley's (2005) work further serve to explain different conceptions by different stakeholders about what mindsets leaders need to have if they are to achieve success.

From the 'machine' perspective, leaders create and maintain 'command and control' systems which aim to increase employees' certainty about and level of accountability for their work. In such systems:

> We can ignore the deep realities of human existence. We can ignore that people carry spiritual questions and quests into their work; we can ignore that people need love and acknowledgement; we can pretend that emotions are not a part of our work lives; we can pretend we don't have families, or health crises, or deep worries. In essence, we take the complexity of human life and organise it away ... People can be viewed as machines and controlled to perform with the same efficiency and predictability. (Wheatley, 2005: 19)

In this reality, teachers are supervised closely, conform to the one 'best' model of teaching, and lists of curriculum 'standards'. (It may, however, be necessary in schools at a particular phase of their development, to adopt this temporarily.) In contrast, the 'living systems' metaphor encourages a view of organization as a process, one involving consistent adaptation and growth that occurs in response to a strong desire for learning and survival. Here, the process of leadership: 'Involves developing relationships from a shared sense of purpose, exchanging and creating information, learning constantly, paying attention to the results of our efforts, co-adapting, co-evolving, developing wisdom as we learn, staying clear about our purpose, being alert to changes from all directions' (Wheatley, 2005: 27). In this school world, perhaps resembling a learning community, structures depend upon purpose and context, cultures are collaborative, responsibilities are delegated or distributed and principals and their staff are highly responsive to and interact actively with the wider stakeholder communities.

The implications for principals who are disposed to one or the other of these ways of thinking may be that:

1 It may be easier to adopt a Newtonian (machine) perspective and, as engineers, design, monitor and evaluate systems. Fewer personal attributes are needed if this approach is taken. However, while this may result in improvements, research on successful leadership shows that they are likely to be limited.

2 It is harder to adopt a quantum or living systems thinking perspective because this demands greater use of personal attributes, principles and attention to others not as a means of achieving functional outcomes but as ends in themselves. Alongside these and complementary to them, would be a number of interrelated or 'layered' systems. This layered approach is a complex process but is more likely to lead to greater improvements.

One of the more remarkable results of both the International Successful Schools Principals Project (ISSPP) and Department for Children, Schools and Families (DCSF) research discussed in this chapter was that even in contexts of high-stakes accountability, successful principals assiduously avoided 'command and control' forms of leadership associated with the 'machine' metaphor. Rather, they frequently acted with compassion and considerable sensitivity in predicting, responding to and managing the human tensions and dilemmas experienced by parents, staff and students. Their conception was of their schools as living systems rather than machines.

So the question for those who educate/train leaders and for leaders themselves is which 'beliefs' and what kinds of values, qualities, strategies and skills do principals need which will make it more possible for them to lead and manage in ways which are responsive to the influences upon and needs of students and the demands of policy, and which express their moral and instrumental purposes of education in order to achieve success. Are they those which focus primarily upon the functional purposes of leadership, the 'machine' metaphor? Are they those which emphasize the interpersonal, interactive processes of personal influence, the 'living systems' metaphor?

Theme 2: Building and sustaining improvement – six pillars of success

What leaders do, is, at least in part, a function of who they are (their identities), their beliefs and values – how they think and feel – and the interactions between these and the contexts in which they work. Complexity theory acknowledges this, emphasizing that, 'the role of leadership ... rather than looking to influence the participants directly, is to foster conditions that enable the participants to face their current difficulties as well as an unspecified future' (Zellermayer and Margolin, 2005: 2).

There seem to be six pillars upon which successful principalship which lasts are built:

1 *Principals' values.* It is the translation of these into practice which will result in relative success or failure.

2 *Combining logic and emotion: the nature of successful leadership.* It is the ways this combination is employed which will determine the extent of principal influence, direct and indirect, upon the 'mindsets', the kinds of commitments to success by staff, pupils and community.

3 *Sharing the leadership: what headteachers do in building and sustaining success.* All leaders must engage with processes of change which will not always be comfortable. Thus, a sense of timing and choice of strategy or group of strategies which meet the needs of school and staff contexts and which enable them to move beyond these are crucial to success.

4 *Continuing learning and development for all.* It is self-evident that staff need to continue to learn in order to avoid slipping into unselfconscious routines, and to respond to changes in understandings of subject and pedagogical knowledge, external social change and policy-led changes in expectations, aspirations and directions.

5 *Layered leadership: managing transitions.* Change is not an event but a process of transition. Successful system change is unlikely without corresponding changes in the hearts and minds as well as the actions and interactions of the people who work in the organization. To achieve successful change is, therefore, complex, often takes time and some will be slower to change than others. It may be more appropriate, then, to think of change in terms of transition and the strategies used to lead change as phased and 'layered' and fit for purpose.

6 *Phases of change for improvement: sustaining the turnaround.*

1. Principals' values: context sensitive, not context dependent

The case studies in the international Successful School Principals' Project (Day and Leithwood, 2007) were drawn from eight countries with a wide range of political, social, cultural and educational histories – from the inclusive, egalitarian and decentralized traditions of social democracy in Scandinavian countries to the discipline and collectivity of the centralized school systems in China and the high-stakes, results-driven accountability cultures of England and the USA. Moreover, each of the eight countries used different criteria for judging school success. Yet despite such differences in social, political and educational contexts, the study concluded that, 'the values, aspirations, qualities, achievements and ways of achieving and sustaining success are startlingly similar across all countries and all school phases, regardless of size' (Day and Leithwood, 2007: 171). Similarities were also found in the ways successful principals in different school contexts across the participating countries worked.

For example, principals in high-poverty schools seem to demonstrate that certain of the qualities, strategies and skills used in combination play a greater role in the success in their schools than in those schools located in areas of relative advantage. It may be concluded, therefore, that: 'Different leadership strategies may be effective in different circumstances but also … the principals' purposes and the ways they act out their beliefs, values and visions in the contexts in which they work make the difference between success and failure' (Day and Leithwood, 2007: 174).

Further confirmation was provided by the results of a national, longitudinal project in England which examined the impact of leadership on student outcomes in schools which had achieved success over time in relation to value-added student test and examination data and under the leadership of the same principal. It found that principals in schools serving disadvantaged communities: (a) face the most persistent levels of challenge; (b) apply greater combinations or clusters of strategies with greater intensity; and (c) use a greater range of personal and social skills than do those in other schools which serve more advantaged communities and are at later stages of professional and whole school development (Day et al., 2007). Whatever the contextually inspired strategies used by successful principals, however, their values remain constant in their exercise of values-led contingency leadership (Day et al., 2000).

Together, these two research projects suggest that:

- successful principals draw upon the same basic repertoire of leadership practices, but

- the ways in which leaders apply these practices – not the practices themselves – demonstrate responsiveness to, rather than dictation by, the contexts in which they work.

The findings have important implications for the recruitment, training, support and renewal of principals. They suggest that schools in different socio-economic contexts and experiencing different levels of success may require principals with values, qualities, strategies and skills which match the nature of the context if they are to improve through responsiveness to context.

2. Combining logic and emotion: the nature of successful leadership

Robust research across a number of countries has shown that successful headteachers are not only highly-skilled diagnosticians, culturally responsive, able to combine and apply clusters of strategies and skills, and highly adept in working with a range of key stakeholders from within and outside of the school for its benefit (Day and Leithwood, 2007), they are also emotionally literate and exercise emotional understandings in their everyday work with colleagues:

> Logic and reason, as important as they are, are not the be all and end all. Unless you deal with how people feel about things, logic and reasoning do not matter. No one is going to buy into what you are leading unless you get past their feelings and emotions. I have always been a very logical and reasoning person, and this is not enough. I always thought it was, but it is not. (Experienced principal)

All schools need the leadership of principals who know how people feel, who possess or are able to develop high levels of self-awareness, knowledge and emotional understandings of the needs and of the minds and hearts of staff, students and community. They recognize that strategic intent will never be fully realized without the emotional commitment of staff and students. Often, the expressions of such knowledge and emotional understandings are to found in principals' exercise of 'relational trust' (Bryk and Schneider, 2003: 23): 'Key in this regard is how conversations take place within a school community. A genuine sense of listening to what each person has to say marks the basis for meaningful social interaction.'

According to Robinson's (2007: 19) report: 'Judgements about the trustworthiness of others are made on the basis of four interpersonal qualities: respect, competence, personal regard for others and integrity.' Her representation and extension of the research of Bryk and Schneider (2002) (Figure 2.1) which found a strong statistical connection between improvements in relational trust and gains in students' academic achievement provides an interesting hypothetical connection between the determinants of relational trust, its consequences for the school as an organization and the academic and social outcomes of students. It also implicitly reinforces the importance to successful principalship of rational and non-rational qualities.

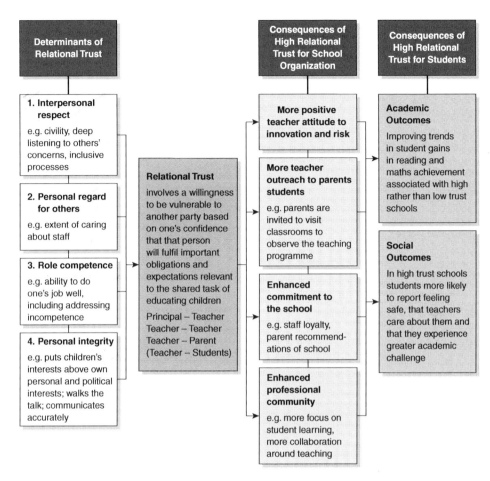

Figure 2.1 How relational trust works in schools (Robinson, 2007). Published by the Australian Council for Educational Leaders (ACEL). Monograph Series Number 41: 20)

In the 64 case studies in the ISSPP project and, more recently, in the emerging findings from, Effective Leadership and Student Outcomes project in English schools, it was clear, also, that the achievement of sustained success is dependent upon the ability of principals to exercise both cognitive and emotional qualities in combination which are timely, fit for purpose and context sensitive: 'Developing emotional fitness ... is not a one-off task – it is about creating a climate in which people feel safe enough to learn and grow in their capacity to value themselves and others, to relate effectively and to lead' (Harris, 2007: 42).

Achieving success is a complex endeavour, which demands skill, courage and resilience. Just as teachers in classrooms must motivate, engage, challenge and nurture students' commitment to learn and achieve through the exercise of a range of intra and interpersonal qualities, so too must principals do so in their work. Cognition and emotion are two sides of the same coin.

3. Sharing the leadership: what headteachers do in building and sustaining success

> Cultures do not change by mandate; they change by the specific displacement of norms, structures and processes by others; the process of cultural change depends fundamentally on modelling the new values and behaviour that you expect to displace to existing ones. (Elmore, 2004: 11)

Particularly interesting in the findings of the English project is that despite the increased consultation, participation and clarity of roles and responsibilities, sense of ownership and 'whole schoolness', the way that leadership was dispersed within many of the case-study schools was hierarchical in the early phases of new principals' work. In that phase, delegation of tasks rather than 'distribution' of responsibilities with accountabilities was the more common pattern in schools. Some principals distributed leadership in ways which provided authority for decision-making alongside responsibilities, but most retained a much closer hold on decision-making. While both strategies represent an increased number of staff involved in leadership functions, distribution implies greater ownership in decision-making than delegation. Thus, what appears to be a more distributed horizontal system on paper may, nevertheless, retain the characteristics of a more traditional hierarchical system. While there can be no doubt, as previous research has also shown, that school leadership has a greater influence upon staff and students' sense of ownership, participation and identity when it is widely distributed (Day et al., 2010; Leithwood et al., 2006), it may be that existing cultures initially demand delegation rather than distribution, at least in the short term, as part of a transition phase from one culture to another.

4. Continuing learning and development for all

> Leadership not only promotes, but directly participates with teachers in, formal or informal learning. (Robinson, 2007: 8)

Another claim in the research literature on successful principal leadership is that, *school leaders improve teaching and learning indirectly and most powerfully through their influence on staff motivation, commitment and working conditions* (Day et al., 2009). Successful heads are those who consistently provide staff with opportunities to engage in regular professional learning activities, related to individual, group and organizational needs both within and outside the school. In the English study, these were of five kinds:

- alignment of the activity with the school improvement plan (for example, new forms of student assessment, teaching approaches, behaviour management)
- building in-house leadership (for example, mentoring, peer observation, in-service training led by colleagues)
- succession planning: preparing colleagues for leadership roles
- building capacity for learning and change
- sustaining commitment.

Alongside these, successful principals were actively engaged in 'talent spotting' as a means of recruiting staff.

Robinson (2007) found from her meta-analysis of the research literature on the effects of leadership on student outcomes that of the five leadership dimensions she identified, that is, (a) establishing goals and expectations; (b) strategic resourcing; (c) planning, coordinating and evaluating teaching and the curriculum; (d) promoting and participating in teacher learning and development; and (e) ensuring an orderly and supportive environment, that it was (d) promoting and participating in teacher learning and development, which had the largest, most significant effect size, at 0.84. However, research has found that in many schools the range of learning and development opportunities provided for teachers and other staff is often too narrow and not built into the infrastructures and cultures (Goodall et al., 2005). Thus its impact on students is often unnecessarily limited. Moreover, principals themselves often do not always model learning.

Crucial to professional learning and development is the provision of time to learn. Lodge and Reed (2003) found that time and space – rare commodities in the busyness cultures of schools – are often hard to find in the press for measurable results caused by the improvement agendas of policy-makers:

> There is paradoxically no time on the improvement agenda for the improvement focus that is badly needed: good contextual analysis, a reconsideration of the purposes of schools, the needs of the future and the curriculum needed to serve the emerging citizens in our schools. These lie at the heart of sustainable improvement capacity ... And compression and disintegration result in damage to the culture of schools and to their school improvement endeavours. (cited in Thomson, 2007: 38)

Yet successful principals in the research on which this chapter draws did exactly that. They found time – for themselves and colleagues. They did not accept compression and disintegration but rather nurtured reflection, broadened participation and, most importantly, engaged others in decision-making processes which resulted in success in different phases of their schools' improvement journeys. They broadened participation in the life of the school by involving parents more in classrooms and school events of all kinds, engaging students more actively in their own learning, in feedback on the quality of education, and through giving them opportunities to participate and sometimes lead in school-wide decision-making through, for example, school councils.

5. Layered leadership: managing transitions

The key qualities of successful principals identified by a range of research are that they are open-minded and ready to learn from others, flexible rather than dogmatic within a system of core values, and persistent, resilient and optimistic. In short, they are able to exercise 'adaptive' leadership (Heifetz, 1994), solving problems in imaginative, creative ways which often lie outside the norms of existing solutions and practices. Kendall et al. (2005) present an interesting and attractive four-stage model for understanding the anatomy of organizational change.

Within these four stages, they describe first-level impacts which change institutional processes, infrastructure and staffing; second-level impacts where the first-level changes begin to influence key players (for example, senior management and other 'gatekeepers'); third-level impacts in which there are observable changes in outcomes (for example, student behaviour, examination results); and fourth-level impacts in which the key changes have become embedded in the schools' cultures and ways of working thus enabling more change to occur in the established direction. Yet even this careful analysis does not quite capture the complexity of creating the conditions, building capacity, creating time and space, and applying the emotional understandings, expertise and effort needed for sustaining change for improvement.

Successful principals acknowledge school as a complex, living, dynamic organism in which a change to one part, for example, the physical environment or student assessment procedures, will not only rely upon other parts for at least tacit support but is also likely to result in both anticipated and unanticipated positive and/or negative effects in other parts. Moreover, in beginning and continuing their stewardship of the school they recognize that they have inherited staff and students who are at a particular phase in the pace of their own development and so are likely to embrace (or not embrace) change in different ways. This perhaps explains why they apply not one but a cluster of strategies simultaneously in a phased and 'layered' approach. More emphasis is placed on some strategies rather than others at any given time or in a particular phase in the development of the school. As some new values or practices become embedded, so they move from the centre of the improvement stage, their place being taken by others. Always, however, they remain on the stage as the improvement play progresses. Thus, how principals conceptualize the situation, how intelligently they analyse contexts of need, how sensitively they manage people, how they respond to existing cultures within and outside the school within a clear articulation of values expectations and aspirations, and how they phase the introduction and implementation of development strategies are all critical factors in their success.

Successful principals, then, contribute actively and significantly to their students' learning, well-being and achievement by:

1 *Understanding* that leadership is a values-led *relational* process which takes place in the interactions of people and their situations (relational trust and relational agency).

2 *Diagnosing and responding* to the development phase of the school in the selection and timing of strategic interventions (layered leadership).

3 *Focusing* upon capacity building of staff (including succession planning) with commitment and classroom learning and teaching as the twin focus.

4 *Prioritizing* improving physical and behavioural conditions for learning.

5 Always working to *break down* barriers to whole-school vision ownership: a key means of achieving this is by widening participation and distributing leadership responsibilities and accountabilities.

6. Phases of change for improvement: sustaining the turnaround

Recently, there has been much writing about principals who 'turn around' schools which are experiencing difficulties or failing to improve standards, particularly schools in challenging or disadvantaged urban contexts. Turn-around is one thing, sustaining turn-around is, however, another. It involves the application of layered leadership in managing transition. Transition is different from change:

> Change is an external procedure that deals with policies, structures, or practices, whereas transition is an internal process of reorientation and transformation that people go through before the change can work. Transition takes longer because it requires three separate phases: departure from the way that things and people used to be; being in a neutral zone, a time when things are not the old way anymore, but are not yet the new way; and a new beginning. (Zellermayer and Margolin, 2005: 2)

An example of leadership and management of transition is to be found in an elementary school in England which was threatened with closure but eight years on was identified as being 'outstanding' by Ofsted (the Office for Standards in Education, the national external school inspection agency). The principal is neither 'charismatic' nor 'heroic' in the classical sense of their meanings. However, her work is illustrative of how successful principals model and draw differentially upon combinations of attributes and strategies which are 'fit for purpose' at their time of use to first 'turn around' the school and then sustain an improvement trajectory.

1. Phase 1: Coming out of 'special measures'

Here the focus was on enriching the teaching and learning environment; providing security for the students; establishing a behaviour policy, gaining community acceptance; and improving classroom teaching.

> I talked a lot about my beliefs and expectations ... I acknowledged that I had just come out of the classroom ... So I knew what it was like, and that there would be flexibility as long as the job's done ... I talked about working habits ... and I brought some examples of the standards of work I would be expecting ... (Headteacher)

2. Phase 2: Taking ownership – an inclusive agenda

Here the emphasis was upon combining five strategies: vision and values to develop the school's mission; distributing the leadership, communicating a belief in practice that many people can take responsibility for leading change and demonstrating that they can be trusted to do so; inclusivity – integrating students from different social and cultural environments so that, for example, incidents of bullying and racism were dealt with fairly and consistently; appraisal and continuing professional development designed to support staff; and a persistent priority placed upon improving teaching and learning although peer observation and the use of student progress and performance data to inform classroom decision-making. 'Teachers watch each other and analyse ... and, slowly, staff attitudes have changed from being self-engrossed and defensive to a professional atmosphere in which teachers are comfortable with observing and supporting each other ...' (Headteacher)

3. Phase 3: Going deeper and wider – sustaining the momentum

As a result of the strategies used in phases 1 and 2 over the previous three-year period, during the next three years the leadership was broadened and its functions reviewed; liaison with community groups increased; students took more owner-ship of their learning through evaluating their progress; staff development and well-being continued to be emphasized; and the horizons for students were widened, with links to schools in other countries. 'She's very good at pacing anything new that comes into school so that staff don't feel overwhelmed ... she's very good at prioritizing ... and everything is brought in for discussion ... so that we all feel as if we matter, that we all count.' (Teacher)

4. Phase 4: Excellence and creativity – everyone a leader

Today, a visitor to the school could be forgiven for appreciating its bright, almost pristine environment. Classrooms are purposeful, the welcome for visitors is genuine, the warmth of relationships is evident and the sense of achievement by staff, students and all connected with the school, palpable. The students seem to be like those in any school in a thriving area of town, city or countryside. It is difficult to believe that many return each evening to homes which are emotion-ally dysfunctional, socially and economically disadvantaged, or that some are involved in crime on a regular basis. Indeed, household income is in the lowest 10 per cent nationally and crime and disorder statistics are in the worst 3 per cent. Pupil mobility is high, with 42 per cent not completing their education pro-gramme in this school, 40 per cent having social services involvement and 35 per cent classified as having 'special educational needs' (SEN). There are 13 different languages spoken and 80 per cent of students are in one parent families. Yet:

> The children want to achieve now. You can feel it ... A few years ago it was quite a struggle. You were up against a lot of negativity from the children ... not despair, but disinterest. And now, because their success is celebrated, they want more of it ... they want to do well for themselves and can see a means of doing it. (Teacher)

Conclusion

The messages for principal educators and policy-makers are clear. First, they need to prepare principals for leading and managing change in schools in a variety of socio-economic settings and in different developmental phases. Second, they need to provide opportunities for principals to develop their knowledge of self, to be clear about their educational values, to further enhance their dispositions towards, and skills in, reflective practice and clarity of values since both are essential to achieving success. Third, principals need knowledge of a wide range of informal and formal learning activities and change contexts and processes so that they can provide these opportunities to others. Fourth, they need to engage principals in situations where they can develop their emotional understandings of self and others and refine their ways of applying these, since relational trust is essential in creating and sustaining conditions for improvement. Fifth, they need to teach the values and practices of, 'layered leadership', as it is a characteristic of the strategic leadership responses of successful principals in all schools.

Reflective Questions

1 What are the qualities, strategies and skills needed by principals if they are to achieve success in managing and leading complex organizations in terms of change and transition?
2 What are the contexts in which principals learn best?
3 How can principals learn emotional understanding?
4 What are the dispositions and strategies which best develop trust and trustworthiness in principals as essential conditions for the enhanced participation of staff and students and the distribution of leadership?
5 What experiences of layered leadership strategies can you identify and how have these contributed to the phasing growth and improvement of your organization?

Further Reading

Day, C. and Leithwood, K. (eds) (2007) *Successful Principal Leadership in Times of Change: International Perspectives*. Dordrecht: Springer.

This book is one of the few which combine both a critical overview of the literature on successful principals with in-country, cross-cultural cases of their work in eight countries. It identifies key themes in leadership values and strategies and highlights the importance of particular values, intra- and interpersonal qualities, diagnostic skills in the effective development of strategies which build and sustain the capacities of teachers and nurturing schools as living systems.

Davies, B. and Brighouse, T. (eds) (2008) *Passionate Leadership in Education*. London: Sage.

In this book, internationally recognized writers on leadership explore what makes leaders passionate about their role and their schools. The contributors show that leadership must move on from 'role' or 'job' towards an energy and commitment for enhancing children's learning and lives. They maintain that passion must be the driving force that moves vision into action. The book is essential for all students on leadership programmes and educational professionals looking to achieve self-improvement and organizational improvement. The book takes the meanings of moral purpose to new levels.

References

Bryk, A.S. and Schneider, B. (2003) *Trust in Schools: A Core Resource for School Improvement*. New York: Sage.

Davies, B. and Brighouse, T. (eds) (2008) *Passionate Leadership in Education*. London: Sage.

Day, C. and Leithwood, K. (eds) (2007) *Successful Principal Leadership in Times of Change: An International Perspective*. Dordrecht: Springer.

Day, C., Harris, A., Hadfield, M., Tolley, H. and Beresford, J. (2000) *Leading Schools in Times of Change: A Multi-perspective Study of Effective Headteachers*. Buckingham: Open University Press.

Day, C., Sammons, P., Harris, A., Hopkins, D., Leithwood, K., Gu, Q., Penlington, C., Mehta, P. and Kington, A. (2007) *The Impact of School Leadership on Pupil Outcomes*. DCSF Interim Report, October.

Day, C., Sammons, P., Harris, A., Hopkins, D., Leithwood, K., Gu, Q., Brown, E., Ahtaridou, E. and Kington, A. (2009) *The Impact of School Leadership on Pupil Outcomes*. Research report, DCFS-RR108. London: Department for Children, Schools and Families.

Day, C., Sammons, P., Harris, A., Hopkins, D., Leithwood, K., Gu, Q., Brown, E. and Antaridou, E. (2010) *Ten Strong Claims For Successful School Leadership in English Schools*. Nottingham: NCSL.

Elmore, R.F. (2004) *School Reform from the Inside Out: Policy, Practice and Performance*. Cambridge, MA: Harvard University Press.

Fris, J. and Lazaridou, A. (2006) An additional way of thinking about organisational life and leadership: the quantum perspective, *Canadian Journal of Educational Administration and Policy*, (48), 5 January: 1–29.

Goodall, J., Day, C., Harris, A., Lindsey, G. and Muijs, D. (2005) *The Impact of Professional Development*. Research report. Nottingham: DfES.

Harris, B. (2007) *Supporting the Emotional Work of School Leaders*. London: Paul Chapman Publishing.

Heifetz, R.A. (1994) *Leadership Without Easy Answers*. Cambridge, MA: Harvard University Press.

Kendall, L., O'Donnell, L., Golden, S., Ridley, K., Machin, S., Rutt, S., et al. (2005) *Excellence in Cities. The National Evaluation of a Policy to Raise Standards in Urban Schools 2000–2003. Research Report 675B*. London: Department for Education and Skills.

Leithwood, K., Day, C., Sammons, P., Harris, A. and Hopkins, D. (2006) *Seven Strong Claims about Successful School Leadership*. Nottingham: National College for School Leadership.

Lodge, C. and Reed, J. (2003) Transforming school improvement now and for the future, *Journal of Educational Change*, 4(1): 45–62.

Möller, J., Eggen, A., Fuglestad, O.L., Langfeldt, G., Preshus, A.-M., Scrøvset, S., Stjernstrøm, E. and Vedøy, G. (2007) Successful leadership based on democratic values, in C. Day and K. Leithwood (eds) *Successful Principal Leadership in Times of Change: An International Perspective*. Dordrecht: Springer.

Robinson, V.M.J. (2007) *School Leadership and Student Outcomes: Identifying What Works and Why*. Australian Council for Educational Leaders, Monograph 41; ACEL Inc. P.O. Box 4368, Winmalee, NSW, Australia.

Senge, P.M. (1990) *The Fifth Discipline*. New York: Currency/Doubleday.

Snowden, D.F. and Boone, M.E. (2007) A leader's framework for decision making, *Harvard Business Review*, November: 69–76.

Thomson, P. (2007) *Whole School Change: A Review of the Literature*. London: Creative Partnerships, Arts Council.

Wheatley, M. (2005) *Finding Our Way: Leadership for an Uncertain Time*. San Francisco, CA: Berrett-Koehler.

Zellermayer, M. and Margolin, I. (2005) Teacher educators' professional learning described through the lens of complexity theory, *Teachers College Record*, 107(6): 1275–304.

CHAPTER 3

How Effective Leaders Reduce Educational Disparities

Russell Bishop

Leaders play a central role in reducing disparities for indigenous and other minoritized peoples. They must have a sound understanding of the theoretical underpinnings of the reform processes so they can inspire a shared vision, model the way forward and, most importantly, challenge the status quo.

This chapter is about the ways that leaders can act to reduce educational disparities for indigenous and other minoritized[1] peoples. Examples will be drawn from Te Kotahitanga,[2] because from our experiences in this large-scale, school reform project, we have come to understand that while classrooms are the most effective initial sites for educational reform (Alton-Lee, 2003; Elmore et al., 1996; Hattie, 1999; 2003), teachers who work in isolation are unlikely to develop and maintain to any significant extent 'new teaching strategies spontaneously and on their own' (Elmore et al., 1996: 7). Therefore, teachers are better able to sustain change when there are 'mechanisms in place at multiple levels of the system to support their efforts' (Coburn, 2003: 6). In other words, teachers are strengthened in their capacity to sustain change if they are supported by a broader systemic focus on reform within the school and at national policy levels (Hattie, 1999). Institutional, organizational and structural changes are necessary to create contexts in which classroom learning can be responded to, supported and enhanced so that student achievement can improve and disparities can be reduced. *It is leaders who drive these changes.* Which raises the question of 'What leaders need to know and do to support teachers in using the pedagogical practices that raise achievement and reduce disparities' (Robinson et al., 2009: 2). This chapter, following Coburn (2003), seeks to address this question by presenting a detailed investigation of the qualities of effective leadership. The framework presented here uses the acronym

GPILSEO where effective leaders establish *goals,* support *pedagogic* change, reform the *institution,* distribute *leadership, spread* the reform, use *evidence* strategically and take *ownership* of the reform.

What effective leaders need to know and do

1. Effective leaders establish and develop specific measurable goals so that progress can be shown, monitored and acted upon

Effective leaders establish explicit academic goals that are 'vital for maintaining a coherent and stable student-centred vision' (McDougall et al., 2007: 53). Robinson (2007: 10) explains that:

> Goal setting works by creating a discrepancy between what is currently happening [and] some desired future state. When people are committed to a goal, this discrepancy is experienced as constructive discontent that motivates goal-relevant behaviour. Goals focus attention and lead to more persistent effort than would otherwise be the case.

Leithwood and Jantzi (2006: 206) argue that people are motivated to set goals and work towards them when individual 'evaluation of present circumstances indicates that it is different from the desired state, when the goals are perceived to be hard but achievable, and when they are short term but understood within the context of longer term and perhaps more important, more obviously valuable purposes'.

For an individual to motivate others, however, the individual must possess a high level of self-efficacy or agency. Leadership, therefore, ought to be based on the assumption that 'the school improvement process must be conceived of as relating to the school, subgroups and individuals simultaneously, yet still leading … to a coordinated, positive set of results' (Lindahl, 2007: 321). For example, effective principals lead individuals and groups as well as institutions (Lindahl, 2007). Principals need to inspire collective efficacy, which means they must see themselves as having a clear sense of purpose. Holloman et al. (2007: 437) argue that a major impediment to implementing large-scale reforms is that '[t]he culture of today's school does not promote permanent fixes. In fact, the cynicism that many educators feel today is a result of years of cyclical changes in programmes and innovations'. Leadership, therefore, begins with a convincing and authoritative introduction to the reform, especially to influential school staff members. The principal sets the school's tone, and the authority vested in the principal makes the office instrumental to reform. Equally, a new principal unconvinced by the reform's objectives or methodologies has considerable power to undermine reform, even where a school's governors direct otherwise.

Leadership, in what the Education Review Office (2002) calls good practice schools for Māori, involves a commitment to improving Māori achievement that is driven by a vision that is shared by New Zealand's governors, principal and all teachers. In this context it is incumbent upon school leadership to (a) understand what is being promoted by reform initiatives, and (b) be simultaneously responsive and proactive in promoting and supporting the reform through institutional and structural change.

Leadership needs to be proactively directed towards a common goal of establishing the school as a high-performing institution where high levels of student achievement and learning are normalized. This means that '[i]f goals are to function as influential co-ordinating mechanisms, they need to be embedded in school and classroom routines and procedures' (Robinson, 2007: 9–10). Leaders of high-achieving schools are more likely to see that their goals and expectations are well understood and to see that academic achievement is recognized and conveyed to the community. Staff consensus about goals is more likely to characterize high-performing schools (2007: 10). Goals need to be specific, because specificity allows self-regulation: 'it's possible to judge progress and thus adjust one's performance … Goal-setting increases performance and learning' (2007: 11).

In Te Kotahitanga, leaders of the educational reform initiative, who are in-school professional development facilitators, themselves are supported by external professional developers to set, and support teachers to set, specific goals rather than unspecified changes or developments. This is because 'the potency of leadership for increasing student achievement hinges on the specific classroom practices which leaders stimulate, encourage and promote' (Leithwood and Jantzi, 2006: 223). Achieving these goals requires leadership that looks beyond short-term solutions to immediate problems: a mixture of long-term and short-term goals being necessary. Schmoker (1999) promotes the setting of short-term goals as being motivational, but Hargreaves and Fink (2006) warn that setting short-term goals may promote the practice of teaching so that students can pass the next test. Focusing on long-term learning gains is necessary and will focus teaching activities on sustainable long-term change designed to eliminate barriers to achievement. Short-term goals are, however, necessary to monitor progress towards the long-term goals.

Goal setting is encouraged at a number of levels in Te Kotahitanga: school wide, among groups and individual teachers, and within classrooms. Boards of trustees, the schools' governance body and principals are supported to set specific measurable goals for those students not currently being served well by the school. Teachers are supported to set individual goals in feedback sessions following formal observations in their classrooms, and group goals during collaborative co-construction meetings. Students are supported to set goals based on examinations of their performance.

2. Effective leaders promote and support pedagogic reform

Effective leadership for sustainable educational reform promotes and is responsive to the development and implementation of pedagogic relationships and interactions in the classrooms that promote the reduction of educational disparities through improvements in student learning and achievement. Effective leaders do this by providing and/or supporting the means/process of professional learning for teachers that allows the embedding of the conceptual depth of the reform into the theorizing and practice of classroom teachers, principals and national

policy-makers: teachers' and leaders' conceptual depth of the theoretical principles that underlie the reform being a major indicator of sustainability. In other
words, teachers and school leaders who have a deep understanding of the underlying theories and principles and who can implement appropriate practices are
better able to respond flexibly to new demands and changing contexts in ways
that will sustain and perhaps deepen the reform over time (Robinson et al.,
2009; Timperley et al., 2007). Reform without depth of understanding will trivi-
alize the initiative, and teachers and schools will soon revert to old explanations
and practices. Two of the dimensions of leadership identified by Robinson et al.
(2009) support this understanding. The first is that which involves leadership of
effective teaching, including how to improve and evaluate it, along with skills in
developing collegial discussions on instructional matters (2009). Their empirical
analysis shows this dimension to have a moderate impact on student outcomes.
It includes such activities as: leaders being actively involved in collegial discussions on how teaching practice affects student achievement; an active oversight
and coordination of the teaching programme; involvement in teacher observation and feedback; leading staff to systematically monitor student progress to
inform their ongoing teaching programme. Coupled with this dimension is leaders'
focus on promoting and participating in teacher learning and development. This
dimension includes actions such as leaders using their own knowledge to help
staff solve teaching problems, and working directly with teachers or subject
department heads to plan, coordinate and evaluate the impact of teachers and
teaching on student learning and achievement through the monitoring of student
progress in relation to what is being taught and how it is being taught. The
evidence gathered by Robinson et al. (2009: ix) showed that: 'leaders who are
actively involved in professional learning gain a deeper appreciation of what
teachers require to achieve and sustain improvements in student learning,
which enables them to discuss the changes with teachers and support them in
making appropriate adjustments to class organisation, resourcing and assessment
procedures'. In short, the more leaders act in an instructional or pedagogic manner
where they focus their relationships, their work and their learning on the core
business of teaching and learning, the greater their influence on student outcomes will be.

The importance of learning relationships

As Robinson et al. (2009: 8) suggest, creating dichotomies in leadership styles can
promote the notion that there is a distinction between tasks and relationships;
that is, between 'leading through progressing tasks and leading through relationships and people'. There is also a danger that we talk about there being a sequence
of, first, developing relationships, then developing tasks; in other words, get the
relationship right then pursue the common task, the educational challenges, the goal
setting and suchlike. In contrast, Robinson et al. argue that 'relationship skills are
embedded in every dimension' 2009: 8). In goal setting, for example, 'effective
leadership involves not only determining the goal content (task focus), but doing
so in a manner that enables staff to understand and become committed to the

goal [relationship focus]' (2009: 8). So whether we are focusing at the level of the classroom, school or system, relationships are part and parcel of everyday activities that seek to improve student outcomes.

At the classroom level we learnt from detailed interviews with 350 Māori students in 2005 and 2006 that the teaching approaches they preferred, and, indeed, within which they could achieve, were not a matter of teachers being either task or relationship oriented, but both simultaneously (Bishop et al., 2007). These Māori students clearly understood that when both were happening at the same time they were able to engage effectively with learning and see their achievement levels improve. They were able to describe a range of scenarios. The first was when a teacher was task oriented but did not clearly show that they cared for the learning of their students, learning did not occur. Second, if the teacher demonstrably cared for the learning of the students but was unable to engage them in meaningful learning interactions, again they were unable to learn. It was only when their teachers were task *and* relationship oriented simultaneously, that they were able to demonstrate on a daily basis that they cared for the learning of their students, set high expectations for performance and classroom management (including their own subject content knowledge), as well as being able to use a range of discursive interactions and strategies, including formative assessment, that Māori students knew they were going to learn and achieve. One student commented: 'She's dedicated to what we do in our class. I think it's just her passion, that she likes seeing kids achieving instead of failing. Feels cool, that we've got someone who's gonna help us get through school' (School 2).

Fullan (2003) notes that this task–relationship intersection is based on what Bryk and Schneider (2002) term 'relational trust', which their research showed was fundamental to improved student achievement. Just as at the classroom level, relational trust is also fundamental to creating an effective school culture. Robinson et al. (2009: xv) suggest that practical steps for developing relational trust include 'establishing norms of integrity, showing personal regard for staff, parents and students; demonstrating role competence and personal integrity through modelling appropriate behaviour, following-through when expectations are not met, demonstrating consistency between talk and action, and challenging dysfunctional attitudes and behaviours'.

Working with educational reform for indigenous students would also suggest adding those qualities created in classrooms and across schools where teachers and leaders create learning relationships wherein learners' culturally generated sense-making processes are used and developed so that they may successfully participate in problem-solving and decision-making interactions. Such relationships must promote the knowledge, learning styles and sense-making processes of the participants as 'acceptable' or 'legitimate'. Leaders should interact with others in such a way that new knowledge is co-created within contexts where all can safely bring what they know and who they are to the learning relationship; and where what participants know, who they are and how they know what they know form the foundations of interaction patterns. In short, where culture counts (Bishop and Glynn, 1999).

Teachers need opportunities in which to learn new ways to teach. One forum for these opportunities is within-school professional learning communities. Robinson and Timperley (2007), referencing Bolam et al. (2005) however, warn that there is little evidence that professional learning communities have a strong impact on student outcomes unless they promote 'the type of teacher learning that makes a difference to their students' through 'an intensive focus on the relationship between what the teacher had taught and what the students had learned' (2007: 11). In other words, leaders focus 'the group on how to move beyond analysis of the data to identifying specific teaching practices to help a particular student or group of students' (Robinson and Timperley, 2007: 12). In this role leaders are facilitators of student learning rather than leaders of collegial discussions.

In Te Kotahitanga, formal 'co-construction' meetings, facilitated by in-school professional developers, are regularly organized for groups of teachers from a range of subject areas who teach a common group of students. The focus on these meetings is not on better subject transmission, but rather on leaders not only supplying or demonstrating how teachers can obtain evidence of student participation and learning, but also lead collaborative problem-solving and decision-making discussions about the relationship between teaching practice and student outcomes based on collaborative analysis of this evidence. As one teacher commented during one such meeting. 'The test results show a significant improvement. The kids are asking more questions, better questions, higher level questions, questions that indicate they're engaged in the topic so there is a certain amount of understanding. You know those kinds of things. They're smiling.' A second: 'We identified a couple of base strategies ... we have learnt as a group that they respond well to lots of positive encouragement ... one of the goals was to continue to increase the positive encouragement we give these kids and not to ignore them'. A third commented: 'so I kept pushing it along seeing they were buying into what we were doing and the cognitive level of the lesson was right at the upper limit ... which was good. It extended me, I was having to be better prepared and be ready for anything that was thrown at me' (Bishop et al., 2007).

3. Effective Leaders redesign the institutional and organizational framework

Effective leadership needs to strategically promote and align organizational and structural changes so as to support and embed pedagogic changes within the everyday practices of the school. This will include changing timetables, meeting times and agendas, staff recruitment procedures, staff promotion criteria, school policies on streaming, discipline and assessment practices, the provision of support and space for in-school professional development staff, the reshaping of the role of the heads of departments, and the reshaping of the composition of the senior management team to include senior professional developers, among others.

New Zealand schools are self-managing. Responsibility for operational decisions, including the provision of professional learning opportunities for the staff of the school, has been devolved to the governance of boards of trustees. This includes the provision and allocation of funds from schools' budgets for the ongoing provision of professional learning opportunities for staff. The prioritizing of the allocation of a significant amount of funding that could be directed towards sustaining the reform, once the externally generated support and funding are withdrawn, is thus in the hands of New Zealand schools.

These conditions mean that, for Te Kotahitanga and similar reforms, once the external support has been withdrawn from the school, the professional development cycle needs to be maintained within the schools, with its attendant staffing and organizational support. For leaders, this means they will need to (re)prioritize and rationalize resource expenditure. For some this will involve conflict as previous resource allocations are challenged, but alignment of resource allocation to the visions and goals of the school is necessary, and unless resource procurement and allocation are strategically handled, the reform will face great challenges and will probably remain as a 'project' on the periphery of the school's activities rather than being centralized, as is necessary for success.

Another example of structural changes is shown where one large school, prior to the implementation of Te Kotahitanga, had a large number of different initiatives being implemented. Three years after the implementation of Te Kotahitanga, the senior management team of this school were working to reduce these to four. In addition, these four had to fit in with the strategic goals set by the school for the reduction of educational disparities within the school through the improvement of Māori students' educational achievement. As their principal explained, one of the main tasks she faced was 'sticking to the knitting'. By this she meant, in Fullan's (2008) terms, the Ministry of Education has 'initiative-itis'; that is, the 'tendency to launch an endless stream of disconnected innovations that no one could possibly manage' (2008: 1). Her concern with the plethora of new projects promulgated by the Ministry is that they need to be worthy:

A lot of time is spent evaluating new initiatives. Staff are very busy so we can't afford to just get involved into any new initiative. We are to look carefully at any new initiative to see how it fits into our school's philosophy and goals. Something new has to rate. We have a ruler now as [to] what is an effective programme and we use that ... Any new initiative has to match up to Te Kotahitanga. (Principal, School 1)

4. Effective leaders spread the reform

Effective leadership that aims to sustain an educational reform needs to develop a means to spread the reform so that parents, *whānau* and community are engaged in a way that addresses their aspirations for the education of their children. Through these actions we would expect to see a reconnection of parents and families with the educational advancement of their children, and an enormous change in the life chances and lifestyles of those people currently underserved by the education system. Communicating the intentions of the reform and signalling that the school is prepared to be accountable to the community are necessary steps in promoting effective relationships with the community. One way this is done in Te Kotahitanga is for the schools to hold annual staff induction workshops at local *marae*, hosted by local Māori families. At these events there are opportunities for the leaders, both formally and informally, to inform the local community, in a very convivial setting, of their intentions to develop and/or persist with the goal of raising the achievement of their children.

Communication of the outcomes of the reform in terms of raised student achievement is also important on a regular basis. Again, in Te Kotahitanga, we find that when students begin to achieve well at school, parents who have previously been absent from parent–teacher report meetings for example, become very visible. This visibility then begins to be seen in other activities of the school's life. Success attracts success. Principals and other school leaders can help the wider school community to understand the changes that are needed to strengthen teaching and learning.

Leaders need to spread its goals and vision to others, within and outside the school, so as to align the new norms within the school, within the norms of supporting institutions, and within communities in association with the school. Holloman et al. (2007) propose a 'purpose-driven' leadership model, which requires an organization to 'define its purpose, maintain integrity ... prevent burnout and sustain vitality' (2007: 438). The model supposes a school culture in which there is constant reflection on why certain methodologies are favoured over others. Leithwood and Riehl (2003) suggest that educational improvement often means making personal changes to the way responses have been undertaken in the past, and in order to achieve this, effective principals must respect staff and show they are concerned for their feelings. Therefore, as Bolman and Deal (2003) note, effective leaders need to learn how to cope with power and conflict, and how to build coalitions, hone their political skills and deal with internal and external politics.

A questioning culture is one that will best support such developments. It is a way of challenging people more inclined to being negative about a reform to refocus their attention on constructive criticism that 'could more clearly define the purpose of the school'. In turn, refocusing resistance can foster 'purposeful dialogue' (Holloman et al., 2007: 438). However, these ideas presuppose reform that is theoretically well-informed and supported by valid empirical data. Robinson (2007) considers that '[p]eople cannot adapt descriptions of effective practice to their own contexts unless they understand the theoretical principles that explain why they work and under what conditions'. Further, '[i]t is the combination of description, practical example and theoretical explanation that makes for powerful professional learning' (2007: 5). To this end, leaders are reliant on robust evidence to support the direction of the reform initiative (see below). This means that any attempts to weaken the connection between research and practice can be expected to seriously compromise school leaders' capacity to support sustainable reform. Whatever the case, it is important that as many teachers as possible are included in the reform, because 'effective professional development is likely to involve teachers investigating pedagogy and analysing data within their own settings' (Alton-Lee, 2004: 10), and because 'quality of teaching is critical to ... a shift' in student achievement (2004: 4).

5. Effective leaders develop the capacity of people and systems to identify, gather and use evidence

Fundamental to Collins's (2001) study of what moves an organization from 'good' to 'great' is the understanding that effective leaders work continuously to select the right people, and to support and develop them. For example, Te Kotahitanga professional development facilitators, as leaders of professional learning within their respective schools, develop the capacity of teachers to identify and continually question their discursive positioning and theories of action by providing professional learning opportunities that use alternative theories, evidence and vicarious experiences. These leaders also provide the necessary resources and tools for teachers to be able to engage effectively with the reform goals and processes.

Robinson et al. (2009) note that leaders of sustainable educational reform are able to reshape the situation in which they work so that others can learn to do their job strategically by selecting, developing and using tools that will assist their own learning and promote student learning. They found that these tools include physical qualities such as classroom furniture and smart whiteboards. However, of primary importance is what they termed 'smart tools', which include software for student management systems to provide teachers with differentiated data about student attendance and achievement, formative assessment packages such as asTTle (assessment tools for teaching and learning) and PAT (Progressive Achievement Tests) school's strategic plans, policy documents, and the means of reporting student progress to the students, their families and the community.

Leaders also support the use of reform-specific smart tools such as those that enable teachers to reflect critically on their practice and theorize in such a way as to bring about changes in practice. One such example from Te Kotahitanga is the PSIRPEG model, which, following the intervention cycle of observations, feedback, co-construction and shadow coaching, affords teachers the opportunity to *plan* for their next learning activities, choose appropriate *strategies*, identify appropriate *interactions*, identify the *relationships* that are likely to develop the *positionings* that will be supported, and the positive student *experiences* that will lead to reaching the *goals* of improved student achievement.

As Te Kotahitanga grows and develops in each school, systemic and institutional developments are necessary to support the changes taking place in the classroom. An area that needs to be developed is that of accurately measuring student attendance data, stand-downs, suspensions, early-leaving exemptions, retention rates and achievement data. There are two reasons for this. First, it allows teachers the opportunity to reflect collaboratively on these data to inform their ongoing practice. Second, they can use the same data for summative purposes to identify if there is a relationship between the implementation of the educational reform in question and positive changes in student participation and achievement. In order for these objectives to be met, it is important that project schools are able to undertake the task of data gathering and processing in real time. To do so they will need to continue to develop the use of electronic student management systems so that the schools can use the data for formative purposes in collaborative settings, and then aggregate the data for summative purposes.

Probably more important than the systems for providing the evidence on the basis of which teachers can collaboratively make practice-changing decisions is the need for capacity building, in the sense of leaders of the reform providing professional learning opportunities for teachers to learn how to both identify and gather appropriate evidence for learning, and to be able to use evidence of student learning to ascertain where and how to modify their classroom practice through the ongoing provision of appropriate and responsive professional learning opportunities.

6. Effective leaders take ownership of the project

Effective leadership that aims to sustain an educational reform takes ownership of the reform. The first characteristic of ownership is a leader taking responsibility for the performance of students who are currently not benefiting from their school/system. One principal described how their school could have continued along the path they were travelling, but they were not satisfied that they were addressing the needs of all their students:

> Twenty per cent of our students are Māori. We had some key issues with Māori achievement. We were in that absolutely luxurious position where we could have sat back and said, 'This isn't about us. We are doing OK as a school. We have no problems.' We have a significant number of Māori students, and their future was in our hands and we have not been meeting their needs. We had been looking for the way to make a difference and had tried several things but we just weren't making the breakthrough that we wanted.

This action also involves careful disaggregation of data to identify the learning outcomes of specific groups of students and the implementation of processes to ensure this information is disseminated and acted upon. To do so, leaders must work towards building a school culture that focuses on an ongoing reduction in educational disparities through the ongoing improvement of student learning and outcomes. To ensure *this* happens in an ongoing way, leaders must take responsibility for ensuring that the integrity of the means of producing increased achievement gains for the target students (such as the cycle and the facilitation teams in the Te Kotahitanga project) is not jeopardised by conflicting and competing interests and agendas.

Leaders also need to take responsibility for building capacity among students, staff and other leaders so that they are able to take responsibility for student outcomes, rather than focusing solely on accountability systems. This aspect of leadership is often at odds with national policies that limit the time available to develop support for the development of in-school capacity. Nevertheless, persistence in pursuit of the goals of reducing disparities is the hallmark of effective leadership. The unrelenting pursuit of goals that will also involve leaders in creating classrooms, a school culture and education systems where new situations are addressed from an in-depth understanding of the reform's aims and approaches rather than from past practice is crucial. Past practices have led us to a situation of educational disparities being based on ethnic lines. Effective leaders express their dissatisfaction with this situation and are prepared to own the consequences of promoting and sustaining educational reforms to reduce disparities through targeting and raising the achievement of students who are currently not well served by the education system.

Conclusion

On the one hand, leading school reform is difficult, basically because '[t]he complexity of interacting contextual variables … is enormous' (Lindahl, 2007: 328). On the other hand, a great deal is known about the conditions that are necessary to support student learning, and this is a good starting point. Among the keys to sustainable reform is leadership that is cognizant of these conditions, and is willing to support the purpose of all school routines, procedures and practices and to shape a school culture centred on reform.

The fundamental changes that are needed in classroom relationships and interactions and in the culture of schools, through the institutionalization of schools as professional learning communities focused on improving student learning, depends on all leaders having a sound understanding of the theoretical underpinning of the reform while simultaneously being responsive and proactive about supporting and promoting reform processes and goals. To this end, principals' leadership is essential. However, principals' leadership to the exclusion of others is ineffective; leadership needs to be distributed. Principals, therefore, in Kouzes and Posner's (2002) terms, need to inspire a shared vision, model the way forward, enable others to act, and challenge the status quo.

Overall, a measure of the effectiveness of leadership will be seen in the actions and beliefs of teachers. Ineffectively-led schools foster and support teachers who are likely 'to attribute student achievement to global factors or student traits, such as experience and knowledge, socioeconomic conditions, inexperience with the English language, academic ability, lack of readiness and inadequate parental involvement' (McDougal et al., 2007: 74). Effectively-led schools are characterized by teachers who attribute 'student achievement toward specific, teacher-implemented, instructional actions and planning processes, and away from teacher and student traits, and non-instructional explanations' (2007: 74). In other words, effective leaders support and foster committed, agentic educators.

Reflective Questions

1 In reducing disparities for indigenous and other minoritized peoples in schools, systemic and institutional developments are necessary to support the changes taking place in the classroom. An area that needs to be developed is that of accurately measuring

student attendance data, stand-downs, suspensions, early-leaving exemptions, retention rates and achievement data. What measures, systems and processes are you involved in, that assist you to become more reflective and aware of the current reality relating to student engagement, retention and learning?

2 Challenging the status quo is an important aspect of educational leadership. In what ways do you question, challenge and support your colleagues in exploring different ways of working to reduce disparities for indigenous and other minoritized peoples.

Further Reading

Elmore, R. (2004) *School Reform from the Inside Out: Policy, Practice and Performance.* Cambridge, MA: Harvard Education Press.

This book provides a strong theoretical and research base about many of the ideas that are in this chapter. What is crucial is that structural reform works most effectively when the reform creates conditions where changes in practice lead to changes in structure, and where school institutions, structures and organizations evolve in a responsive, flexible manner so as to be supportive of classroom reform. Indeed, the main finding from this detailed analysis of the relationship between structure and pedagogy was that 'changing structure did not change practice, it only relabeled existing practices with new names. The schools that succeed in changing practice are those that start with the practice and modify school structures to accommodate to it' (Elmore, 2004: 4).

Ladson-Billings, G. (2006) From the achievement gap to the education debt: understanding achievement in US schools, *Educational Researcher*, 35(7): 3–12.

This article positions the argument about why we need to address educational disparities within an historical time frame. Using the notion of the national debt as a metaphor, Ladson-Billings (2006) suggests that it is the *annual accumulation* of achievement gaps, as has been seen in New Zealand since educational disparities were first identified in the Hunn report in 1960, that needs to be addressed rather than any one gap. By this she means that just as the accumulation of annual fiscal deficits produces an economic debt, so the accumulation of achievement gaps over time has produced an education debt; a debt the education system owes to Māori children who have been short-changed by the education system for generations. In other words, it is the long-term inter-generational effects of the legacies of an education system that is oriented to the interests of the dominant group that has created this education debt.

Notes

1 'Minoritized' is a term used in Shields et al. (2005) to refer to a people who have been ascribed characteristics of a minority. To be minoritized one does not need to be in the numerical minority, only to be treated as if one's position and perspective are of less worth; to be silenced or marginalized. Hence, for example, in schools on the Navajo reservation with over 95 per cent of the population being Navajo, or in Bedouin schools, we find characteristics of the students similar to those we may find among Māori in mainstream schools in which they are actually in the numerical minority.

2 Te Kotahitanga is a large-scale, theory-based educational reform, funded by the New Zealand government which aims at reducing educational disparities for indigenous students. It is currently being implemented in 50 secondary schools in New Zealand.

Parts of this chapter are reproduced with permission from Bishop, R., O'Sullivan, D., Berryman, M. (2010) *Scaling Up Education Reform: Addressing the Politics of Disparity*, Wellington: NZCER Press.

References

Alton-Lee, A. (2003) *Quality Teaching for Diverse Students in Schooling: Best Evidence Synthesis*. Wellington: Ministry of Education.

Alton-Lee, A. (2004) *Using Best Evidence Syntheses to Assist in Making a Bigger Difference for Diverse Learners*. Wellington: Ministry of Education.

Bishop, R. and Glynn, T. (1999) *Culture Counts: Changing Power Relations in Education*. Palmerston North: Dunmore Press.

Bishop, R., Berryman, M., Cavanagh, T. and Teddy, L. (2007) *Te Kotahitanga Phase 3 Whanaungatanga: Establishing a Culturally Responsive Pedagogy of Relations in Mainstream Secondary School Classrooms*. Wellington: Ministry of Education.

Bolman, L.G. and Deal, T.E. (2003) *Reframing Organizations' Artistry, Choice and Leadership*. 3rd edn. San Francisco, CA: Jossey-Bass.

Bryk, A. and Schneider, B. (2002) *Trust in Schools: A Core Resource for Improvement*. New York: Russell Sage Foundation.

Coburn, C. (2003) Rethinking scale: moving beyond numbers to deep and lasting change, *Educational Researcher*, 32(6): 3–12.

Collins, J. (2001) *Good to Great: Why Some Companies Make the Leap and Others Don't*. New York: Harper Business.

Education Review Office (2002) *Māori Students: Schools Making a Difference*. Wellington: Education Review Office.

Elmore, R. (2004) *School Reform from Inside Out: Policy, Practice and Performance*. Cambridge, MA: Harvard Education Press.

Elmore, R., Peterson, P. and McCarthey, S. (1996) *Restructuring in the Classroom: Teaching, Learning, and School Organization*. San Francisco, CA: Jossey-Bass.

Fullan, M. (2003) *The Moral Imperative of School Leadership*. Thousand Oaks, CA: Corwin Press.

Fullan, M. (2008) *The Six Secrets of Change: How Leaders Survive and Thrive*. San Francisco, CA: Jossey-Bass.

Hargreaves, A. and Fink, D. (2006) *Sustainable Leadership*. San Francisco, CA: Jossey-Bass.

Hattie, J. (1999) Influences on student learning, professorial inaugural lecture, University of Auckland, Auckland, August.

Hattie, J. (2003) New Zealand education snapshot: with specific reference to the years 1–13, paper presented at the Knowledge Wave 2003, Leadership Forum, Auckland, February.

Holloman, H., Rouse, W. and Farrington, V. (2007) Purpose-driven leadership: defining, defending and sustaining a school's purpose, *International Journal of Leadership in Education: Theory and Practice*, 10(4): 437–43.

Kouzes, M. and Posner, B. (2002) *The Leadership Challenge*. San Francisco, CA: Jossey-Bass.

Ladson-Billings, G. (2006) From the achievement gap to the education debt: understanding achievement in US schools, *Educational Researcher*, 35(7): 3–12.

Leithwood, K. and Jantzi, D. (2006) Transformational school leadership for large-scale reform: Effects on students, teachers and their classroom practices, *School Effectiveness and School Improvement*, 17(2): 201–27.

Leithwood, K.A. and Riehl, C. (2003) What do we already know about successful school leadership? Paper presented at the annual meeting of the American Educational Research Association, Chicago, April.

Lindahl, R. (2007) Why is leading school improvement such a difficult process?, *School Leadership and Management*, 27(4): 319–32.

McDougal, D., Saunders, W. and Goldenberg, C. (2007) Inside the black box of school reform: explaining the how and why of change at getting results in schools, *International Journal of Disability, Development and Education*, 54(1): 51–89.

Robinson, V. (2007) *School Leadership and Student Outcomes: What Works and Why*. Monograph 41, ACEL Monograph Series. Wimmalee, SA: ACEL.

Robinson, V. and Timperley, H. (2007) The leadership of the improvement of teaching and learning: lessons from initiatives with positive outcomes for students, *Australian Journal of Education*, 51(3): 247–62.

Robinson, V., Hohepa, M. and Lloyd, C. (2009) *School Leadership and Student Outcome: Identifying What Works and Why: A Best Evidence Synthesis Iteration*. Wellington: Ministry of Education.

Schmoker, M.J. (1999) *'Results': The Key to Continuous School Improvement*. Alexandria, VA: Association for Supervision and Curriculum Development.

Shields, C.M., Bishop, R. and Mazawi, A.E. (2005) *Pathologizing Practices: The Impact of Deficit Thinking on Education*. New York: Peter Lang.

Timperley, H., Wilson, A., Barrar, H. and Fung, I. (2007) *Teacher Professional Learning and Development: Best Evidence Synthesis Iteration (BES)*. Wellington: Ministry of Education.

CHAPTER 4

Leadership and Student Learning: What Works and How

Kenneth Leithwood

This chapter brings together two lines of recent research in response to the two most crucial questions now facing leaders, leadership researchers and policy-makers who depend on successful leadership to meet their goals for school reform: 'How does leadership improve student learning?' and 'Which leadership practices account for that improvement?'

This chapter synthesizes two recent lines of inquiry in which my colleagues and I have been engaged as a response to the most crucial question currently facing school leaders, leadership researchers and policy-makers who depend on good leadership to achieve their reform goals. This question is about how successful leadership improves student learning and what it is that successful leaders do to accomplish that goal. The first section of the chapter addresses primarily the 'how' part of the question, while the second part of the chapter is about 'what'.

Figure 4.1 forecasts the approach taken to answer both parts of the question. The far left variable in the figure is a placeholder for the chapter's response to *what* leadership practices nurture improved student learning, while the variables and relationship in the remainder of the figure summarize the chapter's response to *how* successful leadership practices are connected to the experiences and eventually the learning of students.

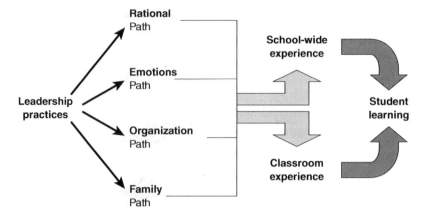

Figure 4.1   Leadership and student learning

How leadership influences student learning

My colleagues and I recently outlined a practically useful, metaphorical conception of how leaders influence student learning (Leithwood et al., in press). This conception synthesizes what is, by now, a substantial amount of evidence, but evidence that has been hard to access and use by practising school leaders because it lacked coherent organization. Our contribution to this need for greater coherence rests on two fundamental assumptions about school leadership. First, such leadership is about the exercise of influence and, second, the effects of such influence on student learning are mostly indirect. Premised on these two assumptions, we identify four distinct paths along which the influence of successful leadership practices flow in order to improve student learning. As Figure 4.1 indicates, these are the rational, emotional, organizational, and family paths.

Each path is populated by distinctly different sets of variables or conditions, each having a more or less direct impact on students' experiences. Such variables might include those relating to school culture, teachers' practices, teachers' emotional states, or parents' attitudes. Selecting the most promising of these variables and improving their status are two of the three central challenges facing leaders intending to improve learning in their schools. As the status of variables on each path improves, through influences from leaders and other sources, the quality of students' school and classroom experiences are enriched, resulting in greater learning. Since exercising leadership influence along one path alone, or just one path at a time, has rarely resulted in demonstrable gains for students, alignment of leadership influence across paths is the third leadership challenge.

Selection and improvement of variables, the first two leadership challenges, are addressed in the next four sections of this chapter, each section focusing on one path. Using the results of recent research, some of the most powerful variables located on each path are identified. One or two of these variables are explored in more detail; evidence of their impact on students is summarized. Alignment of leadership influence across paths is taken up in the fifth section. Hattie's (2009) recent and remarkably comprehensive synthesis of meta-analyses is frequently used to estimate the impact on student learning of selected variables found on three of the four paths.

The rational path

Variables on the rational path are rooted in the knowledge and skills of school staffs about curriculum, teaching and learning. In general, exercising a positive influence on these variables calls on school leaders' knowledge about the 'technical core' of schooling, their problem-solving capacities (Robinson, in press) and their knowledge of relevant leadership practices.

The rational path includes both classroom- and school-level variables. Since there is now a considerable amount of evidence available about the effects on student learning of many such variables, school leaders are able to prioritize for their attention, those known to have the greatest chance of improving their students' learning. In the classroom, Hattie's (2009) synthesis of evidence implies that school leaders carefully consider the value of focusing their efforts on improving, for example, the extent to which teachers are providing students with immediate and informative feedback, teachers' use of reciprocal teaching strategies, teacher–student relations, and the management of classrooms. Effects of these variables on student learning are among the highest reported for all classroom-level variables, whereas some variables currently the focus of considerable effort by school leaders have much less demonstrable impact (for example, individualized instruction).

The emotional path

The rational and emotional paths are much more tightly connected than many leaders believe. Considerable evidence indicates, for example, that emotions direct cognition: they structure perception, direct attention, give preferential access to certain memories, and bias judgement in ways that help individuals respond productively to their environments (Oatley et al., 2006). Exercising influence on variables located along the emotional path depends fundamentally on leaders' social appraisal skills (Zaccaro et al., 2004) or emotional intelligence (Goleman, 2006).

A recent review of more than 90 empirical studies of teacher emotions and their consequences for classroom practice and student learning (Leithwood, 2006; Leithwood and Beatty, 2007) pointed to a large handful of teacher emotions with significant effects on teaching and learning including job satisfaction, organizational commitment, morale, stress/burnout, engagement in the school or profession, and teacher trust in colleagues, parents and students.

The organizational path

Structures, culture, policies and standard operation procedures are the types of variables to be influenced on the organizational path. Collectively, they constitute teachers' working conditions which, in turn, have a powerful influence on teachers' emotions (Leithwood, 2006). These variables constitute both the school's infrastructure and a large proportion of its collective memory.

Hattie's (2009) synthesis of evidence identifies more than a dozen variables located on the organizational path. Some can be found in the classroom (for example, class size, ability groupings), some are school-wide (for example, school size, multi-grade/age classes, retention policies); many are typically controlled by agencies outside the school (for example, school funding, summer school).

The family path

It is often claimed that improving student learning is all about improving 'instruction' (Nelson and Sassi, 2005; Stein and Nelson, 2003). While improving instruction is both important and necessary work in many schools, this claim, by itself, ignores all of the powerful variables found on both the emotional and organizational paths described above. Even more critically, this claim seems to dismiss factors accounting for as much as 50 per cent of the variation in student achievement across schools (for example, Kyriakides and Creemers, 2008). These are variables located on the family path. Since best estimates suggest that everything schools do within their walls accounts for about 20 per cent of the variation in students' achievement (for example, Creemers and Reetzigt, 1996), influencing variables on the family path is a 'high leverage' option for school leaders.

Treating as many variables as possible on the family path as alterable rather than given was considered to be the new work of leaders more than 15 years ago (Goldring and Rallis, 1993). By now, there is considerable evidence about what these variables might be. For example, Hattie's (2009) synthesis of evidence points to seven family-related variables with widely varying but significant effects on learning. At least three of these variables are open to influence from the school, including home environment, parent involvement in school and visits to the home by school personnel.

Alignment of leadership influence across paths

While variables associated with each of the four paths are distinct, they also interact with variables on the other paths; the previous account of variables on several paths pointed to several examples of such interaction. Typically, failure to take such interaction into account severely limits school leaders' influence. This means, for example, that if a school leader decides to improve the status of a school's academic press (a variable on the rational path), she will also need to consider what her teachers' feelings will be, in response (for example, effects on their sense of efficacy).

The need for alignment across paths seems to hugely complicate leaders' work. But picking only one or two powerful variables on a path, and planning for the most likely interactions makes the leadership task much more manageable. This way of thinking about the leadership task, however, does add weight to the argument that leaders' success will typically depend on devoting one's attention to a small number of priorities.

Leadership practices influencing variables on the rational path: improving teachers' pedagogy

This section of the chapter is about leadership practices likely to be useful in improving one key variable on the rational path, teachers' pedagogy, the most obvious and arguably the most powerful variable on this path. Evidence for this section was provided by a much larger research project about leadership and student learning (Leithwood et al., 2004; Louis et al., 2009).[1] This evidence consists of the insights of principals and teachers, similar to earlier strands of leadership research in schools which have generated many useful insights (for example, Blasé and Blasé, 1998).

Starting with the practices used by most successful leaders

Much of the success of school leaders in building school organizations which make significantly greater-than-expected contributions to student learning depends on how well these leaders interact with the specific social and organizational contexts in which they find themselves (for example, Judge et al., 2009). Nevertheless, evidence from district, school, and many non-education organizations points to four broad categories of leadership practices used by successful leaders in many different contexts, but enacted in ways that are quite sensitive to those contexts (Leithwood and Riehl, 2005; Leithwood et al., 2006). These broad leadership categories include: setting directions, developing people, redesigning the organization, and managing the instructional programme. Each of these four categories includes from three to five specific practices,[2] many of which also find support in the comprehensive synthesis of evidence provided by Robinson and her colleagues (2008).

The study reported in this section used the four core categories of successful leadership practices (described below) as a point of departure. The study aimed to determine the extent to which leadership practices identified by principals and teachers as positive influences on classroom pedagogy were encompassed by the four categories, to better understand their enactment for such purposes and to extend or modify the categories as needed. This study also inquired about differences in the value attributed to the four categories of practices by teachers varying in their own pedagogical expertise and by school level (elementary, middle, secondary).

Setting directions

This category of practices carries the bulk of the effort to motivate leaders' colleagues. It is about the establishment of what Fullan (2003) and others call 'moral purpose', a basic stimulant for one's work. Most theories of motivation argue that people are motivated to accomplish personally important goals for themselves.[3] Four more specific sets of practices are included in this category, all of which are aimed at bringing a focus to both the individual and collective work of staff in the school or district. Done skillfully, these practices are one of the main sources of motivation and inspiration for the work of staff. These more specific practices include building a shared vision, fostering the acceptance of group goals, creating high performance expectations, and communicating the direction.

Developing people

Three sets of practices in this category also make significant contributions to motivation. But their primary aim is capacity building, not only in terms of the knowledge and skills staff need to accomplish organizational goals, but also in terms of the disposition to persist in applying the knowledge and skills. Individual teacher efficacy is arguably the most critically necessary disposition, and it is a third source of motivation in Bandura's (1986) model. People are motivated by what they are good at. And mastery experiences, according to Bandura, are the most powerful sources of efficacy. So building capacity leading to a sense of mastery is highly motivational, as well.

Those more specific core leadership practices aimed at developing people include providing individualized support/consideration, intellectual stimulation, and modelling appropriate values and practices. This set of practices, claim Podsakoff et al. (1990), should communicate the leader's respect for his or her colleagues, as well as concerns about their personal feelings and needs. Encompassed by this set of practices are the 'supporting' and 'recognizing and rewarding' managerial behaviours associated with Yukl's (1994) multiple linkages model, as well as Hallinger's (2003) model of instructional leadership and Waters et al.'s (2003) meta-analysis.

Redesigning the organization

The organizational setting in which people find themselves frames much of what they do. There is little to be gained by increasing people's motivation and capacity if working conditions will not allow their effective application. In Bandura's (1986) model, beliefs about the situation form a fourth source of motivation; people are motivated when they believe the circumstances in which they find themselves are conducive to accomplishing the goals they hold to be personally important. The four practices included in this category are about establishing the conditions of work which will allow staff to make the most of their motivations and capacities; these practices include building collaborative cultures, restructuring to organization to support collaboration, nurturing productive relationships with families and communities, and connecting the school to its wider environment.

Managing the instructional programme

Many studies of instructional leadership identify practices included among the three other dimensions of our 'core' practices. For example, Robinson and her colleagues (2008) found that 'establishing goals and expectations' had a significant effect on student outcomes. Hallinger's (2003) instructional leadership model includes 'defining the school's mission', which is encompassed within our dimension 'setting directions' and therefore not included in this part of the framework. The dimension includes only those practices with a focus on teaching and learning not found among the other three core leadership dimensions, including: staffing the programme, providing instructional support, monitoring school activity, buffering staff from distractions to their work and aligning the allocation of resources.

The study

Evidence for this study was provided by a sample of principals (12) and teachers (65) located in 12 elementary, middle and secondary schools serving students from similar mid- to low-socio-economic family backgrounds. The initial selection of the 12 schools was based on the quality of teachers' instructional practices assessed during classroom observations.[4] Six of the 12 schools were designated high-scoring schools (HSS) based on these ratings of classroom instruction, while the remaining six were designated low-scoring schools (LSS).

Teachers whose lesson had been observed were subsequently interviewed about that lesson, their approach to teaching, the principals' role in guiding and supporting their work, factors that had the greatest influence on student learning, district influences, professional development opportunities, the school community, the extent of parental involvement, and what they would tell a new teacher about what it's like to work at this school.

Interviews with principals and vice-principals addressed the principal's leadership in areas such as goals for student achievement, vision for the school, student learning, and decision-making about instruction. These administrators were also asked about leadership distribution in the school, professional development experiences for themselves and their teachers, curriculum and instruction, school culture, state and district influences on administrators' and teachers' work in the school, and the impact of parents and the wider school community.

Practices common across schools

Results indicated that a large proportion of both principals and teachers across all 12 schools agreed on the importance of three specific practices:

- Focusing the school on goals and expectations for student achievement (100 per cent principals and 66.7 per cent teachers).
- Keeping track of teachers' professional development needs (100 per cent principals, 84 per cent teachers). Although professional development was often prescribed, designed, and delivered at the district level, principals were involved in managing teachers' attendance at workshops offered outside the school, as well as planning for, and sometimes providing on-site professional development themselves.

- Creating structures and opportunities for teachers to collaborate (91.7 per cent principals, 66.7 per cent teachers). Principals supported collaboration among teachers by scheduling times for teachers to meet and discuss how they were working through the curriculum.

Other practices attracting support from a smaller but still sizeable number of principals and teachers included:

- Monitoring teachers' work in the classroom (83.3 per cent principals, 37.7 per cent teachers). Principals mentioned formal classroom observations carried out for teacher evaluation purposes, and also less formal ways of monitoring such as classroom visits and checking lesson plans.
- Providing back-up for teachers with student discipline and with parents (25 per cent principals, 23.1 per cent teachers). School safety and student behaviour management were of concern to both administrators and teachers. Teachers were particularly appreciative of administrators who could be relied on to back up teachers when there were challenging situations with parents.
- Providing mentoring opportunities for new teachers (33.3 per cent principals, 26 per cent teachers). Some teachers and principals referred to programmes initiated by the district or the school to support staff members who were new to teaching or new to the school.
- Being easily accessible (50 per cent principals, 27.5 per cent teachers). Principals spoke about how they supported teachers' efforts in the classroom in a general way.
- Staying current was considered to be a very important part of their instructional leadership by most principals (83.3 per cent), although only one teacher seemed to be aware of it.

How do the specific leadership practices described above relate to the four categories with which the study began? For purposes of this comparison, only those practices identified by a sizeable number of respondents were considered (those discussed above) even though the data set, as a whole, identified many more. Table 4.1 reports the frequently mentioned, helpful leadership practices identified in the first part of our analysis (right-hand column) in relation to the four sets of core leadership practices identified as successful in earlier research (left-hand column).

Two sets of activities are closely aligned with the core practices related to *direction setting*. Focusing the schools' and teachers' attention on goals and expectations for instruction and student achievement is part of clarifying the school's vision, building a shared set of goals, and creating high-performance expectations. Four actions teachers believed contributed to improving their skills and abilities are part of enacting the individualized support associated with *developing people*: keeping track of teachers' professional learning needs, being easily accessible to teachers, providing backup for teachers with student discipline and with parents, and providing mentoring opportunities for new teachers. Just one set of

Table 4.1   Connecting principal and teacher voices to core leadership practices

Core leadership practices	Practices identified as instructionally helpful
1 Setting directions	
1.1 Building a shared vision	• Focusing the school on goals for student achievement
1.2 Fostering the acceptance of group goals	• Focusing teachers' attention on goals for student achievement
1.3 Creating high-performance expectations	• Focusing teachers' attention on expectations for student achievement
1.4 Communicating the direction	• Staying current
2 Developing people	
2.1 Providing individualized support and consideration	• Keeping track of teachers' professional development needs • Providing general support/open door • Being easily accessible • Providing backup for teachers for student discipline and with parents
2.2 Offering intellectual stimulation	• Providing mentoring opportunities for new teachers
2.3 Modelling appropriate values and practices	
3 Redesigning the organization	
3.1 Building collaborative cultures	
3.2 Modifying organizational structures to nurture collaboration	• Creating structures and opportunities for teachers to collaborate
3.3 Building productive relations with families and communities	
3.4 Connecting the school to the wider community	
4 Managing the instructional programme	
4.1 Staffing the instructional programme	
4.2 Monitoring progress of students, teachers and the school	• Monitoring teachers' work in the classroom
4.3 Providing instructional support	
4.4 Aligning resources	
4.5 Buffering staff from distractions to their work	

actions associated with *redesigning the organization* was mentioned – creating structures for teachers to collaborate. Finally, monitoring teachers' work was the only action associated with *Managing the instructional programme* mentioned by a sizeable number of respondents.

The results of this analysis, in sum, are twofold. First, a substantial number of core leadership practices were not identified by many of our respondents (seven of the 16). We cannot know with much certainty the actual explanation for this. Principals, for example, might have enacted these practices but they were not visible to teachers; only some of the core leadership practices might have much influence on teachers' classroom practices, or perhaps the principals in our study had a relatively narrow repertoire of leadership tools to work with. But this was a study about leadership practices perceived to influence just one of many variables on only one of the four paths (rational path) we have conceptualized as conduits for leaders' influence on student learning. So it is reasonable also to speculate that only a subset of the core leadership practices would be required for this purpose.

A second result of the evidence reported to this point is that all of the leadership practices frequently identified as helpful in this study are readily associated with at least one of the core leadership practices identified by considerable amounts of earlier research. So this study provided no serious challenge to the core practices as an account of successful leadership. At the same time, the results did clarify how those practices apparently most relevant for instructional improvement purposes were enacted, a step beyond the 'what' of leadership to the 'how'.

Practices in high versus low-performing schools

Were the school leaders in our high- and low- performing schools (as judged by the quality of teachers' observed pedagogy) engaged in different leadership practices? This was the question initially prompting the study and determining the selection of schools. On this question, principal and teacher responses concurred about only one leadership practice. 'Providing instructional resources and materials' was identified as helpful by half of the principals and 25 per cent of the teachers in low-scoring schools, whereas only one principal and 6 per cent of the teachers in high- scoring schools identified this practice as helpful.

When considering principal responses separately, the small size of the sample means that percentage differences in their responses are deceptive. A difference of two principals between the high- and low-scoring samples is evident in the case of only two practices:

- participating in their own professional development (six HSS versus four LSS)
- supporting community involvement in student learning (two HSS versus four LSS).

There were relatively large differences in the opinions of high- and low-scoring teachers in relation to the following practices:

- supporting teacher collaboration for purposes of instructional improvement (85 per cent HSS versus 56 per cent LSS)
- helping to ensure consistent approaches to student discipline (18 per cent HSS versus 38 per cent LSS)

- providing teachers with instructional resources and materials (6 per cent HSS versus 25 per cent LSS)
- supporting parental involvement in student learning (88 per cent HSS versus 72 per cent LSS scoring).

In sum, principals in pedagogically high- and low-performing schools reported doing many of the same things to improve classroom pedagogy although principals in high-performing schools devoted more attention to building their own capacities and less to supporting community involvement. Pedagogically high-performing teachers placed greater value on leaders supporting their collaborative work and the involvement of parents in student learning, whereas pedagogically low-performing teachers placed greater value on principals' helping with student discipline and accessing instructional resources.

Practices across school levels

Comparisons also were made among principals' and teachers' views on instructionally influential leadership practices in elementary, middle, and secondary schools. Results indicated that there was almost no variation in the number of principals at each school level identifying any of the practices. However, most practices were identified by a third or fewer of the 12 principals in the sample. More variation across school levels was evident in teachers' responses:

- 'Monitoring teachers' classroom work' was identified by only 30 per cent of middle school leaders, a slightly larger proportion of high school teachers (34.8 per cent), and fully 54.5 per cent of elementary teachers.
- 'Creating structures for teachers to collaborate' was identified by 78.3 per cent of high school teachers 70 per cent of middle school teachers and 63.6 per cent of elementary teachers.
- 'Allowing teachers flexibility regarding classroom instruction' was a practice identified by 55 per cent of middle school, 43.8 per cent of high school, and 40.9 per cent of elementary school teachers.

These results, in sum, do seem to suggest that there are differences among the three levels of schooling in the leadership practices considered most helpful for improving instruction. But the sample for this study is too small to pinpoint with much certainty what those differences might be. This is an especially promising focus for larger-scale studies in the future.

Conclusion

This chapter has addressed the two most challenging and practically relevant sets of questions about school leadership at the present time: how do school leaders improve the learning of their students and which leadership practices are most likely to stimulate that improvement? A complex and sometimes quite detailed answer to these crucial questions has been developed on the grounds that there are no simple answers that have much potential, and that the 'devil is in the details'. It is unlikely that there are simple and abstract answers that will be of much use.

The first part of the chapter described a relatively novel conception of how school leaders influence student learning. It is a conception designed to make more accessible and usable the 'buzzing confusion' of evidence about this issue in much of the contemporary leadership literature. There were two foundational starting points for this conception: the first was a generic definition of leadership as the exercise of influence; the second was an assumption that most leadership influence on student learning is indirect.

Building on these two starting points, four paths were identified along which leadership influence flows. A key part of a school leader's job, it was argued, is to (a) select variables on each path that both demonstrate considerable power to improve student learning and make sense to focus on, in light of local school circumstances and (b) devote their efforts to improving the status of those selected variables.

Encompassing most components of the school organization, evidence summarized about variables on the four paths indicated, quite clearly, that a narrow focus on classroom instruction (a variable on the rational path), the dominant focus in much current educational policy, will often be necessary but rarely will it be sufficient. Variables on all paths have demonstrably significant effects on student learning. So, over time, successful school leaders will need to build the capacity of their organizations in ways that reflect the importance of all paths.

The second part of this chapter acknowledged the importance of improving classroom instruction, notwithstanding the need for leaders to also attend to many other important variables in their schools. Guided by a set of 'core' practices demonstrably useful for most successful leaders (setting directions, developing people, redesigning the organization and managing the instructional programme), results of a recent qualitative study were summarized. This study aimed at confirming, refining, extending or revising the value of these core practices when instructional improvement is the goal.

Results indicated that almost all leadership practices considered instructionally helpful by principals and teachers were specific enactments of the core practices. Teachers varying widely in the sophistication of their classroom instruction identified as helpful most of the same leadership practices, and these results were roughly the same in elementary, middle and secondary schools. Teachers and principals agreed that the most instructionally helpful leadership practices were 'focusing the school on goals and expectations for student achievement', 'keeping track of teachers' professional development needs' and 'creating structures and opportunities for teachers to collaborate'.

No doubt the answers provided to questions about the how and what of leadership in this chapter will be considered controversial and incomplete by others. But the questions themselves cannot be ignored. The chapter is a challenge for others to work towards better answers.

Reflective Questions ❓

1 Which of the four paths garners the most attention in your own school improvement efforts? Why?
2 What evidence do you have to justify this focus of attention?
3 In your own experience, which leadership practices have contributed most to the improvement of instruction in your school? How do they compare with those identified in this chapter?

Further Reading 📖

Leithwood, K. and Beatty, B. (2007) *Leading with Teacher Emotions in Mind*. Thousand Oaks, CA: Corwin.

This book summarizes empirical evidence about the consequences of teacher emotions for their classroom practices and for student learning. It also examines what it is in the workplace that significantly influences those emotions, Because the major influence on teacher emotions is the leadership practices experienced by teachers, the book describes how those in leadership roles can improve the emotional climate of their schools.

Leithwood, K. and Jantzi, D. (2008) Linking leadership to student learning: the role of collective efficacy, *Educational Administration Quarterly*, 44(4): 496–528.

Collective efficacy or confidence is among the most productive emotions those in organizations can develop. Because it encourages resilience in the face of challenges and persistence in the face of failure, those groups with high levels of collective efficacy give themselves the opportunity to learn their way forward. This article identifies some of the key features of organizations which foster collective efficacy among school leaders.

Notes

1 This mixed methods, five-year study collected two rounds of survey evidence from approximately 180 schools in each round, as well as qualitative, site visit data from administrators and teachers in 32 schools annually over three cycles. Evidence reported in this chapter comes from the third round of site visits.
2 Similar approaches to the classification of successful leadership practices are not difficult to find. See, for example, Hallinger and Heck (1999), Conger and Kanungo (1998) and Robinson et al. (2008).
3 An example is Bandura (1986).
4 These observations were guided by an observation schedule described more fully in Newmann et al. (1995).

References

Bandura, A. (1986) *Social Foundations of Thought and Action*. Englewood Cliffs, NJ: Prentice-Hall.

Blasé, J. and Blasé, J. (1998) *Handbook of Instructional Leadership: How Effective Principals Promote Teaching and Learning*. Thousand Oaks, CA: Corwin Press.

Conger, C. and Kanungo, R. (1998) *Charismatic Leadership in Organizations*. Thousand Oaks, CA: Sage.

Creemers, B.P.M. and Reezigt, G.J. (1996) School level conditions affecting the effectiveness of instruction, *School Effectiveness and School Improvement* (7): 197–228.

Fullan, M. (2003) *The Moral Imperative of School Leadership*. Thousand Oaks, CA: Corwin Press.

Goldring, E.B. and Rallis, S.F. (1993) *Principals of Dynamic Schools: Taking Charge of Change*. Newbury Park, CA: Corwin.

Goleman, D. (2006) *Social Intelligence: The New Science of Human Relationships*. New York: Random House.

Hallinger, P. (2003) Leading educational change: reflections on the practice of instructional and transformational leadership, *Cambridge Journal of Education*, 33(3): 329–51.

Hallinger, P. and Heck, R. (1999) Next generation methods for the study of leadership and school improvement, in J. Murphy and K. Louis (eds), *Handbook of Research on Educational Administration*, 2nd edn. San Francisco, CA: Jossey-Bass. pp. 141–62.

Hattie, J. (2009) *Visible Learning: A Synthesis of Over 800 Meta-analyses Relating to Achievement*. London: Routledge.

Judge, T., Piccolo, R. and Kosalka, T. (2009) The bright and dark sides of leader traits: a review and theoretical extension of the leader trait paradigm, *The Leadership Quarterly*, 20(6): 855–75.

Kyriakides, L. and Creemers, B.P.M. (2008) Using a multidimensional approach to measure the impact of classroom-level factors upon student achievement: a study testing the validity of the dynamic model, *School Effectiveness and School Improvement*, 19(2): 183–205.

Leithwood, K. (2006) *Teacher Working Conditions that Matter: Evidence for Change*. Toronto: Elementary Teachers' Federation of Ontario.

Leithwood, K. and Beatty, B. (2007) *Leading with Teacher Emotions in Mind*. Thousand Oaks, CA: Corwin.

Leithwood, K. and Jantzi, D. (2008) Linking leadership to student learning: the contributions of leader efficacy, *Educational Administration Quarterly*, 44(4): 496–528.

Leithwood, K. and Riehl, C. (2005) What do we already know about educational leadership, in W. Firestone and C. Riehl (eds), *A New Agenda for Research in Educational Leadership*. New York: Teachers College Press. pp. 12–27.

Leithwood, K., Day, C., Sammons, P., Harris, A. and Hopkins, D. (2006) Successful school leadership: what it is and how it influences pupil learning, National College for School Leadership, research report, No. 800.

Leithwood, K., Louis, K.S., Anderson, S. and Wahlstrom, K. (2004) *How Leadership Influences Student Learning*. New York: Wallace Foundation.

Louis, K., Leithwood, K., Wahlstrom, K., Anderson, S., Mascall, B. and colleagues (2009) Learning from leadership: investigating the links to improved student learning, final report of research to the Wallace Foundation.

Nelson, B. and Sassi, A. (2005) *The Effective Principal: Instructional Leadership for High Quality Learning*. New York: Teachers College Press.

Oatley, K., Keltner, D. and Jenkins, J.M. (2006) *Understanding Emotions*. 2nd edn. Malden, MA: Blackwell.

Podsakoff, P., MacKenzie, S., Moorman, R. and Fetter, R. (1990) Transformational leader behaviors and their effects on followers' trust in leader satisfaction and organizational citizenship behaviors, *Leadership Quarterly*, 1(2): 107–42.

Robinson, V., Lloyd, C. and Rowe, K. (2008) The impact of leadership on student out-comes: an analysis of the differential effects of leadership types, *Educational Administration Quarterly*, 44(5): 635–74.

Robinson, V.M. (in press) From instructional leadership to leadership capabilities: empirical findings and methodological challenges, *Leadership and Policy in Schools*.

Stein, M.K. and Nelson, B.S. (2003) Leadership content knowledge, *Educational Evaluation and Policy Analysis*, 25(4): 423–48.

Waters, T., Marzano, R.J. and McNulty, B. (2003) *Balanced Leadership: What 30 Years of Research Tells Us about the Effect of Leadership on Pupil Achievement. A Working Paper.* Aurora, CO: Mid-continent Research for Education and Learning.

Yukl, G. (1994) *Leadership in Organizations*. 3rd edn. Englewood Cliffs, NJ: Prentice-Hall.

Zaccaro, S.J., Kemp, C. and Bader, P. (2004) Leader traits and attributes, in J. Antonakis, A.T. Cianciolo and R.J. Sternberg (eds), *The Nature of Leadership*. Thousand Oaks, CA: Sage. pp. 101–24.

CHAPTER 5

Leadership and Student Learning Outcomes[1]

Philip Hallinger and Ronald H. Heck

This chapter examines the ways in which the field of educational leadership and management has approached the study of leadership impact on student learning over the past several decades. It presents a variety of conceptual models as well as empirical evidence that address whether and how school leadership impacts learning in practice.

Over the past several decades, scholars focusing on educational leadership and management have developed a theoretically-informed, empirical knowledge base concerning leadership effects on learning (Bossert et al., 1982; Hallinger and Heck, 1996). This research generally supports the conclusion that school leadership exerts a measurable, albeit indirect, effect on student learning (Hallinger and Heck, 1996; Leithwood et al., 2006; Robinson et al., 2008). School leadership appears to achieve these effects through strategic actions that focus on *changing* a constellation of sociocultural, structural and academic processes that directly impact student learning outcomes.

This chapter examines the current state of the art with respect to understanding how school leadership is believed to impact student learning outcomes. The main body of the chapter maps the evolution of research on school leadership effects on learning. We present several conceptual frameworks that describe different ways of illuminating the possible ways in which leadership can impact student learning. We discuss each of these conceptual models and then comment on how empirical research has influenced our thinking about their validity for understanding the practice of leadership for learning. We conclude the chapter with a discussion of future challenges with respect to research and practice in leadership for learning.

Conceptualizing leadership effects on learning

Increasingly, educational systems throughout the world are holding the leadership of primary and secondary schools accountable for student performance results. Not surprisingly, and despite acknowledged measurement limitations, *student achievement* has become the key performance indicator favoured by education policy-makers from Hong Kong to Sydney and New York to London. Given the centrality of student achievement in national accountability systems and increased investments in the development of learning-centred leadership, policy-makers and practitioners are increasingly interested in the means by which leadership impacts learning. Several conceptual models have been proposed by scholars studying leadership for learning (Hallinger and Heck, 1996; Pitner, 1988). These include direct effects, mediated effects, reciprocal effects, antecedent effects and context effects models. We will discuss each, paying attention to both conceptual issues and research findings.

Direct effects models of leadership for learning

The first of these models of leadership for learning is a direct effects model, as shown in Figure 5.1. This has been termed by some a 'heroic model' of leadership because it seeks to 'explain' variations in student learning by actions of the leader, usually the principal, alone.

Note that in this model 'school leadership' may be represented by any type of leadership. Indeed, researchers have employed measures of instructional leadership (Hallinger and Murphy, 1985), transformational leadership (Leithwood, 1994) or other forms of leadership in examining direct effects models (Hallinger and Heck, 1996; Robinson et al., 2008).

Numerous studies have sought to investigate this type of model. Researchers have collected data, typically through teacher surveys, and examined the relationship between teacher ratings of the principal and student learning outcomes across some number of schools. In a review conducted in the mid-1990s, we concluded that studies employing direct effects models had not yielded significant findings of leadership effects on learning regardless of the model of leadership employed by the researchers (Hallinger and Heck, 1996). A more recent review of this research has yielded a similar conclusion.

The reasons proposed for the barren fruit yielded by direct effects studies can be traced to its underlying theoretical rationale. First, it should be acknowledged

Figure 5.1   Direct effects model of leadership for learning

that schools account for a relatively small portion of the variation in student achievement outcomes compared with family background or socio-economic status. Thus, studies that seek to identify the impact of leadership on learning are already dealing with a relatively small portion of the total contribution that schools make towards the improvement of student learning.

Second, principals do not teach children, or, if they do, their direct impact will be on a relatively small number of students attending the school. The effects of principals on student learning are achieved primarily through their impact on teachers (Hallinger and Heck, 1996; Leithwood et al., 2006; Robinson et al., 2008). Thus, we assert that the direct effects model starts with an untenable assumption. We have yet to see a strong theoretical rationale to support a direct effects model, and the empirical literature bears this out with a lack of significant results.

Mediated effects models of leadership for learning

School leaders are capable of having significant positive effects on student learning and other important outcomes ... Indeed, enough evidence is now at hand to justify claims about significant leadership effects on students that the focus of attention for many leadership researchers has moved on to include questions about how those effects occur. (Leithwood et al., 2010: 1)

Given the lack of efficacy of direct effects models in explaining patterns of student learning outcomes, researchers began to explore more complex models of leadership for learning. These models began to incorporate more explicitly the *means* through which leadership could be conceptualized to impact learning (Hallinger and Heck, 1996; Kleine-Kracht, 1993; Leithwood et al., 2006; in press; Pitner, 1988). Mediated effects models of leadership for learning begin with the assumption that school leaders obtain results by working through other people (Bossert et al., 1982; Bridges, 1967; 1977). The task then becomes to conceptualize how leaders impact people and their environment to achieve better learning results with students. A mediated effects model of leadership for learning is shown in Figure 5.2.

Mediated effects studies of leadership and learning have conceptualized and examined school leadership, generally that of the principal, in relation to a wide range of mediating school-level variables (Hallinger and Heck, 1996). Mediating

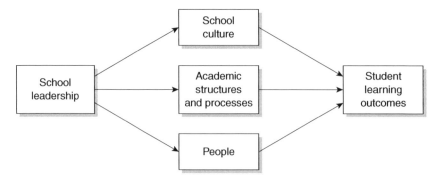

Figure 5.2   Example of a mediated effects model of leadership for learning

variables that have been examined in some depth include school climate, school culture, clear academic mission, academic capacity, curriculum structure, communication, teacher collective efficacy, staff motivation, organizational structure, professional learning of staff, strategic planning and resource allocation, managing the instructional programme, staff participation in decision-making and academic expectations (Hallinger and Heck, 1996; Leithwood et al., 2006).

Mediated effects studies have generally employed similar research methodologies as used in the direct effects studies. The key difference is that the teacher survey is expanded to include items that examine the mediating variables (for example, collective efficacy, school mission, communication, academic capacity) as well as leadership (for example, Hallinger et al., 1996; Heck et al., 1990). Then when the data are analysed the researcher conducts statistical tests that examine the relationships among the variables, in line with the model proposed in Figure 5.2. These tests will determine whether there are direct and/or indirect effects of leadership on learning.

Quite a few published studies have confirmed the greater efficacy of the mediated effects perspective (for example, Heck et al., 1990; Hallinger et al., 1996; Leithwood and Jantzi, 1999; Marks and Printy, 2003). Indeed, over the past decade, the mediated effects perspective has been widely embraced as the dominant view of conceptualizing the means by which leadership impacts student learning. These studies rather consistently report small to moderate indirect effects of leadership acting through the mediating school-level conditions. Notably, these studies do not find direct effects from leadership to learning even when data are analysed within the mediated effects models of leadership for learning.

Figure 5.2 portrays three general 'paths' that mediate leadership effects on learning: school culture, academic structures and processes and people. These were identified in our earlier review of the leadership effects literature (Hallinger and Heck, 1996). Others have proposed other 'paths' or avenues through which leadership works to impact learning. For example, in a recent paper, Leithwood et al. (2010) proposed four paths: rational, organizational, emotions and family. The identification of these paths is considered to be of considerable practical importance. We also wish to note the similarity of this model to a more general leadership model proposed by Kouzes and Posner (2007).

Recently support for the mediated effects perspective received additional support in the form of a meta-analysis of leadership studies conducted by Robinson and her colleagues (2008). Meta-analysis is a statistical method used to synthesize the results of a number of studies. In this instance, the meta-analysis confirmed the efficacy of the mediated effects model of leadership effects on learning. The authors of this meta-analysis reported that empirical evidence supported instructional leadership as the strongest model of leadership for learning (that is, when compared with transformational leadership and other leadership models). The leadership foci reported to be most significant in terms of impact on learning were:

- principal involvement in and support for the professional learning of staff
- academic vision and mission
- managing curriculum and instruction (Robinson et al., 2008).

Our own view is that transformational and instructional leadership share many common features (see Hallinger, 2003). For example, both models emphasize the importance of vision, mission, goals, modelling, high expectations and continuous professional learning. We suggest that the main distinction is that instructional leadership explicitly assumes that mission, goals, expectations and professional learning are organized around an academic learning focus. In contrast, a 'transformational school leader' could be transformational around a set of values and goals that were not explicitly oriented towards student learning. This is a very important point to keep in mind; that is, our notion of leadership for learning is explicitly oriented towards student achievement as the pre-eminent, though not sole, purpose of schooling.

Reciprocal effects models of leadership for learning

> Although administrative man has been described as both the initiator and recipient of action, the dominant focus of the empirical and theoretical work has been on administrative man as an *origin* of his decisions on the one hand, and an *origin* of the behavior of subordinates on the other … The understanding we have, in consequence, is limited to the decision-making behavior of administrative man as products and processes of a person acting on his own and as a person acting as a causal agent to produce certain effects in the organization. (Bridges, 1970: 7)

Although mediated effects studies represented a conceptual advance over earlier direct effects models, mediated effects models continue to assert a *heroic role* for leaders. As such, they fail to take into account the systemic forces and constraints under which leaders operate (Bossert et al., 1982; Bridges, 1967; 1970; 1977; Hallinger and Heck, 1996). This assumption was clearly articulated 40 years ago by Bridges (1970; 1977) when he pointed out that leaders are not only a cause of change in others, but are also influenced by others.

Thus, both direct and mediated effects models ignore the possibility that leadership both *impacts* and *is influenced* by the changing state of school conditions and performance outcomes. The conceptualization of leadership effects on school conditions learning and outcomes as a process of *mutual influence* has been termed a 'reciprocal-effects' model (Pitner, 1988: 107). This model was aptly described by Mulford and Silins: '[S]uccessful school principalship is an interactive, reciprocal and evolving process involving many players, which is influenced by, and in turn, influences the context in which it occurs' (Mulford and Silins, 2009: 2).

This characterization of school leadership as a mutual influence process resonates with practitioners and has strong face validity when viewed in light of theoretical treatises on organizational leadership (for example, Bass and Bass, 2008). Yet, this perspective on leadership is clearly at odds with the preponderance of empirical research on leadership and learning in schools (Hallinger and Heck, 1996; 2010). A reciprocal effects perspective on leadership for learning conceptualizes leadership as *both* a cause and effect of school level conditions (for example, school climate and culture) and student learning outcomes. A simple reciprocal effects model of leadership effects is displayed in Figure 5.3.

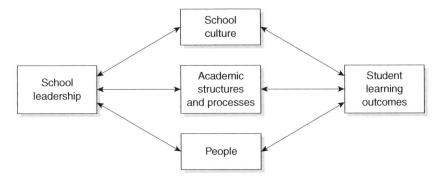

Figure 5.3   A simple reciprocal effects model of leadership for learning

We wish to highlight three features of this model. First, the arrows signalling the direction of effects move in both directions between leadership and the mediating school conditions. This suggests existence of mutual influence between these factors. Second, even within this reciprocal effects model, leadership effects are still *mediated* by the school's internal conditions or capacities. However, the effects of the internal conditions are the sum total of the mutual influence relationship rather than only that of the school conditions as portrayed in Figure 5.3. Finally, Figure 5.3 further proposes that internal school conditions are also part of a feedback or reciprocal relationship with the school's performance outcomes. For example, as a school leadership sees improvement or decline in performance they will take steps to make changes in the school's academic capacity for improvement.

We note in this regard that school improvement is, by definition, a *process* that involves change in the state of the school over time. This observation suggests that the empirical study of leadership for learning requires models that take into account the changing state of schools over time. Indeed, we noted 15 years ago, 'To the extent that leadership is viewed as an adaptive process rather than as a unitary independent force, the reciprocal-effects perspective takes on increased salience' (Hallinger and Heck, 1996: 19).

Progress in examining leadership for learning from the perspective of reciprocal effects models has, however, been hampered by a blind spot in the vision of scholars. Virtually all quantitative studies of school leadership have consisted of one-time cross-sectional surveys of school leaders. This type of research design that seeks to examine relationships among relevant factors at a single point in time has characterized the research in school leadership going back to the 1960s. This feature of research conducted in educational leadership and management is of great salience when we wish to examine the 'effects' of leadership on learning, effects which by definition unfold over time. Ogawa and Bossert (1995: 239–40) succinctly summarize the case for using longitudinal data in studies of leadership effects:

[S]tudies of leadership must have as their unit of analysis the organization. Data on the network of interactions that occur in organizations must be compiled over time … The importance of the dimension of time must be emphasized. If leadership involves influencing organizational structures, then time is important. Only time will tell if attempts at leadership affect organizational solidarity. Also, the time that is required for such effects to occur and the duration of the persistence of the effects may be important variables.

With this in mind, we note that studies employing longitudinal data on school leadership effects have been exceedingly scarce. Nonetheless they are an imperative if we seek to define and test leadership models that propose reciprocal effects. To date, we have only been able to identify a few studies that incorporated longitudinal data into studies of leadership effects and only two employed a reciprocal effects approach to examining the data (Hallinger and Heck, 2010; Heck and Hallinger, 2009; Mulford and Silins, 2009).

Our own study of the effects of 'collaborative school leadership' on learning represents the most explicitly designed test of the reciprocal effects model to date in education (Hallinger and Heck, 2010; Heck and Hallinger, 2009). We employed a longitudinal data set collected annually from about 200 elementary schools over a four-year period to compare the efficacy of a mediated effects model with that of the reciprocal effects model. In our reciprocal effects model, we proposed that leadership both shapes and is shaped by the school's 'academic capacity for improvement'. Academic capacity referred to a constellation of school-level conditions such as sustained focus on improvement of learning, open communication, stakeholder involvement in decision-making, curriculum standards, and student support (Heck and Hallinger, 2009; Saphier and King, 1985).

Using four years of data, we examined the impact of changes in the strength of collaborative leadership on changes in the schools' academic capacity and growth in student learning over time using a *mediated effects* model (see Figure 5.4). We found significant effects of 'change in collaborative leadership' on 'change in academic capacity' which were significantly related to growth in student achievement in elementary school reading and math (Hallinger and Heck, 2010; Heck and Hallinger, 2009). This result was quite encouraging since testing this model with longitudinal data provides much greater confidence that leadership may be 'causing' the change in academic capacity than data obtained from a cross-sectional study.

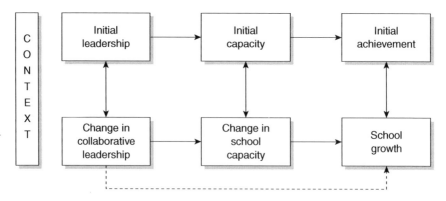

Note: ---▶ Path tested but not expected to be significant

Figure 5.4   Testing a mediated effects model of leadership for learning using longitudinal data

Next we used the same data-set to test the efficacy of the *reciprocal effects* model. Our approach to this more complex analysis is depicted in Figure 5.5. Based on a variety of criteria, the data provided stronger evidence in support of a reciprocal-effects perspective on leadership and school improvement (Hallinger and Heck, 2010; Heck and Hallinger, 2009).

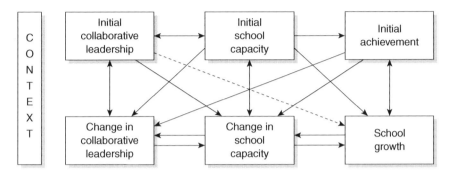

Figure 5.5   Testing a reciprocal effects model of leadership for learning using longitudinal data

Our analysis found that initial academic capacity positively affected subsequent changes in collaborative leadership, and initial collaborative leadership positively affected subsequent changes in academic capacity. This suggests that these constructs were part of a *mutually reinforcing relationship* in which growth in one led to positive change in the other. It was further noted that improvements in the schools appeared to 'gain momentum' over time through changes in collaborative leadership and academic capacity that were organic and mutually responsive. Moreover, it seems important to us to note that the effects of academic capacity on collaborative leadership was *stronger* over time than the corresponding effect of collaborative leadership on academic capacity. This suggests that leadership can act as an important catalyst and supporting factor for the development of the school's capacity for improvement, but that the school's internal conditions (for example, academic capacity) will usually exercise an even stronger influence on leadership (Hallinger and Heck, 2010; Heck and Hallinger, 2009).

Personal antecedent effects on leadership for learning

While in the past researchers often concentrated on one specific potentially effectiveness-enhancing factor (e.g. school leadership), or investigated the influence of several factors on outcomes without taking into account the possibility that factors relate to each other, nowadays there are calls to pay attention to the interrelatedness of factors, the direct and indirect effects of factors, the mediated effects of factors, and to use time-ordered modeling procedures like path analysis or structural equation modelling. So, a plea for more complex models is made (see, for example, Witziers et al., 2003). (Opdenakker and Van Damme, 2007: 179–80).

The next feature to add to our evolving model of leadership for learning concerns the personal values, beliefs, experiences, and knowledge of the school leader(s). As suggested by Bossert and colleagues (1982), as well as Opdenakker and Van Damme above, we believe that understanding leadership for learning requires a fully contextualized model. This would be incomplete without taking into account the individual differences of the leaders themselves. The model shown in Figure 5.6 suggests categories of personal 'antecedents' that we believe to be relevant in understanding how leaders enact leadership in practice.

Moreover, we also wish to highlight the fact that the model of leadership for learning presented in Figure 5.6 is a *values-based, normative model of leadership*. Values define both the ends towards which leaders aspire as well as the desirable means by which they will work to achieve them. Indeed, the model conceptualizes leadership as explicitly aimed at the improvement of student learning (that is, the model presumes a specific thrust that *should* be the aim or goal). Moreover, it also highlights the role of values in shaping leadership.

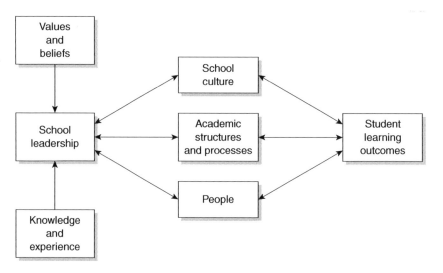

Figure 5.6 Personal antecedents added to the reciprocal effects model of leadership for learning

Beliefs, expectations, knowledge and experience also shape the thinking and actions of leaders. The impact of beliefs on behaviour was illustrated vividly in studies that demonstrated how teacher expectations influence teacher behaviour and student learning (Rosenthal and Jacobson, 1992). Similar findings surfaced in studies of instructionally effective schools where educators appeared to manifest a different set of beliefs about the potential of their students. These findings highlighted the importance of maintaining high expectations for all children, and became codified in the normative statement that 'all children can learn' (Edmonds, 1979; Purkey and Smith, 1983). Beliefs such as these implicitly shape the approach that principals take towards decision-making, resource allocation, curriculum organization, teaching and learning in the school. Space precludes a fuller consideration of the role of these personal antecedents, but the reader is referred elsewhere for more in-depth discussions (Hallinger and Heck, 1996; Leithwood et al., 2006; in press).

School context effects on leadership for learning

As Ronald Edmonds often said, we know far more about the features that characterize an effective school than we know about how a school became effective in the first place. Why, then, do we try to force schools that we don't like, to resemble schools that we do like, by employing means that have little to do with the evolution of the kind of schools that we like? (Barth, 1986: 294)

Twenty-five years hence, Barth's question continues to echo in the halls of academia as researchers seek to understand, interpret, and convey the applicability of their findings to the improvement of practice in schools. For example, even as scholars point to progress in developing a better understanding of the means by which leadership contributes to learning in schools (for example, Hallinger and Heck, 1996; Leithwood et al., 2010; Robinson et al., 2008), we remain highly constrained in our ability to answer a fundamental question posed by school principals: 'Given what you know about leadership for learning, where would you advise me to put my effort as a school leader in order to gain the greatest improvement in learning for students *at my school*?' The appended qualifier, *at my school*, highlights the limitations imposed upon leaders based upon variations in the *contexts* in which they work.

While this is a reasonable question, the answer requires a level of contextualization of research findings that goes beyond the limits of the current literature on leadership and learning. For example, early studies in this domain focused

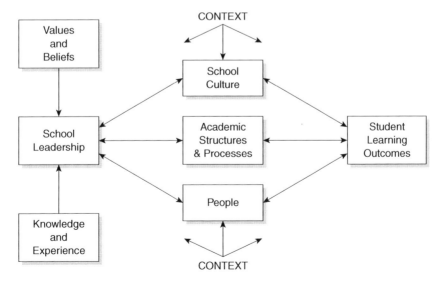

Figure 5.7 A full model of leadership for learning

on leadership in poor urban elementary schools that had been judged to be instructionally effective (Edmonds, 1979; Hallinger and Murphy, 1986). Yet, as suggested by Barth (1986) and others, these schools were atypical in important respects, and the findings while inspiring and important had limited generalizability as a guide for practice in other school settings (Cuban, 1984). Barth's remarks highlight the importance of the school's 'context' as a *moderator* or shaper of leadership effects.

Simply stated, *context* refers to environmental and organizational conditions that moderate the leader's impact on student learning. Relevant contextual conditions include school level, school size, student composition, teacher quality, institutional structure, and societal culture (Bossert et al., 1982; Hallinger and Heck, 1996; Opdenakker and Van Damme, 2007). As observed by Opdenakker and Van Damme (2007: 194):

> Quite often relationships between school characteristics and school outcomes are studied without taking into account possible relations and influences between school characteristics. Effects of school context, school leadership, student composition and school practice on school outcomes are studied without paying attention to possible relations between school characteristics and mediator effects. The consequences of this are inconsistencies in research results between studies and a rather limited understanding of the educational effectiveness of schools.

We suggest that there is no single correct style of leadership for learning that is suitable to all school contexts. Instead, leaders must shape their strategies and styles to meet the needs and constraints of their particular school. For example, when the lead author was a school head in Thailand, his boss once remarked to him that he 'needed to work more on his EQ in working with Thai people'. This referred to how he, an American who was managing a predominantly Thai staff, managed his emotions and relationships with staff. Context makes a difference, in this case context refers to the cultural context of the school.

From the perspective of context effects, each school can be seen to be on its own 'unique journey of school improvement' (Jackson, 2000) that requires different leadership approaches at different times. Our own research suggests that successful principals do indeed adapt their styles and strategies to both internal school conditions (as noted above) and to context conditions (Hallinger and Murphy, 1986; Heck and Hallinger, 2009). Moreover, we wish to note findings from a recent longitudinal study of school improvement in the UK. Day et al. (2010) were able to identify four broad stages of school improvement and differential approaches to leadership for learning during the four stages. For example, they found clear evidence of more directive leadership apparent during the earlier stages of the school improvement journey, especially for schools in challenging circumstances. These results run counter to policy prescriptions which assume that one style of leadership is suitable across all school contexts. These results support assertions that a comprehensive and valid model of leadership for learning must place leadership in a specific context (Bossert et al., 1982; Bridges, 1977; Hallinger and Heck, 1996).

Conclusion

This chapter focused on whether and how leadership makes a difference in student learning. We would be remiss if we did not at this point also note that space limitations precluded us from further unpacking our assumptions about leadership. For example, we did not discuss changing conceptions of leadership for learning as evolving from a traditional focus on principals to a more recent focus on shared (Marks and Printy, 2003), collaborative (Hallinger and Heck, 2010) and distributed (Gronn, 2003; Spillane, 2006) leadership during the past decade. We acknowledge the importance of this development and refer the reader to other chapters for a more explicit discussion of implications these perspectives hold for leadership for learning.

Twelve years ago, Fullan and Hargreaves (1998: 106) suggested the limits of what research could offer in the way of advice for practitioners seeking to improve their schools.

> There is no ready answer to the 'how' question. Singular recipes oversimplify what it will take to bring about change in your own situation. Even when you know what research and published advice tell you, no one can prescribe exactly how to apply it to your particular school and all the unique problems, opportunities and peculiarities it contains.

While this observation is certainly true in a general sense, we assert that research is making important progress in understanding how leadership contributes to school improvement and student learning in different school contexts. We are optimistic that future research will continue to gradually refine the current state of the art as discussed in this chapter so that over time the field is much better equipped to meet Barth's (1986) important challenge to contextualize how leadership contributes to learning across different school contexts.

Reflective Questions

1 Do you believe that school leadership has a positive impact on student learning? If yes, why? If no, why not?
2 What are the most important *means* or *paths* by which you believe school leadership impacts student learning?
3 What *personal characteristics* of school leaders influence how they lead? Why do you think are these particular characteristics are important? Are your beliefs about this relationship supported by research?
4 How does the *context* of the school (for example, school size, school level, community type, student composition) influence how we lead for learning?

5   Is there one best leadership style for improving student learning in schools? If yes, what would that look like? If no, why? If 'it depends' – what would it depend upon?

Reflective Activities

1   Think of the *most effective leader for learning* whom you have observed and/or worked with. Write a list of at least six characteristics that made him or her – in your eyes – a good leader for learning. Then think of the *least effective leader for learning* whom you have observed or worked for/with and write down a list of at least six of his or her characteristics. Compare this list to the principles about leadership for learning discussed in this chapter. Write a reflective essay that synthesizes your personal experience and beliefs with the conceptual perspectives and empirical findings contained in this chapter.
2   Consider the issue of *how the school's context impacts the exercise of leadership for learning*. Watch the film *Lean on Me*, which describes the leadership of a principal who was given less than one school year to 'turn-around' a failing school. Assess his *leadership for learning* in terms of the overall model presented in this chapter. Discuss his leadership in terms of his personal characteristics, the needs and constraints of his school's context, and his leadership strategies. Evaluate whether you believe he was a 'good leader' and discuss why.

Further Reading

Barth, R. (1986) On sheep and goats and school reform, *Phi Delta Kappan*, 68(4): 293–6.
Day, C., Sammons, P., Leithwood, K., Hopkins, D., Harris, A., Gu, Q. and Brown, E. (2010) *Ten Strong Claims about Successful School Leadership*. Nottingham: National College for School Leadership.
Hallinger, P. (2003) Leading educational change: reflections on the practice of instructional and transformational leadership, *Cambridge Journal of Education*, 33(3): 329–51.
Robinson, V., Lloyd, C. and Rowe, K. (2008) The impact of leadership on student outcomes: an analysis of the differential effects of leadership types, *Educational Administration Quarterly*, 44(5): 635–74.
Saphier, J. and King, M. (1985) Good seeds grow in strong cultures, *Educational Leadership*, 42(6): 67–74.

Note

1   The authors wish to acknowledge the funding support of the Research Grant Council (RGC) of Hong Kong for its support through the General Research Fund (GRF 840509).

References

Barth, R. (1986) On sheep and goats and school reform, *Phi Delta Kappan*, 68(4): 293–6.
Bass, B. and Bass, R. (2008) *The Bass Handbook of Leadership*. New York: Free Press.

Bossert, S., Dwyer, D., Rowan, B. and Lee, G. (1982) The instructional management role of the principal, *Educational Administration Quarterly*, 18(3): 34–64.

Bridges, E. (1967) Instructional leadership: a concept re-examined, *Journal of Educational Administration*, 5(2): 136–47.

Bridges, E. (1970) Administrative man: origin or pawn in decision making? *Educational Administration Quarterly*, 6(1): 7–25.

Bridges, E. (1977) The nature of leadership, in L. Cunningham, W. Hack and R. Nystrand (eds), *Educational Administration: The Developing Decades*. Berkeley, CA: McCutchan.

Cuban, L. (1984) Transforming the frog into a prince: effective schools research, policy, and practice at the district level, *Harvard Educational Review*, 54(2): 128–51.

Day, C., Sammons, P., Leithwood, K., Hopkins, D., Harris, A., Gu, Q. and Brown, E. (2010) *Ten Strong Claims about Successful School Leadership*. Nottingham: National College for School Leadership.

Edmonds, R. (1979) Effective schools for the urban poor, *Educational Leadership*, 37: 15–24.

Fullan, M. and Hargreaves, M. (1998) *What's Worth Fighting for Out There*. New York: Teachers College Press.

Gronn, P. (2003) *The New Work of Educational Leaders: Changing Leadership Practice in an Era of School Reform*. London: Sage.

Hallinger, P. (2003) Leading educational change: reflections on the practice of instructional and transformational leadership, *Cambridge Journal of Education*, 33(3): 329–51.

Hallinger, P. and Heck, R. (1996) Reassessing the principal's role in school effectiveness: A review of empirical research, 1980–1995, *Educational Administration Quarterly*, 32(1): 5–44.

Hallinger, P. and Heck, R.H. (2010) Collaborative leadership and school improvement: understanding the impact on school capacity and student learning, *School Leadership and Management*, 30(2): 95–110.

Hallinger, P. and Murphy, J. (1985) Assessing the instructional leadership behavior of principals, *Elementary School Journal*, 86(2): 217–48.

Hallinger, P. and Murphy, J. (1986) The social context of effective schools, *American Journal of Education*, 94(3): 328–55.

Hallinger, P., Bickman, L. and Davis, K. (1996) School context, principal leadership and student achievement, *Elementary School Journal*, 96(5): 498–518.

Heck, R.H. and Hallinger, P. (2009) Assessing the contribution of distributed leadership to school improvement and growth in math achievement, *American Educational Research Journal*, 46: 626–58.

Heck, R.H., Larson, T. and Marcoulides, G.A. (1990) Principal instructional leadership and school achievement: validation of a causal model, *Educational Administration Quarterly*, 26: 94–125.

Jackson, D. (2000) The school improvement journey: perspectives on leadership, *School Leadership & Management*, 20(1): 61–78.

Kleine-Kracht, P. (1993) Indirect instructional leadership: an administrator's choice, *Educational Administration Quarterly*, 18(4): 1–29.

Kouzes, J. and Posner, B. (2007) *The Leadership Challenge*. San Francisco, CA: Jossey-Bass.

Leithwood, K. (1994) Leadership for school restructuring, *Educational Administration Quarterly*, 30(4): 498–518.

Leithwood, K. and Jantzi, D. (1999) The relative effects of principal and teachers sources of leadership on student engagement with school, *Educational Administration Quarterly*, 35: 679–706.

Leithwood, K., Anderson, S., Mascall, B. and Strauss, T. (in press) School leaders' influences on student learning: the four paths, in T. Bush, L., Bell and D. Middlewood (eds), *The Principles of Educational Leadership and Management*. London: Sage.

Leithwood, K., Day, C., Sammons, P., Harris, A. and Hopkins, D. (2006) *Seven Strong Claims about Successful School Leadership*. Nottingham: National College of School Leadership.

Leithwood, K., Patten, S. and Jantzi, D. (2010) Testing a conception of how school leadership influences student learning, unpublished paper, University of Toronto/OISE.

Marks, H. and Printy, S. (2003) Principal leadership and school performance: an integration of transformational and instructional leadership, *Educational Administration Quarterly*, 39(3): 370–97.

Mulford, B. and Silins, H. (2009) Revised models and conceptualization of successful school principalship in Tasmania, in B. Mulford and B. Edmunds (eds), *Successful School Principalship in Tasmania*. Launceston, Tasmania: Faculty of Education, University of Tasmania.

Ogawa, R. and Bossert, S. (1995) Leadership as an organizational quality, *Educational Administration Quarterly*, 31(2): 224–43.

Opdenakker, M. and Van Damme, J. (2007) Do school context, student composition and school leadership affect school practice and outcomes in secondary education?, *British Educational Research Journal*, 33(2): 179–206.

Pitner, N. (1988) The study of administrator effects and effectiveness, in N. Boyan (ed.), *Handbook of Research on Educational Administration: A Project of the American Educational Research Association*. New York: Longman. pp. 99–122.

Purkey, S. and Smith, M. (1983) Effective schools: a review, *Elementary School Journal*, 83: 427–52.

Robinson, V., Lloyd, C. and Rowe, K. (2008) The impact of leadership on student outcomes: an analysis of the differential effects of leadership types, *Educational Administration Quarterly*, 44(5): 635–74.

Rosenthal, R. and Jacobson, L. (1992) *Pygmalion in the classroom*. Expanded edn. New York: Irvington.

Saphier, J. and King, M. (1985) Good seeds grow in strong cultures, *Educational Leadership*, 42(6): 67–74.

Spillane, J. (2006) *Distributed Leadership*. San Francisco, CA: Jossey-Bass.

Witziers, B., Bosker, R. and Kruger, M. (2003) Educational leadership and student achievement: the elusive search for an association, *Educational Administration Quarterly*, 34(3): 398–425.

CHAPTER 6

Connecting Leadership and Learning

Geoff Southworth

This chapter argues that leadership should be strongly focused on learning and teaching, particularly pedagogy. How leaders can do this is described, along with some of the implications for schools and their leaders.

Connecting leadership and learning is easy: school leadership has to be strongly focused on learning. Learning is the core business of schools and therefore it is the primary focus of school leaders. This is not to imply that leaders are not also involved with other aspects of schooling, but it is to say, unequivocally, that learning has to be the number one priority. Connection is not the issue, although disconnection could be the problem, it is a given. School leadership involves keeping close to student outcomes, achievements and progress.

In this chapter I elaborate on what this priority focus on learning means and how it can be achieved. In the first section I start by reviewing what we know about leadership for learning. Then, having set out what I think it means, in the second section I go on to look at *how* such leadership is conducted. In the third section I highlight some of the implications and identify some questions which serving and aspiring leaders should consider if they are to make a positive difference to the quality of learning in their schools. Throughout I shall draw on my own research and work with schools and their leaders, and my knowledge of the relevant literature and international research findings.

What we know about leadership for learning

Although there is a tendency among researchers and commentators to find new ways of describing leadership (for example, strategic, passionate, sustainable) there is agreement that effective school leadership is about improving pupil outcomes. The Organisation for Econoimic Co-operation and Development report

(OECD, 2008) which was a 22-country study looking at improving school leadership concluded that: 'Policy-makers and practitioners need to ensure that the roles and responsibilities associated with improved learning outcomes are at the core of school leadership practice' (2008: 10).

In North America instructional leadership has long been advocated (Blasé and Blasé, 1998; Heck, 1992; Hallinger and Murphy, 1986). In part this advocacy has been because the role of the school principal tended to be more administratively based than classroom focused. However, studies into effective schools showed that instructionally focused principals (and in England, headteachers) made a difference to student outcomes and progress. Therefore, these findings challenged administrative assumptions about the roles of principals and reinforced calls for instructionally focused leadership. Recently there are signs that the instructional focus is being re-badged. Hallinger (2009: 1) argues that instructional leadership is being reincarnated as leadership for learning.

Leadership for learning is the primary focus for school leaders because it makes a difference. There is substantial evidence from the effective schools research in the 1980s, school improvement studies in the 1990s, inspection evidence and research in England (Day et al., 2009) and elsewhere (Robinson et al., 2008) that such leadership enhances pupil outcomes. Indeed, Leithwood and colleagues (2006: 6–7) assert that one of seven strong claims that can be made about school leadership is that school leadership is second only to classroom teaching as an influence on pupil learning. Others drawing on school inspection data say: 'For every 100 schools that have good leadership and management, 93 will have good standards of achievement. For every 100 schools that do not have good leadership and management, only 1 will have good standards of student achievement' (Whelan, 2009: 78). The attention to leadership for learning has, in the last few years taken on a significant emphasis. Advocacy for such leadership begs a number of questions, including: what does it actually mean? One answer to this question is that it involves focusing on both learning and teaching.

Throughout the first decade of the twenty-first century there has been increasing interest at the policy level in improving pedagogy. Much of this interest was stimulated by Michael Barber and Mona Mourshed's study (2007) for McKinsey & Co which examined, to quote the title of their report, 'How the world's best-performing school systems come out on top'. This study was highly influential internationally and stimulated much debate among policy-makers. The study looked at 25 of the world's school systems, including 10 of the top performers. The authors were keen to acknowledge cultural and political differences between the countries and how they organized their school systems. However, their main finding noted a fundamental similarity between the high-performing school systems: they all pay great attention to the quality of teaching. What these high-performing school systems did was:

- get the right people to become teachers
- develop them well, and
- construct a system which provides the challenge, leadership and freedom to enable them to perform to the best of their potential.

Whelan, one of the team working with Barber and Mourshed, puts it like this:

> A school system can have excellent people, leaders, standards and struc-
> tures, but unless its teachers have the knowledge and skills to help every
> child to learn, it will never perform well. Compared to other professions
> and some organisations, many school systems have been remarkably
> unsuccessful both at preparing new teachers for entry into the profession
> and at helping all teachers to access the skills and knowledge of the best.
> However, a few school systems particularly in Asia have developed good
> models for ensuring that teachers have the knowledge and skills they need
> to be effective in the classroom. They do that by making sure that teachers
> have a sound grasp of the content which they are teaching, providing
> them with a strong foundation of pedagogical knowledge, and, most
> importantly, by providing them with multiple opportunities to acquire
> tacit knowledge and practical skills from experienced teachers in schools.
> (Whelan, 2009: 147)

A much quoted finding from the McKinsey report was the comment made by one respondent to their enquiry who said: 'The quality of an education system cannot exceed the quality of its teachers' (Barber and Mourshed, 2007: 16). Although at one level this is a statement of the obvious, at another level it is a powerful reminder of what policy-makers and practitioners alike must never lose sight of. It also seems to me that this statement applies at school level: *a school cannot exceed the quality of its teachers*.

From working with many school leaders I know they agree with this interpretation. The selection and recruitment of teachers to the profession is important. So too their initial training and assessment, but in terms of what school leaders can do, the development and improvement of teaching and teachers' pedagogical practices and knowledge are both highly significant. Leadership which is connected to learning develops teachers' pedagogic practice.

This brief overview of latest thinking both in research and policy circles makes the case for what school leadership should be concentrating on. In this respect it is similar to many other discussions in that it looks at what leadership is, or should be, about. However, the real challenge in connecting leadership to learning is not in saying what it is, rather, it is in describing *how* successful school leaders do this. The next section therefore examines how leaders influence what happens in classrooms.

How leaders influence teachers' practice and what happens in classrooms

For over 10 years I have been strongly interested in how leaders make a difference to pupils' learning outcomes and progress. My work has been reported in a number of places (Southworth, 1998; 2002; 2004; 2009; see also NCSL, 2004; 2005) and in this section I summarize the main findings that have emerged. My long-term research 'project' started with studies in both small and very large primary schools. Later, while at the National College for School Leadership (now National College for School and Children's Services Leadership), the findings were tested for their relevance and applicability in secondary schools. Two sets of studies were conducted, first in high-performing departments and, second, in effective departments in secondary schools serving disadvantaged communities. Further work was also conducted into how very effective middle leaders in primary schools influenced colleagues' classroom practices. In addition, other work outside the UK supports the broad findings. For example, in the USA, Knapp et al.'s (2003) work on leading for learning came to much the same set of conclusions, particularly around the importance of modelling. In all cases the findings were consistent and mutually reinforcing, so it can be said that what follows can be applied, at a general level, to the great majority of schools, although this does not remove the need for contextual differences to be taken into account.

Indeed, all leaders should be contextually sensitive which is why detailed prescription is neither wise nor possible. As Hallinger says: 'Leadership for learning incorporates an awareness that instructional leadership practices must be adapted to the nature and needs of a school's specific context: there is no "one size fits all" model available for quick dissemination and implementation' (Hallinger, 2009: 16). The first thing to note about how leaders influence what happens in classrooms is that a leader's influence on teacher practice and student learning is largely *indirect* (Hallinger and Heck, 1996a; 1996). For example, it involves such things as defining the school's academic mission and fostering capacity for professional learning. The idea that a leader's influence is indirect is consistent with the view that leadership is a social influencing process. Since Hallinger and Heck's work others have conducted systematic reviews and meta-analyses of empirical studies. And

> These reports generally confirm our earlier conclusions concerning both the nature and size of school leadership effects on student learning. Moreover, a larger sample of studies and new methodologies for review allow for a higher degree of specificity in their conclusions and confidence in their interpretation of the evidence than was possible 15 years ago when we (Hallinger & Heck) began our own review. (Hallinger, 2009: 11)

In short, Hallinger remains confident about the veracity of his view that leaders influence indirectly.

The reason why indirect effects are the largest is because leaders work with and 'through' others. Headteachers, deputies, heads of departments and subject leaders all rely on colleagues to put into practice agreed ways of working. As such whatever the leaders wish to see is happening is contingent on others actually putting it into practice. Leaders are reliant on others because their ideas are *mediated* by teachers and other members of staff. Moreover, my own research and discussions with leaders reveals that highly effective leaders know this and work carefully on their indirect effects. In other words:

Effective school leaders work directly on their indirect influence.

They do this through three strategies and processes:

- Modelling
- Monitoring
- Dialogue.

In the following subsections I elaborate on each of these in turn.

Modelling

Modelling is all about the power of example. Teachers and headteachers are strong believers in leading by example because they know this influences pupils and colleagues alike. My own research has repeatedly shown me that teachers watch their leaders closely. Teachers closely observe what leaders do in order to:

- check whether the leaders' actions are consistent over time, and
- test whether their leaders do as they say.

Both of these 'tests' are important to teachers, and indeed most of us when we are 'followers' rather than leaders, because we prefer to follow those who can 'walk the talk' (see also Ofsted, 2009a: 3).

Successful leaders know they must set an example and positively use their actions to show how colleagues should behave. They know they must be prepared to do themselves whatever they ask others to do. This is why heads and deputies and members of the leadership team are often among the first to arrive and the last to leave the school premises; why they put extra effort into their teaching, assemblies or meetings; and why they lend colleagues a helping hand, listen to their concerns and notice their successes.

However, really effective leaders know they are being watched by their followers – that they are 'on show'. This notion of 'on show' fits with a sense of leaders being 'on stage'. They understand that they are being watched and use their visibility to their advantage by playing to their audiences. It is not so much a matter of 'putting on a show' as being aware that they are visible, observed and listened to and therefore choose their words with forethought and care to ensure, as far as they can, that their words and deeds are in harmony. There are dangers here of being either indulgent or disingenuous, but those who can avoid these dangers are likely to be more effective in influencing others.

Not only are leaders closely observed, but what they pay attention to gets noticed. Leaders who do not take an interest in learning and classrooms are quickly judged by their teacher colleagues to be uninterested in teaching. By contrast, leaders who visit classrooms, encourage colleagues to talk about their teaching successes and concerns, ensure that meetings of teachers (and support staff) focus on learning and so on are demonstrating through their actions that they remain strongly connected to classrooms.

The content of a leader's actions and words is important. Learning-centred leaders are role models to others because they are interested in learning, teaching and classrooms, and want to know more about them and keep in touch with what is happening in these key areas across the school. Moreover, the Office for Standards in Education (Ofsted, 2009a; 2009b) work on outstanding secondary and primary schools which are excelling against the odds says very much the same things.

The idea of being an exemplar to others can be daunting to some aspiring leaders. Moreover, some think that leaders are born not made. Neither idea finds favour with me. Once one accepts any position of responsibility in a social setting you are visible to others. Teachers, of course, are responsible for their pupils and are highly visible to them, so they should be accustomed to being 'on stage'. As for leaders being born and not made, I think the evidence, as well as personal experience, shows that we can all benefit from training, mentoring and coaching. We can become more self-aware of our strengths, preferences, habits and weaknesses. Coaching can especially help us to see ourselves as others perceive us, and we can become more sensitive to others.

Monitoring

Monitoring includes analysing pupil progress and outcome data (for example, assessment and test scores, school performance trends, parental opinion surveys, pupil attendance data, pupil interview information). At the same time, it involves visiting classrooms, observing teachers at work and providing them with feedback. There is a legitimate quality assurance role to be played here, which the best schools employ (see Ofsted, 2009b: 19), although in the great majority of cases the goal is not to be inspectorial, but to make these processes as educative and developmental as possible for all concerned, including the leaders.

Monitoring classrooms is now an accepted part of leadership. The Office for Standards in Education found that there is a strong link between very good monitoring and good or better teaching (Ofsted, 2003: 20). Where monitoring is effective, the quality of teaching is noticeably higher than in schools where monitoring is poor and infrequent.

Monitoring enables leaders not only to keep in touch with colleagues' classrooms, but also to develop, over time, knowledge of teachers' strengths and development needs. It is a diagnostic assessment of pedagogic skills, strengths and talents. It enables leaders to answer the questions: whose classroom practices are worthy of emulation by others? Who could coach another colleague because they are especially skilled in some aspect of their pedagogy (for example, open-ended questioning; group work; assessment for learning)?

If one teacher needs support in an aspect of their teaching which another colleague is experienced and skilled in, then it makes sense for them to work together and for one to coach the other. However, such an arrangement cannot be brokered unless and until there is an audit of pedagogic strengths across the school. In other words, monitoring plays a crucial role in peer coaching and professional support. Monitoring enables leaders to look at:

- the performance trends across the school
- identifying high-quality teaching which should be spread to all the staff
- who could lead and support other teachers' pedagogic development and in which respects.

Dialogue

Dialogue is all about creating opportunities for teachers to talk with their colleagues and leaders about learning and teaching. Both classrooms and staffrooms are places where there is a lot of talk. Indeed, there is no shortage of talk and conversation in schools. Yet, there is sometimes too little talk about teaching and learning.

The kind of dialogues which influence what happens in classrooms are professional conversations focused on learning and teaching. Leaders create the circumstances to meet with colleagues and discuss pedagogy and pupil learning. Often these dialogues appear to be informal. They can occur in corridors, offices or by the photocopier. Typically, though, they take place in classrooms and they often follow a particular structure.

When leaders visit classrooms, say at the end of the school day, they can encourage teachers to describe and analyse what they have done that day or week. They might ask about a specific pupil, or group, or follow up an aspect of teaching which staff have agreed is an area for development, such as questioning, marking or children with special learning needs. The leader's opening questions are an invitation to the colleague teacher to describe what has been going on. When we describe something, we have to organize what actually happened into an account which makes sense to the listener. In the process of describing, we analyse what happened. And if the listener asks a few questions during the retelling then this usually aids the analysis. Therefore, the depiction of classroom events is not purely descriptive; it is an analytic description.

Describing to a colleague what you did and analysing what happened often requires us to make explicit what we think. This process is often insightful both to the listener and the speaker because we can learn from our retelling things we had not previously been aware of. Recounting such 'stories' is revealing to the story teller. Often we are only aware of something we thought when we hear ourselves say it out loud to someone else. That is when we realize – 'I didn't know I knew that': that is when we learn.

Dialogue, then, is not simply talking – it is *professional learning* and it is sometimes profound professional learning. This discovering of self-knowledge is called articulation. When we explain classroom incidents and events to an interested colleague, we articulate for them and ourselves our thinking, understanding and assumptions. We make our tacit knowledge explicit. Once we have made our knowledge explicit we can 'work on it'. While it remains implicit we can neither share it, nor use it as a resource for ourselves and others.

Earlier I cited Whelan's views on how to improve the quality of teaching. One thing he said was that we need to find 'multiple opportunities to acquire tacit knowledge and practical skills from experienced teachers in schools'. What I am describing here are some of the ways leaders can increase opportunities for teachers and learning assistants to share and spread their tacit, craft knowledge. It is all about making the tacit explicit and using the conversations and presentations as the basis for staff to learn with and from one another.

Although some of these processes occur informally there is a need to structure and organize such opportunities. Initially, and at certain points in the school year, they need to be planned and formal, when participants come prepared to talk, have an agreed subject and focus, and know they are expected to share, listen and learn. These arrangements also help to establish some 'ground rules' for how we will behave and to make clear the purpose of the exercise. Ground rules are important so that everyone knows what is expected of them, how to conduct themselves and that some preparation and follow-up is necessary.

It is vital that one expectation is very clear, namely, that all involved should utilize the knowledge they are creating and sharing with one another. The purpose of these dialogues is not simply to have a 'good talk'; it is to increase our understanding, knowledge and skills of teaching and learning, and to use that knowledge to enhance our teaching practice. Professional dialogues should produce practical, actionable knowledge. Knowledge which makes me better, in some way, as a teacher. And in gaining this knowledge I must be ready and willing to try it out – to put it into my practice.

Some argue that much of what I am arguing for can be done by individuals learning from their own experience. However, I am less convinced of this. Classrooms are such dynamic arenas there is always a great deal to make sense of, to process and to refine into professional craft knowledge. Without dialogue and interested listeners who help us to set out our experience we often do not process the day-to-day actions and learn from them as much as we might. We all learn from experience, but not all of us learn as much as we might. Without leaders and other colleagues acting as mentors or coaches to facilitate our learning we sometimes learn little from our work. In fact, research in the USA (Blasé and Blasé, 1998) shows that leaders often overestimate what teachers learn from their classroom experiences and therefore do not provide the very support they need to increase their learning about their teaching.

Dialogues with teachers include encouragement, feedback and questioning about teaching. It is more powerful when based on classroom observation. Teacher and leader dialogues enhance teacher reflection about teaching methods and expected pupil outcomes, as well as informing teachers' classroom behaviours (Blasé and Blasé, 1998: 93). Professional conversation enables teachers to expand their teaching repertoires and to improve their understandings of their teaching practices.

It should not go unnoticed that the conversations I have been describing involve the construction and co-construction of professional knowledge. This notion of constructing learning is important because increasingly contemporary thinking about learning for both children and adults alike shows that it is a process of constructing meanings and understanding, rather than transmitting knowledge from one to another (Lambert, 2009). Therefore, the beauty of this approach, to my thinking, is that it practises what it preaches. It makes the process of professional development and learning consistent with what we presently know about learning and thereby the medium becomes the message.

Modelling, monitoring and dialogue are the three strategies leaders use to influence others. The three overlap and reinforce one another so that together they enable powerful professional learning to take place and expertise to grow and spread: it is a learning model in every respect. However, in addition to the three strategies, certain organizational conditions need to be in place to maximize their effect.

Organizational conditions and culture

Leadership, especially leadership for learning, takes place within the school; the school as an organization is the environment for the improvement of pedagogic practice. As such, the school is a learning environment for teachers and classroom assistants, as well as pupils. Not every school leader I have met sees, or thinks of, the school in this way – as a learning environment for adults. If and when we do, then we need to ask ourselves is it a good learning environment? Could it be improved?

There are a number of ways by which schools can be productive learning environments for adults. The literature on learning communities is extensive and detailed on this topic, but from experience and research I can offer a small number of ideas which seem to help. These ideas are not exhaustive, but they help to make a start. Other points should be added which reflect specific contexts, experience and needs.

The ideas itemized below are really principles of procedure:

1 Professional learning should be talked about, and leaders (and school governors) should demonstrate they value it.

2 Improvement of practice should be the goal of professional learning. Professional development is valuable, but teaching is a practical task and professional learning needs to enable better practice. Therefore, leaders should enquire and prompt colleagues who undertake the many and different ways of developing themselves to put into practice their new knowledge and enhanced skills.

3 Improving one's practice is necessary not because we are poor practitioners, but because we can all get better. Learning the craft of teaching is a lifelong process; that is what being an educator means. Teachers have to be learners too, this is neither a contradiction nor a paradox, it is what ensures excellence in practice throughout our careers and it is the responsibility of those who serve students to be the very best they can be.

4 On-the-job learning should be seen as part of working in any school. There should be an expectation that we are all learners and that we all learn from our work: the workplace is our learning workshop.

5 Professional learning is collaborative as well as individual; we have a responsibility for one another's learning as well as our own.

6 Professional collaboration involves and requires all to share their skills and talents, to be honest about their pedagogic concerns and challenges, and to support one another.

These principles of procedure are further supported when leaders and managers create time and opportunities for colleagues to meet, to visit one another's classrooms, to lead discussions, to run in-service events for staff groups and to take part in external professional development activities. Joint lesson-planning arrangements have become very common today, so too sharing assessment information and analysing data by departments, key stage, year groups and so on. All of these, and others, create opportunities for professional collaboration. But some of these should not occur instead of talking about teaching. Leaders as chairs of discussion groups, working parties, action research teams or whatever groups and meetings they are leading should ensure that time is used to consider the pedagogic and practical changes needed in classrooms.

Together these principles and procedures help to create a school culture which prizes professional and pupil learning alike. It is powerfully focused on pedagogy. It is also improvement oriented. It is about action – changing classroom practice in order to improve pupils' progress and achievements.

We should aim to ensure, at the very least, that every teacher in a school is as good as the best teachers in that school. This is not to crudely say there are good and poor teachers; it is to acknowledge that some of us are better at some parts of our practice than others. If those of us less competent (but not incompetent) can learn with and from those more experienced or skilled in specific aspects of their teaching, then we can all, over time, get better. In turn, those who have benefited from a colleague or two on one thing will have something to give back on another aspect of our practice. There is a principle of reciprocity (Elmore, 2008: 57) here. Many schools are doing this (for example, Ofsted, 2009b: 34) and some are now developing clusters of schools which work together to share their skills and knowledge among themselves. There are many encouraging signs, but we should ensure that it becomes both common practice and is sustained over time.

Implications

Although there are many implications to highlight from the foregoing, space dictates I highlight just three:

1 Leadership of learning and teaching is distributed.
2 Distributed leadership must be developed.
3 Support is needed to ensure leaders have the resources to hand to lead teaching and learning.

Leadership of learning and teaching is distributed

Leadership of learning and teaching has to be distributed. While the role of headteacher remains very important: 'Leadership for learning as an organising construct for school leadership is not limited to the principal, as was the case with instructional leadership. It incorporates the notion of shared instructional leadership' (Hallinger, 2009: 16). Increasingly in large and medium-sized schools in England headteachers are taking on more strategic leadership of the school. This is often right and proper, but part of being a strategic leader is to ensure that there is a strategy inside the school to lead teaching and learning, and to improve it.

Without doubt middle leaders – heads of departments and faculties, subject leaders and unit leaders – are key players in leading teaching and learning. We have seen in the last decade or so that many of these individuals have moved from managing things (materials, budgets) to leading people. Moreover, we also know that as the improvement of practice spreads, so too does leadership flow 'outwards' and others begin to take on leadership roles:

> As improvement advances, it becomes clearer that role-based definitions of leadership are inadequate, both because teachers who take improvement of their own practice seriously become more expert on instructional issues than their supervisors and because the flow of work through the organization becomes too demanding and too complex to manage exclusively from the top. So the work of leadership tends to flow out into the organization. (Elmore; 2008: 52)

Elmore goes on to illustrate how this can be managed and led. For example he says:

> Every new teacher should have a supervisor who is an experienced teacher who modelled not just excellent teaching but also practices of observation, analysis, problem solving and work with peers that characterise successful approaches to improvement

> Every intermediate teacher (e.g. after their NQT year) would be given some leadership responsibility in some aspect improving teaching, under the guidance of a mentor and be provided with continuous feedback on their practice including the practices of improvement (working with peers, leading groups, creating and demonstrating teaching solutions to pressing problems of performance, etc). (Elmore, 2008: 59)

Also, and very importantly given what was said in the previous section, such leadership development 'follows the contours of expertise' (Elmore, 2008: 59).

We know that some forms of distribution are more effective than others (Leithwood et al., 2006: 13). Laissez-faire approaches are not as effective as more coordinated forms. This is why principles of procedure are important and why the roles of senior leaders and headteachers need to be shaped to ensure that the more they distribute leadership the more they must ensure it is coordinated.

Distributed leadership must be developed

The idea that distributed leadership must be developed follows from what has just been said. Indeed, distribution and development are two sides of the same leadership coin. Three things have struck me from my reading and research around distributed leadership in the last few years. First, that the more leadership is distributed the more leadership development moves from being an option to an obligation the school and senior leaders in it have to honour. Second, when leadership is distributed we have to ask: what kind of leadership is being distributed? I doubt many schools would benefit markedly by having lots more strategic leaders. However, all schools would and should benefit from having as many leaders of teaching and learning as possible. Indeed, Hallinger has argued that there is empirical support for distributed leadership, over time, being a driver for school improvement (Hallinger, 2009: 14). Therefore, it is the leadership of learning which should be distributed. Third, as leadership is distributed we have to move from thinking of leadership as an individual exercise to leadership as a collective activity. This means asking:

- What is the sum total of leadership in the school?
- Who is leading the practice of improvement?
- Who is leading teaching and learning?
- How well is the leadership of learning integrated into a whole school approach which supports and strengthens the school's vision and pace of improvement?

Support is needed to ensure leaders have the resources to hand to lead teaching and learning

Headteachers, deputy heads and assistant headteachers need support in leading and managing the distribution and development of middle leaders. There is some dedicated provision both nationally and locally in England and that is necessary, but not yet sufficient. What is needed is ready access to the latest thinking and key insights into effective classroom practices and pedagogy. However, there is room for more and better provision and access. Hill (2002) wrote an insightful paper entitled 'What principals need to know about teaching and learning'. This title encapsulates what I am now arguing should be provided for them. National agencies, research universities and government departments should liaise and jointly produce succinct and accessible information about effective teaching, latest evidence and research, inspection findings and so on. Currently much of this material remains piecemeal and scattered. It may be timely now for central government to take the lead and sponsor much better collation, reporting and communication of what works in teaching and learning.

Conclusion

Leadership and learning are connected because learning is the core purpose of schools and thereby school leadership. How it is connected and conducted is by senior leaders strategically organizing the distribution of leadership to middle leaders who through their excellence as teachers and their skills as leaders lead by example, monitor pedagogy, learning and the development of colleagues, and through coaching, mentoring and focused dialogue spread the best practice within their schools to colleagues and draw in excellent practice from elsewhere. Senior leaders support middle leaders by building a school culture which values professional collaboration and learning, and by creating the organizational conditions and capacity for staff to work together in their departmental teams and other groupings to concentrate on pedagogic improvements, analysis of learning outcomes and trends and share their practical knowledge of what works.

In other words, what this chapter outlines is what school improvement looks like in action. I say this because 'the greatest gains come from a sustained and strategic approach to improving the quality of teaching' (Hill, 2009).

All of which leads to three main conclusions. First, leading learning means focusing on teaching and learning and, in particular, developing pedagogy. Second, the ideas sketched out in this chapter play a critical part in showing how leaders can enable their schools to become holistic, learning organizations. It is in these ways that they become professionally 'joined up' – coordinated and integrated organizations. Such ways of working are important because 'great schools are more than the sum of their parts' (Ofsted, 2009b: 5). Third, leadership of this kind is essentially a 'human investment enterprise' (Elmore, 2008: 58). Leadership in this view is a knowledge-based discipline focusing on the quality of instruction and the performance of pupils. Furthermore, such leadership ensures schools have a modern, twenty-first century approach to human resource management; a topic largely ignored to date in school leadership writing, and now worthy of concerted attention. Part of human resource management is ensuring there is a systematic approach to leadership development, including the identification of potential and talent, systematic opportunities to lead and feedback, assessment and coaching. Schools should, indeed, must invest in all their human and social capital.

Reflective Questions

Throughout I have posed some questions. Here I set out three of the main ones for school leaders:

1 What is the sum total of leadership in your school?
2 Do leaders in your school collectively know which teachers are excellent in which aspects of their pedagogy?
3 How effective is the development of learning-centred leadership in your school?

Additionally, you might reflect on these two issues:

- Give the school a score out of 10 for how well excellent teaching practices are spread across the teaching group. Given that score, what needs to be done to improve it, and if it is the highest score, what should now be done to sustain it?
- What do you perceive to be the major barriers to establishing or improving the school's culture so that it can support the leadership of learning and teaching? Having identified these, what can *you* do about them and what can the team of leaders do to make things better?

Further Reading

Southworth, G. (2009) Learning-centred leadership, in B. Davies (ed.), *The Essentials of School Leadership*. 2nd edn. London: Sage. pp. 91–111.
This chapter looks at how leaders make a difference to the quality of teaching and learning through the explicit use of modelling, monitoring and dialogues and goes on to consider the implications of these strategies for school leaders.
Elmore, R. (2008) Leadership as the practice of improvement, in OECD *Improving School Leadership: Volume 2*. Paris, OECD. pp. 37–67.
Elmore argues that the in times of high accountability leadership is the practice of improvement and this involves: building leadership capacity; the sharing of knowledge and skill; and treating leadership as a human investment enterprise.

References

Barber, M. and Mourshed, M. (2007) *How the World's Best-performing School Systems Come Out on Top*. London: McKinsey & Co.

Blasé, J. and Blasé, J. (1998) *Handbook of Instructional Leadership: How Really Good Principals Promote Teaching and Learning*. Thousand Oaks, CA: Corwin Press.

Day, C., Sammons, P., Hopkins, D., Harris, A., Leithwood, K., Gu, Q., Brown, E., Ahtaridou, E. and Kington, A. (2009) *The Impact of School Leadership on Pupil Outcomes: Final Report*. Research report, DCSF-RR108. London: DCSF.

Elmore, R. (2008) Leadership as the practice of improvement, in OECD, *Improving School Leadership: Volume 2*. Paris: OECD. pp. 37–67.

Hallinger, P. (2009) Leadership for 21st century schools: from instructional leadership to leadership for learning, public lecture paper, Hong Kong Institute of Education.

Hallinger, P. and Heck, R. (1996a) Reassessing the principal's role in school effectiveness: a review of empirical research 1980–1995, *Educational Administrative Quarterly*, 32(1): 5–44.

Hallinger, P. and Heck, R. (1996b) The principal's role in school effectiveness: a review of methodological issues 1980–1995, in K. Leithwood, J. Chapman, D. Lorsen, P. Hallinger and A. Hart (eds), *The International Handbook of Educational Leadership and Administration*. Dordrecht: Kluwer. pp. 723–84.

Hallinger, P. and Murphy, J. (1986) Assessing the instructional behaviour of principals, *Elementary School Journal*, 86(2): 217–48.

Heck, R. (1992) Principal instructional leadership and the identification of high- and low-achieving schools, *Administrators' Notebook*, 34(7): 1–4.

Hill, P. (2002) What principals need to know about teaching and learning, unpublished paper, University of Melbourne, Australia.

Hill, P. (2009) Reducing variability, PowerPoint presentation at NCSL's international invitational seminar on variability, achievement gaps and sustainable leadership, Nottingham, June.

Knapp, M., Copeland, M., Ford, B. and Markholt, A. (2003) *Leading for Learning Sourcebook: Concepts and Examples*. Seattle, WA: Centre for the Study of Teaching and Policy, University of Washington.

Lambert, L. (2009) Constructivist leadership, in B. Davies (ed.), *The Essentials of School Leadership*. 2nd edn. London: Sage.

Leithwood, K., Day, C., Sammons, P., Harris, D. and Hopkins, D. (2006) *Seven Strong Claims About Successful School Leadership*. Nottingham: National College for School Leadership.

NCSL (2004) *Learning-centred Leadership*. Nottingham: NCSL.

NCSL (2005) *Learning-centred Leadership II*. Nottingham: NCSL.

OECD (2008) *Improving School Leadership: Volume 1 – Policy and Practice*. Paris: OECD.

Ofsted (2003) *Leadership and Management: What Inspection Tells Us*. London: Office for Standards in Education.

Ofsted (2009a) *Twenty Outstanding Primary Schools: Excelling Against the Odds*. London: Office for Standards in Education.

Ofsted (2009b) *Twelve Outstanding Secondary Schools: Excelling Against the Odds*. London: Office for Standards in Education.

Robinson, V., Lloyd, C. and Rowe, K. (2008) The impact of leadership on student outcomes: an analysis of the differential effects of leadership types, *Educational Administration Quarterly*, 44(5): 653–74.

Southworth, G. (1998) *Leading Improving Primary Schools*. London: Falmer.

Southworth, G. (2002) Instructional leadership in schools: reflections and empirical evidence, *School Leadership and Management*, 22(1): 73–91.

Southworth, G. (2004) *Primary School Leadership in Context: Leading Small, Medium and Large Sized Schools*. London: Routledge Falmer.

Southworth, G. (2009) Learning-centred leadership, in B. Davies (ed.), *The Essentials of School Leadership*. 2nd edn. London: Sage.

Whelan, F. (2009) *Lessons Learned: How Good Policies Produce Better Schools*. London: Whelan.

CHAPTER 7

Realizing the Potential of System Leadership

David Hopkins

In making the case in this chapter for the potential of systemic reform to enable every student to reach their potential and for every school to be great, and the consequent role of system leader, I:

- clarify the central policy conundrum of balancing national prescription with schools leading reform
- identify the four key drivers that underpin system change
- outline the concept of and a model for system leadership
- describe the internal and external aspects of the system leadership role
- conclude by proposing some questions and suggesting a reflection on the role of system leadership.

For a country to succeed it needs both a competitive economy and an inclusive society. That requires an education system with high standards, which transmits and develops knowledge and culture from one generation to the next, promotes respect for and engagement with learning, broadens horizons and develops high expectations. We want to ensure all young people progressively develop the knowledge, understanding, skills, attitudes and values in the curriculum, and become effective, enthusiastic and independent learners, committed to lifelong learning and able to handle the demands of adult life. This is a pretty good description of an educational system committed to ensuring that every school is at least a good school and that most are on the journey to becoming great.

This aspiration reflects the now almost global concern over standards of student learning and achievement. It is also becoming increasingly clear that the critical factor in ensuring student success is the role of the school leader. Indeed in our summary of research on this topic – *Seven Strong Claims about Successful School Leadership* (Leithwood et al., 2007) – we claim that, 'School leadership is second only to classroom instruction as an influence on student learning'. It is this that leads me to a simple proposition:

If our goal is 'every school a great school' then policy and practice has to focus on system improvement. This means that a school head or principal has to be almost as concerned about the success of other schools as he or she is about his or her own school. Sustained improvement of schools is not possible unless the whole system is moving forward.

The concept of 'system leadership is one that has recently caught the educational imagination. System leaders are those head teachers who are willing to shoulder system wide roles in order to support the improvement of other schools as well as their own. As such, system leadership is a new and emerging practice that embraces a variety of responsibilities that are developing either locally or within discrete national networks or programmes that when taken together have the potential to contribute to system transformation.

The crucial policy conundrum

The centrality of the role of school leader in the process of educational change has quickened of late particularly as a consequence of various national experiments with large-scale reform (Fullan, 2009). The argument goes something like this (Hopkins, 2010a):

- Most agree that when standards are too low and too varied that some form of direct state intervention is necessary. Typically, the resultant 'national prescription' proves very successful in raising standards in the short term.

- But progress soon tends to plateau and whilst a bit more improvement could be squeezed out especially in underperforming schools, one had to question whether prescription still offers the recipe for sustained large-scale reform into the medium/long term.

- There is a growing recognition that schools need to lead the next phase of reform. But, if the hypothesis is correct, it must categorically not be a naive return to the not so halcyon days when a thousand flowers bloomed and the educational life chances of too many of our children wilted.

- The implication is that we need a transition from an era of prescription to an era of professionalism – in which the balance between national prescription and schools leading reform will also change.

However, achieving this shift is not straightforward. As Michael Fullan (2003) has commented, it takes capacity to build capacity, and if there is insufficient capacity to begin with it is folly to announce that a move to 'professionalism' provides the basis of a new approach. The key question is 'how do we get there?' because we cannot simply move from one era to the other without self-consciously building professional capacity throughout the system. It is this progression that is illustrated in Figure 7.1 and is discussed at length in my book *Every School a Great School* (Hopkins, 2007a).

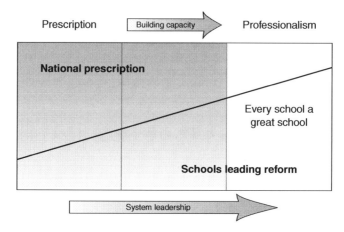

Figure 7.1   Towards system-wide sustainable reform

It is worth taking a little more time to unpack the thinking underlying Figure 7.1. Four further points need to be made:

1 The first is to emphasize that this not an argument against 'top-down' change. Neither 'top-down' nor 'bottom-up' change works just by themselves, they have to be in balance – in creative tension. The balance between the two at any one time will of course depend on context.

2 It must be realized that in many countries at the start of any change process more central direction is needed. This reflects the balance towards national prescription as seen in the left-hand segment of the Figure 7.1. If we assume that time moves from left to right in the diagram, then it is most probably correct to say that, in terms of both policy and practice, high-performing educational systems have over time made progress from the left-hand into the right-hand segment of the diagram.

3 Third it should be no surprise to realize that the right-hand segment is relatively unknown territory. It implies horizontal and lateral ways of working with assumptions and governance arrangements very different from what we know now. The main difficulty in imagining this landscape is that the thinking of most people is constrained by their experiences within the power structure and norms of the left-hand segment of the diagram.

4 Finally, it needs to be made clear that it is leadership, more precisely system leadership, that provides the energy and dynamic to move from an era of prescription to one of professionalism. Despite the rhetoric of politicians and civil servants both local and national, their default position is to maintain their authority and by that token the status quo. It is therefore up to our system leaders to lead policy through their practice. These system leaders often in the face of contrary policy pressure are creating a new more collaborative and lateral landscape of schooling as presaged by the right segment in Figure 7.1. It is the professionals who are now taking the power.

Four drivers for system reform

As has already been intimated, the transition from 'prescription' to 'professionalism' requires strategies that not only continue to raise standards but also build capacity within the system. This point is key, one cannot just drive to continue to raise standards in an instrumental way, and one also needs to develop social, intellectual and organizational capital. Building capacity demands that we replace numerous central initiatives with a national consensus on a limited number of educational trends. The four drivers of personalized learning professionalized teaching, networks and collaboration and intelligent accountability provide the core strategy for systemic improvement. They are the canvas on which system leadership is exercised. As seen in Figure 7.2 the 'diamond of reform', the four trends coalesce and mould to context through the exercise of responsible system leadership.

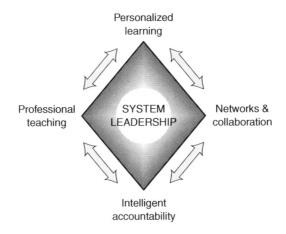

Figure 7.2   Four key drivers underpinning system reform

Personalized learning

The current focus on personalization is about putting students at the heart of the education process so as to tailor teaching to individual need, interest and aptitude in order to fulfil every young person's potential. Many schools and teachers have differentiated curriculum and teaching methods to meet the needs of children and young people with great success for many years. What is new is the drive to make the best practices universal. A successful system of personalized learning means clear learning pathways through the education system and the motivation to become independent, e-literate, fulfilled, lifelong learners. Personalized learning demands both curriculum entitlement and choice that delivers a breadth of study and personal relevance, as well as emphasizing the development of the student's meta-cognitive capacity, in other words 'learning how to learn'.

Professionalized teaching

Significant empirical evidence suggests that teaching quality is the most significant factor influencing student learning that is under the control of the school. It is also clear that the forms of teaching that promote high levels of student learning vary in some instances quite dramatically from country to country. The phrase 'professionalized teaching' implies that teachers are on a par with other professions in terms of diagnosis, the application of evidence-based practices and professional pride. The image here is of teachers who use data to evaluate the learning needs of their students, and are consistently expanding their repertoire of pedagogic strategies to personalize learning for all students. It also implies schools that adopt innovative approaches to timetabling and the deployment of increasingly differentiated staffing models.

Intelligent accountability

Because of the resilience of external forms of accountability, it is often necessary to compensate by increasing the emphasis on internal forms of accountability. The most common approaches would be the use of teacher assessment, bottom-up target setting, value-added measures of school performance and the school holding itself publicly accountable through publishing its own profile of strengths and weaknesses and benchmark comparisons giving a more rounded picture of the schools performance. It is these forms of accountability that (a) allow a sharper fix on the focus of personalization; and (b) develop the professional skill of the teaching staff involved. As a consequence, when the balance between external and internal accountability become more even, it also becomes more 'intelligent'. The assumption also is that over time, as schools increasingly lead reform, internal forms of accountability will become the more important.

Networking and collaboration

This relates to the various ways in which networks of schools can stimulate and spread innovation as well as collaborate to provide curriculum diversity, extended services and community support. The prevalence of networking practice supports the contention that there is no contradiction between strong, independent schools and strong networks, rather the reverse. Nor is there a contradiction between collaboration and competition – many sectors of the economy are demonstrating that the combination of competition and collaboration delivers the most rapid improvements. Although evidence of effectiveness is still accumulating, it is becoming clear that networks support improvement and innovation by enabling schools to collaborate on building curriculum diversity, extended services and professional support to develop a vision of education that is shared and owned well beyond individual school gates.

Although these key drivers provide a core strategy for systemic improvement, it is system leadership that adapts them to particular and individual school contexts. This is leadership that enables systemic reform to be both generic in terms of overall strategy and specific in adapting to individual and particular situations.

It is system leaders who reach beyond their own school to create networks and collaborative arrangements that, not only add richness and excellence to the learning of students, but also act as agents of educational transformation.

System leadership

As we have already noted, 'system leaders' are those headteachers or principals who are willing to shoulder system leadership roles: who care about and work for the success of other schools as well as their own. In England, where our original research was conducted, there appears to be an emerging cadre of these headteachers who stand in contrast to the competitive ethic of headship so prevalent in the 1990s. It is these educators who by their own efforts and commitment are beginning to transform the nature of leadership and educational improvement in this country. Interestingly there is also evidence of this role emerging in other leading educational systems in Europe, North America and Australia (Pont et al., 2008).

The first thing to say is that system leadership as has been argued is imbued with moral purpose (Fullan, 2003). Without that, there would not be the passion to proceed or the encouragement for others to follow. In England for example, where the regularities of improvement in teaching and learning are still not well understood, where deprivation is still too good a predictor of educational success and where the goal is for every school to be a great school, the leadership challenge is surely a systemic one. This perspective gives a broader appreciation of what is meant by the moral purpose of system leadership.

In *Every School a Great School* (Hopkins, 2007a), I argued that system leaders express their moral purpose through:

- Measuring their success in terms of improving student learning and increasing achievement, and striving to both raise the bar and narrow the gap(s).

- Being fundamentally committed to the improvement of teaching and learning. They engage deeply with the organization of teaching, learning, curriculum and assessment in order to ensure that learning is personalized for all their students.

- Developing their schools as personal and professional learning communities, with relationships built across and beyond each school to provide a range of learning experiences and professional development opportunities.

- Striving for equity and inclusion through acting on context and culture. This is not just about eradicating poverty, as important as that is. It is also about giving communities a sense of worth and empowerment.

- Realizing in a deep way that the classroom, school and system levels all impact on each other. Crucially they understand that in order to change the larger system you have to engage with it in a meaningful way.

Although this degree of clarity is not necessarily obvious in the behaviour and practice of every headteacher, these aspirations are increasingly becoming part of the conventional wisdom of our best global educational leaders.[1]

Building on these key capabilities, and combining them with the range of identified roles, it is possible to offer a model of system leadership practice that has emerged inductively from the research we have done with outstanding educational leaders (Hopkins, 2007a). This is set out in the Figure 7.3.

The model exhibits a logic that flows from the 'inside-out.' At the centre, leaders driven by a moral purpose related to the enhancement of student learning, seek to empower teachers and others to make schools a critical force for improving communities. This is premised on the argument already made, that sustainable educational development requires educational leaders who are willing to shoulder broader leadership roles: who care about and work for the success of other schools as well as their own.

It is also clear from our research that system leaders share a characteristic set of behaviours and skills. As illustrated in the second inner ring of Figure 7.3 these are of two types. First, system leaders engage in 'personal development' usually informally through benchmarking themselves against their peers and developing their skill base in response to the context they find themselves working in. Second, all the system leaders we have studied have a strategic capability; they are

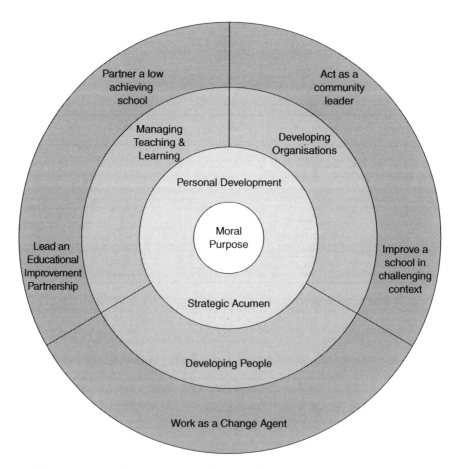

Figure 7.3   A model of system leadership practice

able to translate their vision or moral purpose into operational principles that have tangible outcomes. Taken together these two central circles of the diagram reflect the core practice of 'setting directions' as noted in the table opposite.

As is denoted in the third ring of Figure 7.3, the moral purpose, personal qualities and strategic capacity of the system leader find focus in three domains of the school detailed below – managing the teaching and learning process, developing people and developing the organization.

Finally, although there is a growing number of outstanding leaders that exemplify these qualities and determinations, they are not necessarily 'system leaders'. A system leader not only needs these aspirations and capabilities but in addition, as seen in the outer ring of the model, works to change other contexts by engaging with the wider system in a meaningful way. We have included in the outer ring the range of roles, identified from the research, that focuses on improving other schools, sharing curriculum innovations, empowering communities and/or leading partnerships committed to enabling all schools to move forward.

The nature of the practice implied in this model is described in detail in *System Leadership in Practice* (Higham et al., 2009). In the remaining available space the best I can do by way of illustration is to focus briefly on the *internal* and *external* aspects of system leadership.

Internal aspects of system leadership

A helpful way of focusing on the internal aspects of system leadership is to draw on Leithwood and Reihl's (2005) conceptualization of the central tenets of successful school leadership on which the model just outlined builds. Table 7.1 sets out these practices (see also Hopkins and Higham, 2007). This analysis reinforces the argument that enhancing learning and teaching is a key priority for school leadership. Contemporarily, trends towards personalizing education to individual student needs and interests, coupled with a greater responsibility for student welfare, represent real challenges for school leaders as they attempt to continue to raise school standards and offer a broad and balanced education.

In any discussion of the 'internal system leadership', it is important to realize that at the heart of personalized learning is its impact, not just on test scores and examination results, but on the students' learning capability. If the conditions can be created in the school where the teacher can teach the student how to learn at the same time as assisting them to acquire curriculum content, then the twin goals of learning and achievement can be met at the same time. This point was made in our book *Models of Learning – Tools for Teaching* (Joyce et al., 2009) where we argued that it is the teacher's task not simply to 'teach', but to create powerful contexts for learning. We expressed the essence of personalized learning in this way:

> Learning experiences are composed of content, process and social climate. As teachers we create for and with our children opportunities to explore and build important areas of knowledge, develop powerful tools for learning, and live in humanising social conditions.

Table 7.1   A conceptualization of the capabilities for system leaders

Core practice	Key system leadership actions
Setting direction	Total commitment to enable every learner to reach their potential with a strategic vision that extends into the future and brings immediacy to the delivery of improvements for students
System implication	Ability to translate vision into whole-school programmes that extend the impact of pedagogic and curricular developments into other classrooms and schools
Managing teaching and learning	Ensure every child is inspired and challenged through appropriate curriculum and a repertoire of teaching styles and skills that underpin personalized learning
System implication	Develop a high degree of clarity about, and consistency of, teaching quality to both create the regularities of practice that sustain improvement and to enable sharing of best practice and innovation across the system
Developing people	Enable students to become more active learners, develop thinking and learning skills and take greater responsibility for their own learning. Involve parents and the communities to minimize the impact of challenging circumstances on expectations and achievement
System implication	Develop schools as professional learning communities, with relationships built and fostered across and beyond schools to provide a range of learning experiences and professional development opportunities for staff
Developing the organization	Create an evidence-based school, with decisions effectively informed by student data, with self-evaluation and external support used to seek out approaches to school improvement

It is the integration of curriculum content, teaching and learning strategies and the school cultures that enhance self-confidence that provides the parameters for the work of skilled teachers. But there is a significant barrier to progress in this area: despite the contemporary emphasis on the importance of classroom practice, the language or discourse about teaching remains in general at a restricted level. There is a need for a far more elaborate language in which to talk about teaching and more sophisticated frameworks against which to reflect on practice. Even in those instances where more precision of language is achieved, say in the debate on whole-class teaching, there are few operational definitions against which teachers can assess their own practice and thereby develop and expand their range of classroom practices. The key leadership challenge here is to ensure that quality teaching and learning is underpinned by more elaborate and explicit frameworks for learning and teaching. Teaching for personalizing learning is an important focus for leadership committed to ensuring that every student reaches their potential and that their school is on the path to greatness. Although the impact of leadership on student achievement and school effectiveness has been acknowledged for some time, it is only recently that we have begun to understand more fully the fine-grained nature of that relationship. A reasonably elegant summary of this evidence is as follows:

- The leadership develops *a narrative for improvement.*
- The leadership is *highly focused on improving the quality of teaching and learning* (and student welfare).
- The leadership explicitly *organizes the school for improvement.*
- The leadership creates:
  - *clarity (of the systems established)*
  - *consistency (of the systems spread across school)*
  - *continuity (of the systems over time).*
- The leadership creates *internal accountability and reciprocity.*
- The leadership works to *change context as a key component of their improvement strategy.*

There are two relatively new features to this profile. The first is the emphasis on narrative and its impact on both strategy and culture. It is student learning that is the central focus of the narrative that then presents a series of complex and interacting initiatives within a unifying story around the image of a journey. This is strategic in so far as it integrates a wide variety of initiatives and projects forward, and cultural in so far as it speaks both to the individual and collective contribution and the moral purpose of schooling. The second is the emphasis on 'systems' and the transferability and sustainability of best practice that we discuss in the following section.

The external aspects of system leadership

The characteristics of the 'effective school' have been known for some time, but at a rather high level of generalization. Again we have recently acquired more textured understanding of what these effective practices look like and how they combine together in a 'whole-school design'. We are now at a point when all of the key practices can be presented in an implementable and action-oriented form. It is these practices that provide the currency of interaction between system leaders as they increasingly engage with schools other than their own. It is the exchange of excellent and increasingly precise practices for the personalization of learning that is becoming the stock in trade of the new breed of system leaders and that informs the roles that they are adopting.

We have recently identified a variety of system leader roles emerging in England that is consistent with such a moral purpose (Higham et al., 2009). At present these are:

- Develop and *lead a successful educational improvement partnership* across local communities to support welfare and potential, usually as a result of the ECM agenda.

- Choose to *lead and improve a school in extremely challenging circumstances* and then sustain it as a high valued-added institution over a significant period of tlme; the Academies movement has proved important in this regard.
- *Partner another school facing difficulties and improve it.* This category includes executive heads of 'hard' federations and leaders of more informal improvement arrangements.
- Act as a *curriculum or pedagogic innovator* who with their staff develop exemplary and increasingly precise curriculum, teaching and assessment practices and systematically share them with others.
- Work as *change agents* or experts' leaders as, for example, in England, National Leaders of Education, School Improvement Partners or Consultant Leaders.

No doubt these roles will expand and mature over time and I believe that they have applicability to a wide range of other educational systems. What is particularly significant about them is that they have evolved in response to the adaptive challenge of system change. If we want to transform systems as well as schools, then the pedagogic knowledge encapsulated in the previous discussion is necessary but not sufficient. It is necessary, indeed essential, because the practices related to the 'instructional core' are the critical currency of school improvement (Hopkins, 2010b). This is the language of school reform and indeed should be the only focus of the conversations between system leaders. It also, however, has to be coupled to a strategy for system-wide change.

It is important to realize, though, that this aspiration of system transformation being facilitated by the degree of segmentation existing in the system only holds when certain conditions are in place. There are two crucial aspects to this:

1 That there is increased clarity on the nature of intervention and support for schools at each phase of the performance cycle.
2 That schools at each phase are clear as to the most productive ways in which to collaborate in order to capitalize on the diversity within the system.

A summary of this 'segmentation' approach is set out in Table 7.2. In the right-hand column is a basic taxonomy of schools based on their phase in the performance cycle. The number of categories and the terminology will vary from setting to setting, the crucial point being that not all schools are the same and each requires different forms of support. It is this that is the focus of the second column, where a range of strategies for supporting schools at different phases of their development is briefly described. Again these descriptions are grounded in the English context, but they do have a more universal applicability. There are two key points here:

1 One size does not fit all.
2 These different forms of intervention and support are increasingly being provided by schools themselves, rather than being imposed and delivered by some external agency. This approach to system transformation relies fundamentally on school-to-school support as the basis of the improvement strategy.

Table 7.2 The 'segmentation approach' to school improvement

Type of school	Key strategies – responsive to context and need
Leading schools	Become leading practitioners Formal federation with lower-performing schools
Succeeding, self-improving schools	Regular local networking for school leaders Between-school curriculum development
Succeeding schools with internal variations	Consistency interventions: such as Assessment for Learning Subject specialist support to particular departments
Underperforming schools	Linked school support for underperforming departments Underperforming pupil programmes: catch-up
Lower-attaining schools	Formal support in federation structure Consultancy in core subjects and best practice
Failing schools	Intensive support from new or consultant school leader New provider or 'Restart' with new name and leaderships

This approach to system transformation requires a fair degree of boldness in setting system level expectations and conditions. There are four implications in particular that have to be grappled with:

1 All failing and underperforming (and potentially low-achieving) schools should have a leading school that works with them in either a formal grouping federation (where the leading school principal or head assumes overall control and accountability) or a more informal partnership. Evidence from existing federations suggests that a national system of federations would be capable of delivering a sustainable step-change in improvement in relatively short periods of time.

2 Schools should take greater responsibility for neighbouring schools so that the move towards networking encourages groups of schools to form collaborative arrangements outside of local control. This would be on the condition that these schools provided extended services for all students within a geographic area, but equally on the acceptance that there would be incentives for doing so. Encouraging local schools to work together will build capacity for continuous improvement at local level.

3 The incentives for greater system responsibility should include significantly enhanced funding for students most at risk to counter the predictive character of poverty noted earlier. Beyond incentivizing local collaboratives, the potential effects for large-scale, long-term reform include:

(a) A more even distribution of 'at risk' students and associated increases in standards, due to more schools seeking to admit a larger proportion of 'at risk' students so as to increase their overall income.

(b) A significant reduction in 'sink schools' even where 'at risk' students are concentrated, as there would be much greater potential to respond to the social-economic challenges (for example, by paying more to attract the best teachers, or by developing excellent parental involvement and outreach services).

4 A rationalization of national and local agency functions and roles to allow the higher degree of national and regional coordination for this increasingly devolved system. At present there are too many national and local organizations acting in a competitive, uncoordinated and capricious way.

In concluding, it is worth briefly reflecting on the distinction between system leaders working in regional or national programmes and those working in locally organized often ad hoc roles. In our experience, the majority of system leaders operate in national programmes that incentivise activity through organization, funding and professional development that in turn create new opportunities for headteachers.

A greater degree of freedom exists however where roles are identified as being locally developed, ad hoc and contextually responsive. In such activity, professionals not only deploy their experience and skill to lead improvements, they also define the terms on which such activity is undertaken and sustained. With no single framework or protocol, a range of models is developed in relation to specific needs (and times). Some centrally driven momentum is sacrificed, but on the principle that system leadership must inherently be a professionally-led agenda.

There are, of course, variations to this bottom-up/top-down distinction. Happily, many local and regional authorities are now imaginatively creating the conditions for schools to support each other. For instance, strategic local leadership partnerships already exist between headteachers, principals and local authorities in many jurisdictions. In one such model the authority retains legal responsibility for value for money while delegating decision-making to a partnership of headteachers who bring coherence and accountability to local collaboration.

As I hope has been demonstrated in this chapter, system leadership represents a powerful combination of practices that gives us a glimpse of leadership in a new educational landscape. The collective sharing of skills, expertise and experience creates much richer and more sustainable opportunities for rigorous transformation than can ever be provided by isolated institutions. Realizing this landscape, however, may also require a bigger shift within the broader education system, in particular by giving school leaders more agency to take the lead – in short, to light their own fires. The future is certainly theirs.

Reflective Questions

1 Respondents in our study saw a wider pool of system leaders as a means to improve student success and address a declining supply of heads. In your region what advantages would come from this and how might you go about it?

2 Our respondents agreed that development should be responsive to need and context, and promote a range of practices not a single style. They questioned whether training should be mainly informal, for instance a toolkit of guidance and materials or peer mentoring by existing system leaders, or more formalized, with a formal qualification or a national framework to ensure standards and progression, leading up to regional or national status. What are your views?

Further Reading

Higham, R., Hopkins, D. and Matthews, P. (2009) *System Leadership in Practice*. Maidenhead: Open University Press/McGraw-Hill.

>This book presents a comprehensive picture of the state of system leadership in England at time of publication. Given that the authors were both central to developing the policy direction and then researching it, one can assume that the book presents an authoritative picture. It is also worth noting that the practice of 'system leadership' in England is probably the most advanced of any OECD country at this present time.

Fullan, M. (2003) *The Moral Imperative of School Leadership*. London: Corwin Press; Fullan, M. (2004) *System Thinkers in Action: Moving Beyond the Standards Plateau*. London and Nottingham: DfES Innovation Unit/NCSL.

>Michael Fullan is both the Dean and Guru of educational change and its most prolific global advocate. In both these extremely important and complementary monographs Fullan sets out the personnel requirements for those educators and policy-makers who are instrumental in making the shift from educational systems dominated by prescription to those that espouse a professional ethic. Fullan's narrative sets the scene for many subsequent policy initiatives around the world.

Note

1   For a detailed discussion, see Hopkins (2007b).

References

Fullan, M. (2003) *The Moral Imperative of School Leadership*. London: Corwin Press.

Fullan, M. (2009) 'Large-scale reform comes of age', *Journal of Educational Change*, 10(2): 101–13.

Higham, R., Hopkins, D. and Matthews, P. (2009) *System Leadership in Practice*. Maidenhead: Open University Press/McGraw Hill.

Hopkins, D. (2007a) *Every School a Great School*. Maidenhead: McGraw-Hill/Open University Press.

Hopkins, D. (2007b) *Transformation and Innovation: System Leaders in the Global Age*. London: Specialist Schools and Academies Trust.

Hopkins, D. (2010a) *Taking Educational Reform to Scale*. Research Report, Department of Education and Early Childhood Development, State of Victoria, Australia.

Hopkins, D. (2010b) 'Confronting the elephant in the classroom – strategies for addressing the instructional core', *School Leadership Today* (in press).

Hopkins, D. and Higham, R. (2007) 'System leadership: mapping the landscape', *School Leadership and Management*, 27(2): 147–66.

Joyce, B.R., Calhoun, E.F. and Hopkins, D. (2009) *Models of Learning – Tools for Teaching*. 3rd edition. Maidenhead: Open University Press/McGraw-Hill Education.

Leithwood, K. and Riehl, C. (2005) 'What we know about successful school leadership', in W. Firestone and C. Riehl (eds), *A New Agenda: Directions for Research on Educational Leadership*. New York: Teachers College Press.

Leithwood, K., Day, C., Sammons, P., Harris, A. and Hopkins, D. (2007) *Seven Strong Claims about Successful School Leadership*. Available from: http://www.npbs.ca/2007-elements/pdfs/seven-strong%20claims.pdf.

Pont, B., Nusche, D. and Hopkins, D. (2008) *Improving School Leadership: Volume 2 – Case Studies on System Leadership*. Paris: OECD.

Section II

Challenges in Developing Learning-Focused Leadership

CHAPTER 8

Leading Professional Learning Communities

Louise Stoll

This chapter examines professional learning communities – what they are, what needs to be considered in thinking about their impact and what is involved in leading their development.

Educational leadership's moral purpose should be to enhance every child's and young person's learning in the broadest sense. In a fast-changing world, ensuring that all children's and young people's learning experiences and outcomes are of high quality – 'raising the bar and closing the gap' as it is expressed in several countries – is a major challenge for leaders, teachers and others supporting students' learning. These adults need the capacity to take charge of change and learn continuously themselves. Capacity, itself, is not a straightforward concept. It is a complex blend of motivation, skill, positive learning orientation, organizational conditions and culture, and an infrastructure of support that is not easy to come by. But, in coalescing, it gives individuals, groups and, ultimately whole-school communities and systems the power to get involved in and sustain learning. Creating and developing capacity is therefore an imperative for anyone passionate about improvement and transforming learning.

What has this got to do with professional learning communities? Research suggests that such communities may hold a critical key to capacity building. Rather than focusing on superficial quick fixes of change, professional learning communities appear to generate and support sustainable improvements because they build the capacity that helps keep schools progressing.

In this chapter I explore the following questions:

- What are professional learning communities?
- What difference do they make?
- How do you lead their development?

What are professional learning communities?

Despite nuances of interpretation, there is increasing international consensus that the term 'professional learning community' refers to an inclusive and mutually supportive group of people with a collaborative, reflective and growth-oriented approach towards investigating and learning more about their practice in order to improve pupils' learning.

What's in a word?

As language is important in conveying meaning, it may be helpful to think about the three words making up this expression. It is not chance that they have been used in association.

Community – the idea of community suggests that the focus is not on individual teachers learning but on learning within a collaborative community context – collective learning in a community of practice (Wenger, 1998). Features of communities – shared beliefs and understandings, interaction and participation, interdependence, concern for individual and minority views, and meaningful relationships through personal connections – are important to a professional learning community. Chris Watkins (2005) uses the letters ABCD to describe how members of communities are Active participants, in a community where Belonging has developed, Collaboration is frequent and Diversity is embraced.

Learning – the focus was originally on what has become known as professional community, emphasizing the context and nature of work relations between teachers. Inserting the word 'learning' coincided with greater emphasis on the objective of improvement: a learning community with a collective purpose of enhancing student learning. Learning refers both to collaborative learning and collective learning. Traditional forms of professional development generally focus on opportunities for individuals to hone their knowledge and skills. But collaborative learning in and beyond the workplace – including peer observation, coaching, collaborative forms of research and enquiry and learning conversations – reinforces how learning within professional learning communities is not a solitary experience. Collective learning is different. It involves working together to develop shared meaning of concepts and practices. It is not just learning together; it is a joint process of generating new and common understandings and creating knowledge of value and use to all involved. In addition, it is a community that is collectively learning about its processes of learning.

Professional – the word 'professional' highlights that the community's work is underpinned by a specialized knowledge base, an ethic of service orienting members towards client needs, strong collective identity through professional commitment, and professional autonomy through collegial control over practice and professional standards. Professionalism is more closely linked now with school development; in other words, to be a professional is to see your part in the whole picture and to play a role beyond your own immediate sphere of influence. The word professional also means that the emphasis is on developing adults as a learning community. This does not mean that students are unimportant, or that their learning is not the reason for having professional learning communities. Professional learning communities are a means to an end: the ultimate aim is not to be a professional learning community. Collaborative work is the process, but the key purpose is to enhance teacher effectiveness as professionals, in order to improve students' learning, progress and achievement.

Think about creating capacity among adults that will make a difference for students:

> By using the term *professional learning community* we signify our interest not only in discrete acts of teacher sharing, but in the establishment of a school-wide culture that makes collaboration expected, inclusive, genuine, ongoing, and focused on critically examining practice to improve student outcomes ... The hypothesis is that what teachers do together outside of the classroom can be as important as what they do inside in affecting school restructuring, teachers' professional development, and student learning. (Louis et al., 2003: 3)

Who's in the community?

Traditionally, such communities were thought of as being the province of leaders and teachers within a particular school. Such a view, however, is potentially limiting of professional learning opportunities. Diversity of views and learning opportunities may be increased through including other members of the school community such as support staff or governor school council members. The main idea is that the entire school's culture is one oriented to developing a professional learning community but within this larger community there may be smaller communities: for example, groups of teachers who scrutinize their practice related to particular topics; sometimes described as teacher learning communities (Wiliam, 2007).

Similarly, extending the community to include members beyond the school or even internationally may bring to bear new knowledge. In an increasing networked society, many schools participate in a wider professional learning community, cluster or network. Some professional learning communities also involve people in other community agencies. These can be seen as professional learning communities when there is an unrelenting focus on students' learning and when headteachers (principals), teachers and other staff are networked in purposeful ways (Katz et al., 2009) such that their joint activity challenges members to break down boundaries in their own thinking and supports professional learning community activity within their individual schools. Whatever the composition, what is important is that the community is focused on learning in ways elaborated below.

How do you recognize a professional learning community?

Professional learning communities appear to share six intertwined characteristics or features that operate together. These are:

1 *Shared values and vision.* Having a shared vision and sense of purpose means there is 'an undeviating focus' on all students' learning because individual autonomy potentially reduces teacher efficacy when teachers cannot count on colleagues to reinforce objectives. In some professional

learning communities, the focus is more general – with professional learning community (PLC) as 'a way of being'. Elsewhere, specific areas of focus are selected over time by the PLC.

2 *Collective responsibility.* Members of a professional learning community consistently take collective responsibility for students' learning and for each other's learning. Such collective responsibility seems to help sustain commitment, puts peer pressure and accountability on those who do not do their fair share, and eases isolation.

3 *Reflective professional enquiry.* This includes: 'reflective dialogue', conversations about serious educational issues or problems involving applying new knowledge in a sustained manner and 'deprivatization of practice' (Louis, Kruse and Associates, 1995), frequently examining teachers' practice through mutual observation and analysis, joint planning and development; seeking new knowledge; constantly converting tacit knowledge into shared public knowledge through interaction; and applying new ideas and information to problem-solving and solutions addressing students' needs (Hord, 1997).

4 *Collaboration.* Staff are involved in developmental activities with consequences for several people that go beyond superficial exchanges of help, support or assistance. Feelings of interdependence are central to such collaboration: a goal of better teaching practices would be considered unachievable without collaboration that links collaborative activity with achievement of shared purpose. Micropolitics may exist, but conflicts are managed more effectively: difference, debate and disagreement are considered essential. Diversity brings a richer perspective to collaborative challenges, 'stretching the professional repertoire beyond usual, habitual, or comfortable practice' (Mitchell and Sackney, 2007: 33).

5 *Group, as well as individual, learning is promoted.* All teachers are learners with their colleagues. In 'learning enriched schools' (Rosenholtz, 1989), teachers' professional self renewal is communal rather than solitary. Collective learning is also evident, as the school learning community interacts, engages in serious dialogue, deliberating about information and data, interpreting it communally and sharing it.

6 *Trusting relationships.* Effective professional learning communities are characterized by what Bryk and Schneider (2002) describe as 'relational trust'. This includes respect, belief in colleagues' competence, personal regard for others – caring about each other – and knowing that people will do what they say; integrity. Trust is sometimes also seen as a precondition for developing professional learning communities.

What difference do professional learning communities make?

Changing what goes on in schools and classrooms is demanding and time-consuming, so there is little point in doing something that does not make a difference. The impact of professional learning communities can be seen at several levels. Historically, the main focus was on improving teachers' practice and morale, and interest in the difference professional learning community might make for the whole organization. That is not where I start.

A difference for students

The ultimate impact has to be the difference that professional learning communities make for children and young people.

The evidence of links between professional learning community and student learning outcomes is still relatively modest. A review of PLCs' impact on teaching practice and student learning found eight robust research studies that explored the connection between PLCs and student outcomes. In all cases, student learning improved. The key to increased achievement was a 'persistent focus on student learning and achievement by the teachers in the learning communities' (Vescio et al., 2008: 87). An international review by Helen Timperley and colleagues in New Zealand (2008) of teacher professional learning and development that makes a difference to student outcomes concludes that in professional learning communities that promote student learning, teachers focus on analysing the impact of their teaching on student learning and are supported to process new understandings and their implications for teaching. The evaluation of Networked Learning Communities, a major programme in England, also found a link between improvements in students' academic results and the number of people in a school actively participating in a network that appeared to be related to the network's influence on teachers' thinking and changing their practice (Earl and Katz, 2006).

Would broader measures of student engagement with the school as a learning community be more appropriate indicators of impact? This issue is little explored. Whatever measures are chosen, the point is that while teacher learning is extremely important, the purpose of promoting staff learning must always be to maximize the learning of students.

Enhancing teacher morale, learning and practice

Enhancing morale and job satisfaction is clearly important. Professional learning community can act as a buffer against the kind of issues causing teachers to leave the profession. Being able to feel part of a school-wide community may be particularly significant in today's world characterized by greater change and uncertainty about meaning and values.

Improving teachers' practice is a major goal of professional learning communities. Teachers' knowledge base can be enhanced and there is an impact more generally on teachers' classroom work, although it's more difficult to find specific changes to teaching practice as a result of participation in a professional learning community. So, in schools with a genuine sense of community, an increased sense of work efficacy leads to increased classroom motivation and work satisfaction, with subsequent increases in collective responsibility for student learning. Where professional learning community is stronger, the influence of professional development programmes on teachers' knowledge and practice is also greater (Ingvason et al., 2005). The path between professional learning community and improvement in practice is not necessarily direct. Instead, it appears to foster change in practice by creating an environment that supports innovation and experimentation, and this is what promotes teacher learning.

Organizational capacity building and improvement

Improvements in individual teachers' practice does not change practice in whole schools. Professional learning communities may provide some answers to the question of how learning and development is dispersed throughout schools, because, where they are functioning at a high level, they appear to have the capacity for learning, enquiry, change and innovation. It is generally thought that this is because they are a means to achieving long-term cultural change in an organization. Establishing lasting collaborative cultures that constantly focus on building the capacity for continuous learning and improvement are critical in a complex and fast-changing world. They are also particularly important in helping spread and sustain improvements in individual teachers' practice and morale.

An emerging aspect of organizational capacity is the ability to engage more effectively with the outside world. Members of more effective professional learning communities are more outward looking and better able to connect productively with outside partners and bring the knowledge from these partnerships back to their community.

In summary, the closer the professional learning community gets to affecting and enhancing teachers' practice, the more likely it is that student outcomes will be influenced. Broader benefits of PLCs are important, however, in developing the culture of learning and enquiry throughout the community that acts as a supporting and energizing condition and stimulus for the focused and deeper work of community members.

How do leaders develop learning communities?

Developing professional learning communities depends on working on a number of processes. These depend on leadership. The idea of professional learning communities should be appealing to principals and headteachers because we know that these leaders have a largely indirect impact on students' progress (Leithwood et al., 2008) and that their greatest power on enhancing student learning can be found in their involvement in and commitment to the learning of teachers (Robinson et al., 2009). Developing professional learning communities creates the culture within which powerful teacher professional learning can take place.

Figure 8.1 shows the development processes that are all connected, as highlighted by the broken lines; they are not mutually exclusive.

Sharing a student learning focus

Collectively clarifying the community's purpose, and then sharpening this to focus on improving or transforming mutually agreed-on areas of student learning gives a PLC its *raison d'être*. Professional learning communities are concerned with

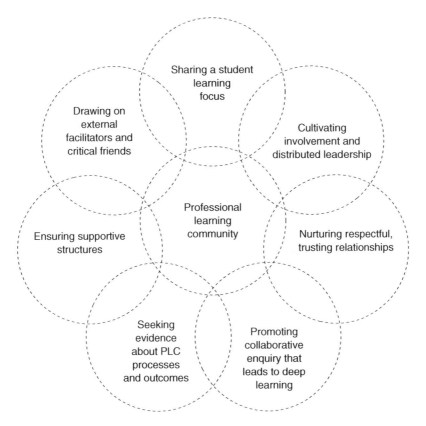

Figure 8.1   Processes involved in leading professional learning communities

improving student learning and practice in the here and now and also preparing students and themselves for a rapidly changing world. This can present a balancing act for leaders: both gathering and paying attention to evidence about strong learning and teaching practice, and encouraging new approaches inspired by fast-emerging knowledge about twenty-first century learning, new understandings about intelligence and their implications for education (Stoll et al., 2010).

Cultivating involvement and distributed leadership

Wide involvement of community members in activities that make a difference to people's practice and student learning needs to be promoted. Commitment to distributed leadership ensures active engagement of colleagues at different levels in leadership practice. This is both leadership within and between school professional learning communities and networks. Headteachers have a major role to play here in distributing the leadership and ensuring engagement and involvement of colleagues (Harris and Jones, 2010). Distributed leadership fits well with the notion of collective responsibility. Interest is also increasingly focused on finding ways for support staff and governors/school council members to contribute actively and lead various activities.

Nurturing trust and collaboration

Developing professional learning community is a human and emotional enterprise with the associated complexity of bringing about change. Working together productively depends on positive relationships and collegiality, and interdependence between colleagues that allows serious challenge and adjustment of practice. Very often, trust-building starts with those in senior leadership positions inviting others to share in the leadership of the school and engaging them in collective learning which is meaningful to them. This helps build trust with each other (Fleming and Thompson, 2004).

Promoting collaborative enquiry that leads to deep learning

For professional learning communities to be intellectually vigorous, members need a solid basis of expert knowledge and skills. Where should decisions come from about the focus for professional learning? Increasingly, it seems that key activities within PLCs are collaborative forms of enquiry where groups systematically and intentionally investigate and explore issues related to student learning with implications for their practice (see Kaser and Halbert, 2009 and McLaughlin and, Mitra, 2003, for two examples). Collaborative enquiry can also identify areas of focus for professional learning. Based on their synthesis of research evidence on professional learning, Timperley and colleagues (2008) developed an enquiry cycle that starts by asking what educational outcomes are valued for students and how students are doing in relation to those outcomes. Other questions follow: What knowledge and skills do teachers need to support students in achieving these outcomes? How do leaders promote teacher learning related to these desired outcomes? Other deep learning opportunities can then be developed to help build the necessary knowledge and skills before asking the final questions: what changes are made for students and what is the impact?

Collaborative enquiry has particular potential to stimulate evidence-based learning conversations. This type of professional dialogue causes a learning community to reflect on and challenge their existing practice; to rethink what they know and do. Developing learning conversations isn't easy. As Lorna Earl and Helen Timperley (2008) explain, they involve negotiating the terrain of trusting relationships, honestly examining relevant evidence and using a set of powerful enquiries *all at the same time*, as well as an undeviating focus on student learning which is sometimes a challenge for teachers.

Seeking evidence about PLC processes and outcomes

Professional learning communities focus on results that are important. Tracking the benefits to see a positive difference in student learning may be methodologically challenging but it is essential. In addition to existing impact studies, members of PLCs themselves can identify indicators related to the ultimate outcomes they are seeking, as well as intermediate outcomes related to theories they have about how they expect their community's activities to make a difference. A broad perspective needs to be taken to examining outcomes in order to avoid the narrowness and 'negative space' issues involved with using single test measures as indicators.

Ensuring supportive structures

Structures shape organizations' capacities to develop learning communities. At their best, structures enable better and deeper communication between members of learning communities. Coordination, communication mechanisms, interdependent roles, joint governance structures (in the case of more than one school) and collaborative plans are all important. Here I focus on two particular structures: time and space.

When you're thinking about stimulating meaningful learning, you have to consider *time* (Stoll et al., 2003). Talk, exchange about and joint reflection on professional issues are key elements of the collaborative activity necessary to develop and connect professional learning communities. These require time, which does not only mean being able to cover staff who engage in enquiry and development activities or attending meetings, but planning and organizing time such that learning with and from a small number of colleagues in one school or several schools can be fed back into the school's wider learning community and reconstructed to create new knowledge. Meeting agendas focused on learning and team teaching increase time for professional learning community development. The challenge is to find creative ways to deal with the perennial challenges of time, or else PLC activities just become an 'add on' to an already overloaded agenda.

Space can also be a facilitator, and one with interesting shifts in meaning. In schools, professional exchange is facilitated by physical proximity, for example teachers in a department in neighbouring classrooms and with interdependent teaching roles, such as team teaching and joint planning. In learning networks, ensuring equality and equal access between partners suggests that meetings and school and classroom visits need to be rotated around schools, whilst similar concerns in extended learning communities implies that meetings should either be rotated around the different community partner locations or held within neutral locations such as community centres or coffee shops. Eighteenth-century coffee houses were known as places for stimulating and sociable conversations, offering a combination of intimate and private spaces and ones that were public and open to speakers of all status, wealth or power. In the coffee house, everyone's contributions were treated as equal.

Community space now also includes the virtual space through which networks of Internet users connect and communicate. In this world of mass collaboration, networks of individuals are sharing, adapting and updating knowledge. The Internet also provides a connecting communication mechanism when time to meet is hard to find.

Drawing on external facilitators and critical friends

While formal and informal leadership of professional learning communities can stimulate, oversee and coordinate many of the development processes, external facilitation can also play a significant role. In the same way that effective professional learning can be enhanced by external input that challenges existing assumptions, an external perspective to a learning network may be necessary to challenge the natural group think that tends to develop amongst the network leaders (Hadfield and Chapman, 2009). A key activity for these facilitators is finding ways to help PLC members engage with external knowledge so that it stimulates dialogue that makes their presuppositions, ideas, beliefs and feelings explicit and available for exploration.

Does the development process change over time?

Bringing about change does not just require knowledge of processes and skills involved. Better understanding of how they blend together and change over time is also needed. Change in professional learning communities isn't linear; as a headteacher in the *Creating and Sustaining Effective Professional Learning Communities* project described it, it goes through 'ebbs and flows' (Stoll et al., 2006). The path is more fluid than fixed, as PLCs perennially evolve with accumulating collective experience. Nonetheless, it seems they go through broad phases of development, generally connected to stages of educational change and levels of use of innovations. People are beginning to map out how the characteristics and processes change over time as professional learning communities broadly move through the phases. Source materials based on the Creating and Sustaining Effective Learning Communities project outline four 'phases' of the journey:

1 *Starting out*: acquiring information and beginning to use ideas.
2 *Developing*: experimenting with strategies and building on initial commitment.
3 *Deepening*: well on the way, having achieved a degree of mastery and feeling the benefits.
4 *Sustaining*: introducing new developments, and re-evaluating quality – professional learning community as 'a way of life'.

Perhaps communities have to be at a certain stage of readiness before they can engage in the collective learning that characterizes professional learning community.

Two stories

Here are stories of two schools at different stages of their journeys as they were developing their professional learning communities. These stories come from the Creating and Sustaining Effective Professional Learning Communities project (Bolam et al., 2005; Stoll et al., 2006). At the start of the project, the headteacher of the first, Highdown, primary school viewed it as 'starting out'. The second story is quite different: it is about a secondary school that, in terms of the phases above, would be seen, at least, to be already 'deepening' when the project began.

Highdown Primary School – starting out and developing a PLC

Highdown was a maintained primary school for 300 boys and girls aged 3–11, 35 per cent of whom were entitled to free school meals, almost twice the national average. Its spacious 1950s buildings were set in an outlying area of a large city on a council housing estate in an area of high unemployment.

The previous head had been in the school for over 25 years. Staff had supported each other through an external inspection that the school had failed. The new headteacher, in post for under two years, who had been deputy head in a multi-cultural, inner city school in the same local authority, saw the school as an 'early starter' PLC in transition.

> I came into a school that is ripe. The staff are lovely, but there's no fire. There's massive potential.

At that time, she thought there was no overall community feeling, although some subgroups demonstrated mutual respect and trust.

> I want all of us to be a learning community. I am head learner. I want teachers really engaging in professional learning and to be part of the network of support staff. I want to grow my own classroom assistants. I want my parents to be involved as part of the community ... Collective responsibility is not school wide ... They are getting the ethos right but not the learning ... There were great results for Key Stage 2 [ages 7–11] but they set low targets – they had low expectations ...

She saw herself as 'lighting fires with lots of initiatives and opportunities' but wanted more initiatives to come from staff. The senior management team (SMT) was 'taking some initiatives' and the staff did 'come on board but do not initiate things of their own'. A PLC was consciously promoted by, for example: the allocation of changed responsibilities to the new deputy head; an enhanced role for teaching assistants; improving the school environment; making strategic staff appointments; working with the governing body; coaching and mentoring of staff by the headteacher; performance management and student targets linked into the school improvement plan; and continuing professional development.

Some staff were critical of insufficient delegation; one teacher thought that the school seemed more of a PLC than some other local schools; staff in one key stage said they were all friends and that was one reason they worked together so well. Two years later the Key Stage 2 coordinator described staff in general as:

> fantastic and as having the same philosophy about children. It made the meetings very easy. We're all singing from the same hymn sheet. The classroom assistants are as good as any teacher. They really do take on board all the ideas that have come along.

The school seemed to be moving well on its journey to develop a PLC.

Princeland High School – deepening and sustaining a PLC

Princeland was in a rural location 10 miles outside a large city. It had about 1,000 students, aged 13–18, 60 teaching and eight support staff. Student achievement was above average. External inspectors noted that the headteacher and senior staff provided very good leadership and promoted an inclusive and engaging spirit, encouraging staff to believe they could affect the school's direction. Staff had been focusing on improving learning and teaching for several years. A deputy headteacher, with a brief for learning development, explained:

> the school is developing emotional intelligence, interpersonal skills and strategies to raise achievement. We've been doing it for a long time and the last two and a half years we have been looking at learning. We've been looking at people skills for seven years ...

The headteacher described the school as a thriving community when he arrived four years earlier:

> there was a lot going on. The previous head had done a fantastic job and had created a vision and direction for the school ... as an organization leading the community through regeneration ... very significant and very unusual ... We wanted to continue that work and embed it.

He was committed to promoting learning and to a distributed style of leadership:

> there is a lot of delegated authority but not delegated responsibility ... I think it's a belief in outcomes rather than process, we know where we want to go and that's shared and accepted by everybody but how we get there is a decision that we take and that's really a decision that people will take in teams.

The senior leadership team were encouraging staff to take a whole-school view of learning. The deputy headteacher with curriculum responsibility said: 'virtually every policy that we write we put the emphasis on teaching and learning'. Three successful strategies were: the Learning Forum, a voluntary, half-termly, after-school meeting where learning and teaching were discussed and good practice shared; the Learning Leader initiative whereby teachers bid for internal resources to develop a learning project – within two years 10 projects were under way; and increasing classroom observation and feedback as a means of professional development and learning. Of this, a deputy headteacher said:

> the big leap that's been able to help us in the last two or three years is people are no longer defensive about being observed or intermingling with each other – there's a whole new culture.

Day-to-day administration tasks were well handled, with sound administrative systems. Relationships between staff had been good for many years and staff felt it was a caring school. Systems for mentoring, coaching and facilitation for staff had also been introduced. Comments from several teachers indicated that they felt professionally supported and encouraged to develop: 'You're encouraged to take risks and be a bit more creative and to work together and develop and share good practice.' Staff were increasingly using information and communication technology (ICT) which facilitated exchange of information and ideas within the school and beyond. The school was involved in several external partnerships and networks and was the lead school in a large networked learning community. It was also leading on initiatives with the local community, for example, a partnership had been developed to secure funding to build a state of the art football facility which could be jointly managed and used by the school and the community. Funding was being sought to set up a virtual college for vocational training which would serve five secondary schools in the area.

What about sustainability?

Sustainability is the elusive elixir of educational change and professional learning communities. Is Princeland still as vibrant a professional learning community as it was a few years ago? The paucity of longitudinal research on professional learning communities means we still know relatively little about the potential for establishing enduringly effective ones and need to keep learning more. Tony Bryk and colleagues (1999) suggest that when internal socialization routines are working properly, they may provide a self-renewal mechanism for professional communities, but much evidence suggests that effective PLCs often subsequently decline. This is likely to be exacerbated in jurisdictions where becoming a professional learning community, originally voluntary and invitational, is now mandated. Paying regular and serious attention to the processes of development appears to be a good start.

Using the ideas

Several resources are now available to help people explore and develop their professional learning communities. A set of materials colleagues and I created (Stoll et al., 2006), arising out of the research project Creating and Sustaining Effective Professional Learning Communities, are designed to promote understanding of and engagement with the idea and practice of professional learning communities with particular reference to people's own contexts; and to stimulate professional learning communities by promoting self-evaluation, reflective enquiry, dialogue, collaborative learning and problem-solving. In other words, the intention is to provide practical support for those wishing to develop and sustain themselves as effective professional learning communities, using an enquiry-oriented approach, in line with definitions of a professional learning community.

Professional learning communities are places, sometimes even spaces, where dialogue and reflection is part of the everyday fabric of their existence. In the spirit of professional learning communities, I conclude with questions for you to consider together within and between your professional learning community contexts.

Reflective Questions ❓

1 What is your story of professional learning community development? What have been your high points in developing your professional learning community? What about your challenges? How have you addressed these?
2 How should a professional learning community's effectiveness be evaluated? How do you know your professional learning community/communities is/are effective?
3 What strategies do you have to sustain your professional learning communities?
4 Is true collective responsibility for enhancing learning across all schools in a district or local region cluster possible?

Further Reading 📖

Hipp, K.K. (ed.) (2006) Leadership and student learning in professional learning communities, *Journal of School Leadership*, special issue, 16(5).

The entire issue of this journal is devoted to a set of international articles that focus on setting the stage for promoting school development using PLCs, building leadership capacity to promote sustainable PLCs, engaging in large-scale sustainable change, and inclusive learning communities.

Stoll, L. and Louis, K.S. (eds) (2007) *Professional Learning Communities: Divergence, Depth and Dilemmas*. Maidenhead: Open University Press.

This international collection explores three of the most challenging dilemmas facing professional learning communities. The authors provide pointers on why these challenges exist, offering rays of hope for ways forward. It is valuable reading for anyone interested in building capacity and harnessing their community as a resource for change.

References

Bolam, R., McMahon, A., Stoll, L., Thomas, S., Wallace, M., Greenwood, A., Hawkey, K., Ingram, M., Atkinson, A. and Smith, M. (2005) *Creating and Sustaining Effective Professional Learning Communities*. DfES Research Report RR637, University of Bristol. Available at: www.dfes.gov.uk/research/data/uploadfiles/RR637.pdf

Bryk, A.S. and Schneider, B. (2002) *Trust in Schools: A Core Resource for School Improvement*. New York: Russell Sage.

Bryk, A., Camburn, E. and Louis, K.S. (1999) Professional community in Chicago elementary schools: facilitating factors and organizational consequences, *Educational Administration Quarterly*, 35 (Supplement): 751–81.

Earl, L. and Katz, S. (2006) *How Networked Learning Communities Work*. Seminar Series Paper No 155. Jolimont, Victoria: Centre for Strategic Education.

Earl, L. and Timperley, H. (2008) *Professional Learning Conversations: Challenges in Using Evidence for Improvement*. Dordrecht: Springer.

Fleming, G.L. and Thompson, T.L. (2004) The role of trust building and its relation to collective responsibility, in S. Hord (ed.), *Learning Together, Leading Together: Changing Schools Through Professional Learning Communities*. New York: Teachers College Press, and Alexandria, VA: ASCD.

Hadfield, M. and Chapman, C. (2009) *Leading School-based Networks*. Abingdon: Routledge.

Harris, A. and Jones, M. (2010) Leading learning for school effectiveness, *Improving Schools*, 13(2) 172–81.

Hipp, K.K. (2006) Leadership and student learning in professional learning communities, *Journal of School Leadership*, special issue, 16(5).

Hord, S.M. (1997) *Professional Learning Communities: Communities of Continuous Inquiry and Improvement*. Austin, TX: Southwest Educational Development Laboratory.

Ingvarson, L., Meiers, M. and Beavis, A. (2005) *Factors Affecting the Impact of Professional Development Programmes on Teachers' Knowledge, Practice, Student Outcomes and Efficacy*. Camberwell, Victoria, Australian Council for Educational Research. Available at: www.research.acer.edu.au/professional_dev/1

Kaser, L. and Halbert, J. (2009) *Leadership Mindsets: Innovation and Learning in the Transformation of Schools*. London: Routledge.

Katz, S., Earl, L. and Ben Jaafar, S. (2009) *Building and Connecting Learning Communities: The Power of Networks for School Improvement*. Thousand Oaks, CA: Corwin.

Leithwood, K., Day, C., Sammons, P., Harris, A. and Hopkins, D. (2008) *Seven Strong Claims about School Leadership*. Nottingham: National College for School Leadership.

Louis, K.S., Anderson, A.R. and Riedel, E. (2003) Implementing arts for academic achievement: the impact of mental models, professional community and interdisciplinary, teaming paper presented at the Seventeenth Conference of the International Congress for School Effectiveness and Improvement. Rotterdam, January.

Louis, K.S., Kruse, S. and Associates (1995) *Professionalism and Community: Perspectives on Reforming Urban Schools*. Thousand Oaks, CA: Corwin.

McLaughlin, M. and Mitra, D. (2003) The cycle of inquiry as the engine of school reform: lessons from the Bay Area School Reform Collaborative. Available at: www.springboardschools.org/research/studies/UV_Leader (accessed 3 June 2009).

Mitchell, C. and Sackney, L. (2007) Extending the learning community: a broader perspective embedded in policy, in L. Stoll and K.S. Louis (eds), *Professional Learning Communities: Divergence, Depth and Dilemmas*. Maidenhead: Open University Press.

Robinson, V., Hohepa, M. and Lloyd, C. (2009) *School Leadership and Student Outcomes: Identifying What Works and Why. Best Evidence Synthesis Programme*. Wellington: New Zealand Ministry of Education.

Rosenholtz, S.J. (1989) *Teachers' Workplace: The Social Organization of Schools*. New York: Longman.

Stoll, L., Bolam, R., McMahon, A., Thomas, S., Wallace, M., Greenwood, A. and Hawkey, K. (2006) *Professional Learning Communities: Source Materials for School Leaders and Other Leaders of Professional Learning*. London: Innovation Unit, NCSL and GTC. Available at: www.innovation-unit.co.uk/about-us/publications/professional-learning-communities.html

Stoll, L., Fink, D. and Earl, L. (2003) *It's About Learning (and It's About Time)*. London: RoutledgeFalmer.

Stoll, L. and Louis, K.S. (eds) (2007) *Professional Learning Communities: Divergence, Depth and Dilemmas*. Maidenhead: Open University Press.

Stoll, L., Halbert, J. and Kaser, L. (2010) Deepening learning in school-to-school networks, in C. Day (ed.), *International Handbook on Teacher and School Development*. London: Routledge.

Timperley, H., Wilson, A., Barrar, H. and Fung, I. (2008) *Teacher Professional Learning and Development: Best Evidence Synthesis Iteration*. Wellington: New Zealand Ministry of Education.

Vescio, V., Ross, D. and Adams, A. (2008) A review of research on the impact of professional learning communities on teaching practice and student learning, *Teaching and Teacher Education*, 24(1): 80–91.

Watkins, C. (2005) *Classrooms as Learning Communities: What's in it for Schools?* London: Routledge.

Wenger, E. (1998) *Communities of Practice: Learning, Meaning and Identity*. New York: Cambridge University Press.

Wiliam, D. (2007) Content then process: teacher learning communities in the service of formative assessment, in D.B. Reeves (ed.), *Ahead of the Curve: The Power of Assessment to Transform Teaching and Learning*. Bloomington, IN: Solution Tree.

CHAPTER 9

Leading Teachers' Professional Learning

Helen Timperley

This chapter identifies how leaders can assist their teachers meet changing job demands through promoting professional learning in ways that impact on entrenched problems of teaching and learning. It describes the shifts in thinking and practice required for teachers and leaders to engage in cycles of evidence-informed inquiry for improvement.

Every day teachers face the challenges of introducing new curricula, assessment approaches and technologies into their classroom practices. In many situations they are also faced with changing student populations that do not necessarily respond to instructional practices in familiar ways. Teacher professional learning has become the multimillion dollar solution. School leaders are faced with how to support teachers to meet these challenges of change and are expected to ensure such opportunities are effective and result in anticipated improvement to teaching practice and student outcomes.

Unfortunately much of this investment has failed to meet its goals, particularly with respect to advancing improved student learning and engagement (Timperley and Alton-Lee, 2008). Typical of many research articles is the opening paragraph by Correnti: 'In the past several decades, many policies have sought changes in teacher practice that would stimulate improvements in student learning. In large part, these policies have provided disappointing and variable results' (Correnti, 2007: 262).

There are several reasons for these outcomes. One is the hope that new ways to teach can easily be learned, so one-off courses abound with little evidence that they make any real difference. Unfortunately change is more complicated than this. Teachers teach in holistic ways that involve beliefs about students and how they learn combined with beliefs about the worth of particular curricula and the most effective ways to teach it. Past experiences of being both a student and a teacher underpin many of their beliefs and these are not easily put to one side to accommodate new ideas.

An alternative approach to one-off courses involves giving teachers time to reflect together about their practice and how to improve it. Regardless of how long or how often, there is little evidence that reflection without input from expertise external to the group leads to the kinds of changes to practice that have a substantial impact on student learning. Most teachers reflect daily on their practice as they go about their work. If they knew how to change in ways to improve their effectiveness, they would have already done so. Much more is needed.

Even when external experts are engaged to work with teachers over a period of time, success is far from guaranteed. The knowledge imparted is not necessarily that which makes the difference to students. In the USA, for example, the most popular professional development project designed to address teachers' expectations of students from low socio-economic communities showed little evidence it made a difference to these expectations or to student outcomes (Gottfredson et al., 1995). Even when the knowledge itself may have the potential to make a difference, it is not necessarily imparted in ways that are meaningful to teachers (van der Sijde, 1989).

This chapter is about the kinds of professional learning that do make a significant difference to student outcomes and the implications this has for school leadership. It is based on a synthesis of the international evidence of the conditions under which teachers can learn to make this difference (Timperley et al., 2008). Over a number of years the veracity of these constructs has been tested through a professional development project in literacy that has involved over 300 primary schools in New Zealand. In this project, visiting facilitators work with schools throughout the country. The achievement of the students whose teachers have been involved in the project has accelerated, on average, twice what would be expected over the two years of the schools' involvement compared with business as usual. Those students achieving among the lowest 20 per cent at the beginning of the project demonstrated improvements threefold to fourfold than expected over the two-year period (Timperley and Parr, 2009). Follow-up studies in a sample of schools have demonstrated that most schools have sustained the rate of gain for their next student cohorts (O'Connell et al., 2008). Achieving these changes, however, has required some fundamental shifts in thinking about professional development, leadership and classroom practice. These shifts include a move from thinking in terms of professional development to thinking in terms of a more intentional, systematic process of professional learning (Guskey, 2000). Another shift is the active involvement of leaders in the promotion and participation in teachers' professional learning rather than leaving this important part of school organization to others. Finally, the greatest shift has involved the development of systematic evidence-informed inquiry into the effectiveness of practice and the building of pedagogical content knowledge. The literacy project demonstrating the high gains for students' literacy learning will be used to illustrate key ideas throughout this chapter.

Building knowledge through teacher inquiry

Competent teachers inquire into the effectiveness of their practice every day as they observe which parts of lessons students appear to understand and what continues to cause them difficulty. Competent leaders support and assist teachers to inquire through structured opportunities to reflect by reviewing relevant assessment information and considering the effectiveness of practice. This inquiry, however, usually takes place within the frameworks of existing knowledge. To make a substantive difference to student outcomes, new frameworks and knowledge need to be brought to bear through the inquiry process. Typically the development of this knowledge involves specialist expertise. However, the quality of this expertise and the ways in which those involved engage with teachers are critical to success.

The synthesis of the evidence of professional development that makes a difference to student outcomes (Timperley et al., 2008) showed that the most effective approach to professional learning involves teachers in cycles of inquiry that begin with what students need to know and do to meet curricula and other goals valued by the communities in which students live and are educated (see Figure 9.1). When profiles of students' achievement are well understood, teachers then inquire into the knowledge and skills they need if they are to be more effective in addressing the learning needs of individuals and groups of students, particularly those not achieving as well as others. From there, teachers engage in new professional learning that deepens their knowledge and refines their skills so they can engage students in new learning experiences in classrooms. Given that the effectiveness of all teaching practice is influenced by context and no particular practices can be guaranteed to result in particular outcomes, the final stage of the inquiry involves examining the impact of changed actions on the outcomes for students that were the focus of the inquiry. The purpose is to understand what has

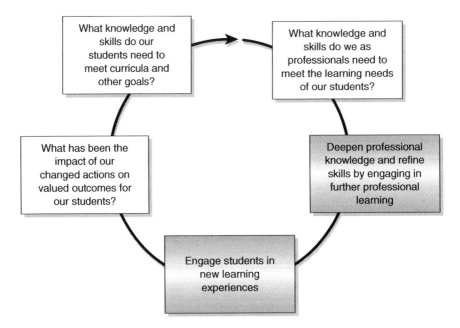

Figure 9.1   Teacher inquiry and knowledge-building cycle to promote valued student outcomes

been effective and what has not. The findings from this examination then lead to another cycle of inquiry.

In this way, teachers develop the adaptive expertise required to retrieve, organize and apply professional knowledge when old problems persist or new problems arise. They have the capability to identify when known routines do not work and to seek new information about different approaches when needed (Bransford et al., 2005). This same concept can be applied to leaders at the level of the school as an organization. They also inquire systematically into school processes that meet their students' needs so that these can be maintained, but they know when they as leaders need to expand the depth and breadth of current expertise because it is not as effective as it might be.

The next sections of this chapter detail the processes involved in developing leaders' and teachers' knowledge and skills through cycles of inquiry and knowledge-building. They are followed by a discussion of what is involved for school leaders when promoting the learning of their teachers in ways that impact positively on their students' learning. How each part of the cycle can work in practice is illustrated by reference to the Literacy Professional Development Project described earlier that has demonstrated improved outcomes for students over the three cohorts of schools between 2004 and 2009.

Identifying students' knowledge and skills

In order to have an impact on student outcomes, the inquiry cycle begins and ends with students. Teaching is a highly contextualized activity with teachers constantly responding to the students in front of them. These classroom experiences, together with the overall school environment developed by leaders, greatly influences what teachers learn and how they think about their teaching. Professional development that focuses on new practices decontextualized from the immediate demands of classroom teaching and learning is not likely to be translated into that environment. Teachers might find the information interesting but rarely apply it given the competing and immediate demands of their students and the curriculum to be taught when they return.

The process of unpacking the question in Figure 9.1, 'What knowledge and skills do our students need to meet curricula and other goals?' involves asking some specific additional questions that might include:

- What do they already know?
- What sources of evidence have we used and how adequate are they?
- What do they need to learn and do?
- How do we build on what they know?

To answer these questions, leaders and teachers need deep knowledge of how to assess students' knowledge and skills for the purposes of diagnosis, particularly for those students who do not respond readily to existing instructional practices. For many leaders and teachers this is the first phase of their professional learning – how to undertake such assessments and how to interpret the information to identify teaching/learning puzzles. In many cases, it involves taking a whole new perspective on the purposes of assessment as one of professional inquiry rather than one of grouping, labelling or credentialling students. How this first phase of the inquiry cycle worked in the Literacy Professional Development Project is described below.

This phase of the inquiry cycle involved undertaking a detailed diagnosis of students' achievement on the deep and surface features of reading or writing. This diagnosis enabled them to relate the students' profiles of achievement to progressions on the curriculum. Most leaders and teachers needed to develop more sophisticated notions about texts and how they worked before they could develop an accurate interpretation of students' achievement profiles. From there, target students were identified in each class to make the change process manageable. These target students provided the focus for the first cycle of inquiry. The prospect of teaching these students in ways that might accelerate their achievement provided the motivation for the teachers to engage in further professional learning to acquire new knowledge and skills.

Identifying teachers' knowledge and skills

This second part of the cycle asks teachers to identify what it is they need to know and do to be more effective, particularly with those students achieving less well than others. In this way, engaging in professional learning has immediate application and is motivated by the *need to know*. Much professional development about effective teaching practices is motivated by the *desire to tell*. Policy-makers, researchers or professional development providers believe or have evidence that some kinds of teaching practices are more effective than others. They then create professional development opportunities to inform teachers about these practices without creating the need to know beyond compliance or teacher interest. As with most learners, the need to know provides a stronger motivation to engage than someone else's desire to tell.

Sometimes leaders address issues of motivation by calling for volunteers. The synthesis of the evidence on professional learning and development found that student outcomes did not depend on whether teachers volunteered or were expected/directed to be involved (Timperley et al., 2008). In some situations the expectations of volunteers were not met, particularly when the extent of change was greater than they had anticipated. In some other situations the expectations of those who were directed were exceeded. What was more important than initial volunteering was that teachers became engaged in the process at some point. Most engaging was the opportunity to solve puzzling teaching and learning problems related to individual students in the teachers' classrooms.

The process of identifying one's own professional learning needs is not easy and usually involves the assistance of others because it is difficult to step outside one's own frame of reference. This person may be a school leader or outside facilitator. Specific questions for teachers to answer with a professional learning facilitator might involve:

- How have we contributed to existing student outcomes?
  - With whom are we most effective?
  - With whom are we not connecting and why?

- What do we already know that we can use to promote better outcomes?
- What do we need to learn and do to promote better outcomes?
- What sources of evidence/knowledge can we utilize?

To answer these questions, teachers need to link their findings from the first inquiry into students' profiles of achievement to specific teaching practices. This process is not easy because examination of teaching practice and its impact needs to be undertaken through a process of unpacking teachers' preconceptions about how students learn and how best to teach them. Why are particular aspects of practice valued? Is what is valued most effective? In order to move on, some key assumptions underpinning existing practice and how they fit with new practice may need to be challenged. Spillane (1999: 154) found, when investigating a mathematics reform in the USA, for example, that if teachers 'are to get to the core reform ideas, [they] have to question, unlearn and discard much of their current, deeply rooted understandings of teaching, learning and subject matter'. Without this kind of examination, suggestions for new practice are likely to be forgotten if they do not fit existing beliefs, or to be assimilated into existing knowledge and practice without a deep understanding what it is that needs to change and why (Hammerness et al., 2005). Hammerness and colleagues refer to this process as one of over-assimilation whereby teachers make superficial changes believing they are making appropriate adjustments to their practice but do not really understand what this involves so are unable to do so.

This process of examining and critiquing beliefs underpinning particular practices can be uncomfortable for those involved because such scrutiny for the purpose of professional learning starts to shift the spotlight from students to teachers. Here leadership is central because teaching and learning to teach are as much about emotional practices as the acquisition of new knowledge (Hargreaves, 1998). Expectations to change may touch raw nerves because they are likely to impinge on teachers' sense of professional identity and competence while they ask themselves, 'Has what I have done before been ineffective?' Stoll et al. (2003: 85) describe how 'neglecting emotions can close people up to learning, and lead teachers to behave defensively to protect themselves from situations that they feel might expose their "inadequacies"'. Elmore (2004) notes one of the strongest social norms in schools is that everyone is expected to pretend that they are equally effective in what they do even when they feel they are unable to do it. Having to pretend is antithetical to professional learning.

The second phase of the cycle of inquiry and knowledge building in the Literacy Professional Development Project is described below:

While students were being assessed, two other kinds of evidence were sought to engage initial understandings and identify teacher learning needs. These included systematic classroom observations using an effective practice framework and responses to a scenario of relatively ineffective teaching practice. In the scenario, lesson activities and feedback were misaligned to the aim of the lesson. Then through collegial discussions teachers' beliefs underpinning their teaching practices and reasons for their particular choices on the scenario formed the basis for identifying beliefs about effectiveness and teacher learning needs. The practice-based nature of the teaching profession means that many teachers had difficulty identifying why they taught in the ways they did and considerable skill on the part of the facilitators was required to help teachers to express them so their adequacy and impact could be examined.

While Figure 9.1 implies a sequential identification of student learning needs and teacher learning needs, in practice, this process, and all others in the cycle, may occur alongside one another. Engagement of teachers' initial understandings occurs throughout the professional learning experience as information is understood more deeply and challenges arise. Learning is iterative rather than sequential.

Deepening professional knowledge

This phase of the cycle is referred to as '*deepening* professional knowledge and *refining* skills by engaging in further professional learning' because it is assumed that the teachers involved have some experience rather than starting as novices. One-day professional development courses do little more than raise teachers' awareness of new information and rarely lead to changes in practice because much deeper learning is required to change practice sufficiently to make a difference to student outcomes.

The knowledge identified as important in the synthesis of the kinds of professional learning associated with high impact on student outcomes typically involved the integration of knowledge of assessment, the curriculum and relevant aspects of the underlying discipline and how to teach it (Timperley et al., 2008). It is only when this knowledge is understood within an overarching conceptual framework of teaching and learning that teachers are able to retrieve and apply it in the moment-by-moment decisions they need to make everyday in classrooms.

As with other professions, teaching is practice based, so new knowledge is usually insufficient on its own to create change. Ways to translate knowledge into practice needs also to be given attention so that the theoretical understandings become the basis for making ongoing, principled adjustments to practice in response to students' learning needs.

When substantial change is required, such as new ways of teaching reading comprehension or scientific reasoning, integration of the different kinds of knowledge together with their translation into practice means that teachers need multiple opportunities to learn. Through this process, partially understood ideas are revisited as they are tried out in classroom contexts. Over time, understandings are deepened and knowledge becomes more easily retrieved and skills enacted in the face of daily classroom challenges. Such opportunities to learn require extended time, typically a year and more, for it to become a part of the routines of practice. It is possible to make superficial changes in less time than this, but typically these relate to narrow discrete areas of learning, not the kind that makes a substantive difference to student outcomes.

The specific approaches developed depend partly on the level and kind of professional learning required. Teachers are as diverse in their knowledge and beliefs as their students. If the changes advocated are consistent with existing beliefs and can be readily integrated into existing practice, then less time and engagement is needed than when existing beliefs are dissonant with the ideas promoted through the change. In the latter case, much closer engagement is needed.

How this process looked in the Literacy Professional Development Project for this phase of the cycle is summarized in the following description:

> Following from discussion of the evidence related to student and teacher learning needs, a plan to support their learning was developed with those involved. Some activities such as workshops included everyone. Others, such as individual classroom observation with follow-up conversations to analyse the effectiveness of practice were individualised. All these activities were focused on the integration of theory about students' progressions through the curriculum, how texts work and how students learn and how this might all look in practice.

> When teachers were observed, for example, they were assisted to construct the important principles underpinning effective practice in the area of focus prior to the observation. When analysing practice following the observation, the analysis was related to these principles with underpinning teachers' beliefs engaged through the observer asking questions like, 'What led you to do ... .' The co-construction of new practice emerged from these conversations with ongoing checking to ensure that the more theoretical ideas could be translated into practice.

Engaging students in new learning experiences

Little is likely to change for students if classroom teaching and learning activities do not change as a result of the inquiry and knowledge development because it is teachers who make the difference to student learning (Cuttance, 1998; Muijs and Reynolds, 2001; Nye et al., 2004). Changes within the instructional core are those that matter (Elmore, 2004). Making changes to organizational routines and structures may help to impact on the instructional core but do not do so on their own.

Leaders play a central role in this process as they observe and support the learning of their teachers. It is important that leaders take a problem-solving and learning focus to these activities rather than one of compliance if teachers are to engage constructively. Accountability systems should be focused on learning and trying to implement new practices rather than on compliance (Timperley, 2005).

The kinds of change expected and the ways in which teachers were supported to make these changes in the Literacy Professional Development Project are summarized in the following description:

> One change asked of teachers was to be more deliberate in their teaching practices, particularly for those students not achieving as well as others. They were asked to draw on their knowledge of what students knew and could do, together with their newly acquired pedagogical content knowledge, to design and implement these deliberate acts of teaching.

Teachers' attempts to change their classroom practices were supported by the ongoing observations and follow-up conversations. These observations were oriented towards problem-solving rather than compliance with criteria for effectiveness shared. There were no secrets.

Assessing impact

The final question in the inquiry and knowledge-building cycle asks teachers and leaders to assess the impact of any changes on the outcomes valued for the students. This question asks:

- How effective has what we have learned and done been in promoting our students' learning?

Impact should be judged on both a lesson-by-lesson basis and more long term. The contextualized nature of teaching practice – this teacher with this group of students in this school – means there can be no guarantee that any specific activity will have the anticipated result. The lesson-by-lesson check assesses immediate understandings of the lesson. Longer-term assessment ensures that the progress made is adequate against agreed benchmarks and identifies which areas of the curriculum need further work.

Teachers, therefore, need to develop self-regulatory skills to judge the impact of their teaching on student outcomes that are valued by the community, such as those described in relevant curricula. The ability to make this assessment is central to ongoing improvement and the development of adaptive expertise whereby teachers know what to keep as part of their regular routines and know how to identify what needs to change and how to access the expertise to develop more effective practice (Bransford et al., 2005). As old problems are solved, new problems become evident because teachers become more skilled at recognizing them and teachers take more control over their own learning.

The following description briefly describes how leaders and teachers assessed the impact of their efforts to improve:

Teachers were encouraged to identify their own learning goals and how they will monitor them. Progress on these goals was assessed through observation of teachers working with students.

The impact on student outcomes was monitored both informally and formally. Informal monitoring usually involved interviewing students to gauge their understanding of the learning intent of particular lessons and the examination of student work. More formal monitoring involved collecting achievement data on a regular basis and holding 'monitoring meetings' where leaders and teachers graphed student progress. Particular attention was given to the speed with which target students were catching up with their peers and discussing how to work with those students not making the necessary progress.

The development of this kind of expertise focuses on developing self-regulated learning processes for teachers and allows them to take 'control of their own learning by defining learning goals and measuring their progress in achieving them' (Donovan et al., 1999: 23). In the inquiry and knowledge-building cycles, this approach encourages teachers not only to define learning goals and progress, but also to judge their impact on the outcomes for students.

Assessing impact is not the end of the cycle. As Figure 9.1 shows, the arrows keep cycling. If assessing impact shows old problems persisting, then different approaches to professional learning need to be taken. On the other hand, if the desired shifts are achieved, new ones are usually identified because the demands of teaching are rarely static.

Implications for school leaders

Developing school routines to support teachers to engage in cycles of inquiry and knowledge building may seem overwhelming for some school leaders. Like teachers, when faced with such a challenge the temptation is to continue with previous practice. In many cases this will involve engaging experts for one-off sessions with staff, sending them on courses of choice, or establishing professional learning communities within the school with little monitoring of changes made to practice as a result. Weighed against these options is the lack of evidence of substantive impact on teaching practice or on student outcomes (Correnti, 2007; Hanushek, 2005; Sparks, 2004).

The brief description throughout the chapter of the engagement of teachers in the Literacy Professional Development Project provides some insights into how professional learning that makes a difference might be achieved. Not only were substantial gains in student achievement made, but they were sustained over the two-year monitoring period after the visiting facilitators had left the school as those involved maintained their inquiry focus.

If depth of learning is to be promoted, it is important to identify what activities should cease, otherwise leaders and teachers will become overwhelmed with all that needs to be done. The challenges of change outlined in the introduction have led many school leaders to engage in multiple innovations and professional learning initiatives throughout their schools. Sometimes teachers choose according to their interests, at other times everyone from the school is involved. Usually the problem with such an approach is there is little coherence among the innovations that demand considerable time and resources for both individuals and groups of teachers. Under such circumstances, learning usually remains superficial and teachers become burnt out as they struggle to put everything into practice. Substantive change remains an illusion.

In the same way that teachers are expected to have a learning plan for their class, leaders need a learning plan for their teachers that systematically builds important knowledge and skills with a focus on depth rather than breadth. As learning is progressed through engagement in one kind of professional development, it needs to be connected to and further developed in the next focus which might be a different curriculum area with similar underlying pedagogical approaches. The qualities of effective feedback, for example, remain the same across the curriculum.

Professional learning plans need to begin by identifying the strengths and learning needs of the teachers as is expected of teachers when working with students. At its most basic this process takes into account the gap between existing knowledge and skills of teachers and student outcomes, and new knowledge and skills required to achieve desired outcomes.

One of the greatest challenges leaders face is to overcome resistance and to increase the motivation for teachers to engage in deep professional learning. A focus on students together with a vision for new possibilities – new ways to teach mathematics, science or literacy with better outcomes for students becomes a central leadership role. Most important, however, is to provide the kinds of opportunities that will realize the vision. This involves:

- a focus on students
- ensuring worthwhile content
- engaging in meaningful processes
- having skills and opportunities to check impact.

These leadership challenges can be framed in a leadership inquiry and knowledge-building cycle which asks leaders to think and act on the answers to their inquiry questions.

- What knowledge and skills do the teachers need for students to meet students' curricula and other goals?
- What knowledge and skills do I as a leader need to meet the teachers' learning needs?
- What kinds of professional learning do I need to deepen my leadership knowledge and refine my skills?
- What do I need to do differently to engage the teachers in new learning experiences?
- How will I assess the impact of my changed actions on those outcomes I value?

Conclusion

If the multimillion dollar solution of professional learning is to meet the demands of change, then the conditions that promote professional learning need to be given as much consideration as those of students. It is not enough to send teachers off to courses or to leave them to their own devices to construct their learning experiences.

Leading teachers' professional learning requires those involved to know the important elements of process so optimal conditions can be created. Coherent professional learning plans are likely to promote access to the relevant content. The development of rigorous inquiry processes ensures that valuable professional learning time is not wasted, but rather focused on what needs to be learned to achieve better outcomes for students.

Reflective Questions ?

Throughout I have posed some questions and here I have identified two central ones:

1 To what extent do you as a leader promote evidence-informed inquiry processes specifically focused on building professional knowledge for your teachers?
2 What important professional learning needs have you identified for yourself so you can better support your teachers?

To answer these questions it may be useful to reflect on recent activities designed to promote professional learning in your organization and to trace around the cycle of inquiry and professional knowledge-building to identify the extent to which each part of the cycle is evident.

Further Reading 📖

Donovan, M.S., Bransford, J.D. and Pellegrino, J.W. (eds) (1999) *How People Learn: Bridging Research and Practice*. Washington, DC: National Academy Press.

This book provides a strong theoretical basis about how people learn that underpins many of the ideas in this chapter. Although the book focuses on student learning, the processes of how people learn are similar, whether school leaders, teachers or students. Learning involves the engagement of preconceptions about how the world works, the development of a deep foundation of factual knowledge that is organized in cognitive frameworks, and the promotion of metacognitive processes that allow learners to take control of their own learning.

Timperley, H. and Parr, J. (2009) Chain of influence from policy to practice in the New Zealand Literacy Strategy, *Research Papers in Education*, 24(2): 135–54.

This paper focuses on leadership at all levels of the system (from government agencies to teachers) that need to be attended to for systemic learning to take place. In our education systems, considerable emphasis has been placed on teachers making a difference, but for teachers to learn they need the environments in which they work to promote their learning. The paper places teacher learning within this wider system, drawing on the Literacy Professional Development Project as case material.

Acknowledgements

The author wishes to acknowledge the funding provided by the New Zealand Ministry of Education to support two aspects of the research underpinning this chapter, my co-researcher, Associate Professor Judy Parr on the LPDP and the involvement of the leaders and teachers in the schools studied.

References

Bransford, J., Derry, S., Berliner, D. and Hammerness, K. (2005) Theories of learning and their roles in teaching, in L. Darling-Hammond and J. Bransford (eds), *Preparing Teachers for a Changing World*. San Francisco, CA: John Wiley & Sons. pp. 40–87.
Correnti, R. (2007) An empirical investigation of professional development effects on literacy instruction using daily logs, *Educational Evaluation and Policy Analysis*, 29(4): 262–95.

Cuttance, P. (1998) Quality assurance reviews as a catalyst for school improvement in Australia, in A. Hargreaves, A. Lieberman, M. Fullan and D. Hopkins (eds), *International Handbook of Educational Change*. Dordrecht: Kluwer. Part Two, pp. 1135–62.

Donovan, M.S., Bransford, J.D., and Pellegrino, J.W. (eds) (1999) *How People Learn: Bridging Research and Practice*. Washington, DC: National Academy Press.

Elmore, R. (2004) *School Reform from the Inside Out: Policy, Practice, and Performance*. Cambridge, MA: Harvard Education Press.

Gottfredson, D., Marciniak, E., Birdseye, A. and Gottfredson, G. (1995) Increasing teacher expectations for student achievement, *Journal of Educational Research*, 88(3): 155–64.

Guskey, T.R. (2000) *Evaluating Professional Development*. Thousand Oaks, CA: Corwin Press.

Hammerness, K., Darling-Hammond, L., Bransford, J., Berliner, D., Cochran-Smith, M., McDonald, M. and Zeichner, K. (2005) How teachers learn and develop, in L. Darling-Hammond (ed.), *Preparing Teachers for a Changing World: What Teachers Should Learn and be Able to Do*. San Francisco, CA: John Wiley & Sons. pp. 358–89.

Hanushek, E. (2005) *Economic Outcomes and School Quality*. Education Policy Series. International Academy of Education & International Institute for Educational Planning, UNESCO. Available at: www.smec.curtin.edu.au/iae/

Hargreaves, A. (1998) The emotions of teaching and educational change, in A. Hargreaves, A. Lieberman, M. Fullan and D. Hopkins (eds), *International Handbook of Educational Change*. Dordrecht: Kluwer. pp. 558–75.

Muijs, D. and Reynolds, D. (2001) *Effective Teaching: Evidence and Practice*. London: Paul Chapman Publishing.

Nye, B., Konstantanopoulos, S. and Hedges, L.V. (2004) How large are teacher effects?, *Educational Evaluation and Policy Analysis*, 26(3): 237–57.

O'Connell, P., Timperley, H., Parr, J. and Meissel, K. (2008) Is sustainability of educational reform an article of faith or can it be deliberately crafted?, paper presented at, the British Educational Research Association Conference, Edinburgh, 3–6 September.

Sparks, D. (2004) Focusing staff development on improving the learning of all students, in G. Cawelti (ed.), *Handbook of Research on Improving Student Achievement*. 3rd edn. Arlington, VA: Educational Research Service.

Spillane, J.P. (1999) External reform initiatives and teachers' efforts to reconstruct their practice: the mediating role of teachers' zones of enactment, *Journal of Curriculum Studies*, 31(2): 143–75.

Stoll, L., Fink, D. and Earl, L. (2003) *It's about Learning*. London: RoutledgeFalmer.

Timperley, H.S. (2005) Distributed leadership: developing theory from practice, *Journal of Curriculum Studies*, 37(6): 395–420.

Timperley, H.S. and Alton-Lee, A. (2008) Reframing teacher professional learning: an alternative policy approach to strengthening valued outcomes for diverse learners, in G. Kelly, A. Luke and J. Green (eds), Disciplines, knowledge and pedagogy, *Review of Research in Education*, Vol. 32. Washington, DC: Sage.

Timperley, H. and Parr, J. (2009) Chain of influence from policy to practice in the New Zealand Literacy Strategy, *Research Papers in Education*, 24(2): 135–54.

Timperley, H., Wilson, A., Barrar, H. and Fung, I. (2008) Best evidence synthesis on professional learning and development, report to the Ministry of Education, Wellington, New Zealand.

van der Sijde, P. (1989) The effect of a brief teacher training on student achievement, *Teaching and Teacher Education*, 5(4): 303–14.

CHAPTER 10

Leadership and Student Outcomes: Are Secondary Schools Unique?

Viviane M.J. Robinson, Linda Bendikson and John Hattie

Research on instructional leadership tells us what it looks like and the impact it has on student learning. But do these findings apply equally to primary and secondary schools? This chapter reviews the research and concludes that secondary principals' instructional leadership is exercised more indirectly than that of their primary counterparts. In addition to direct work with classroom teachers it also involves overseeing the instructional leadership of middle leaders and organizing the school to support the work of improving teaching and learning. Despite these differences, the research suggests that, as in primary schools, more and less effective secondary schools are distinguished by the extent of principal instructional leadership.

The past 20 years have seen a remarkable turnaround in leadership research. From deep scepticism, at least among quantitative researchers, about leaders' impact on student outcomes (Purkey and Smith, 1983), we now have evidence that they can make a considerable difference to the learning and achievement of students (Robinson et al., 2008). Whether or not they do make a difference, however, depends on the particular leadership practices they employ, because different types of leadership have, on average, very different impacts on student outcomes.

The impact of leadership type: transformational versus instructional

One way of characterizing types of leadership is by their theoretical origins. The two leadership theories that have had the most influence in education are transformational and instructional leadership. Transformational leadership refers to that type of leadership which elicits unusually high levels of commitment, loyalty and energy from followers, particularly under conditions of radical or transformational change. The influence processes associated with strong transformational leaders include high levels of individual consideration, intellectual stimulation, encouragement of creativity and inspirational motivation. The latter usually involves the development and communication of an attractive vision (Bass and Avolio, 1994; Burns, 1978).

Instructional leadership, unlike transformational leadership which has its origins in business, has its origins in empirical studies of schools in high-poverty areas that succeeded above the odds (Edmonds, 1979; Hallinger, 2005). In such schools, leaders were more closely involved with the core business of teaching and learning, held high expectations of both staff and students, ensured high-quality opportunities to learn, and engaged parents and community in the educational work of the school. While there have been separate reviews of the relationship between each of these types of leadership and student outcomes, (Hallinger and Heck, 1998; Leithwood and Jantzi, 2005), they had not been systematically compared until the recent meta-analysis by Robinson et al. (2008). Their analysis of 22 studies showed that the impact on students of those types of leadership that are characterized as instructional are three to four times greater than those characterized as transformational. The reason is that measures of instructional leadership are more likely to capture variation in the particular knowledge and skills required to drive improvement in teaching and learning. For example, while transformational and instructional leadership theories and their associated measures both focus on shared goals, instructional leadership research is more likely than transformational to assess, not just the presence of shared goals, but the extent to which they are focused on improved academic or social outcomes for students. It is this educational specificity that may account for the stronger relationship between instructional leadership and student outcomes.

The impact of leadership type: specific practices

In order to dig more deeply into the particular practices responsible for these leadership effects, Robinson et al. (2008) conducted a more detailed analysis of a subset of 12 of the 22 studies that had been included in their comparison of instructional and transformational leadership. The 199 leadership indicators were grouped into five categories, or leadership dimensions, and an average effect size[1] calculated for each. The analysis showed that some leadership dimensions made a considerable impact on student outcomes. The dimension described as 'promoting and participating in teacher learning and development' had the largest average effect on student outcomes. The 0.84 effect size for this dimension can be broadly interpreted as meaning that for every one unit increase in this type of leadership, there is a 0.84 increase in the relevant student outcome. Moderate effects were also found for two other leadership dimensions – establishing goals and expectations (0.42) and planning, coordinating and evaluating teaching and the curriculum (0.42). Small, but still educationally significant effects were found for the two broad sets of practices described as strategic resourcing (0.31) and establishing a safe and orderly environment for both staff and students (0.27).

The main findings of the Robinson et al. (2008) meta-analyses confirm and extend several previous reviews of the published evidence on the links between leadership and student outcomes. In a review of 40 empirical studies published between 1980 and 1995, Hallinger and Heck (1998) concluded that principals have a small indirect effect on student achievement and that the dimensions of leadership that were most powerful were: establishing shared academic goals; building social networks and structures that enable goal achievement; being directly involved in instructional supervision and support; building teacher capacity and providing high-quality opportunities for teacher learning; caring for staff as individuals; and being skilled in problem solving and conflict resolution.

Given that the Hallinger and Heck review was confined to studies of principalship, while the Robinson et al. meta-analyses incorporated studies of both principalship and of other school leaders (for example, deputies), the overlap in their findings suggests that the five leadership dimensions identified by Robinson et al. are important regardless of who carries them out. There is, however, one set of practices identified by Hallinger and Heck (1998) that is different from those identified by Robinson and that may suggest an aspect of instructional leadership that is particularly germane to principal leadership. Principals make an impact on student outcomes not only by setting academic goals but by also building social networks and structures that enable goal achievement. Such school-wide leadership contributions are more likely to be led by the individual with responsibility for the whole organization than by other position holders. This emphasis on leadership as structuring the organization is also found in the work of Leithwood, who described it as a process of establishing policies and procedures such as timetabling, staff assignments and the deployment of resources in ways that support the achievement of educational goals (Leithwood and Riehl, 2005).

In summary, the literature on the links between leadership and student outcomes suggests that 'the more leaders focus their relationships, their work, and their learning on the core business of teaching and learning, the greater their influence on student outcomes' (Robinson et al., 2008: 636). It is perhaps this focus, sustained over a range of different leadership practices that best characterizes what has come to be known as instructional leadership.

Secondary schools: a special case?

Despite the new consensus about the importance of instructional leadership, there are many important questions still to be asked about the links between leadership and student outcomes. One of the more obvious ones is whether instructional leadership operates differently in secondary and primary schools. The meta-analysis reported by Robinson et al. was based on 27 studies, 16 of which were conducted in primary schools, four in secondary and the remaining seven involved mixed school samples. The limited number of studies precluded separate meta-analyses for the primary and secondary samples. Thus the question of primary and secondary differences in instructional leadership remains unanswered. A second unanswered question is about the specific role of the principal. The

Robinson et al. meta-analyses focused on leadership behaviours regardless of who carried them out. Thus, questions about the unique contribution of the principal cannot be answered from these data. The purpose of this chapter, therefore, is to analyse the published evidence to determine (a) the extent to which secondary principals engage in instructional leadership and (b) the impact of such leadership on student outcomes.

Before pursuing these two purposes, we discuss why, on theoretical grounds alone, we might expect the extent and nature of instructional leadership to differ in primary and secondary schools. In the subsequent section of the chapter we check our suppositions, by reviewing the available empirical evidence about the extent and impact of instructional leadership in secondary schools. In the final section we discuss the ambiguity, in both the concept and the measures of instructional leadership, between leadership that involves direct engagement with classroom teachers about teaching and learning and leadership that creates the organizational and social conditions that make such leadership possible.

Our position is that instructional leadership involves both direct engagement with classroom teachers about their teaching (direct instructional leadership) and the development of the organizational conditions that enable such direct engagement (indirect instructional leadership).The principal's school-wide responsibilities mean that he or she has a particular role to play in the latter.

Instructional leadership in secondary schools: the theoretical arguments

Numerous researchers have warned that research carried out in primary schools should not be generalized to the secondary school setting (Bossert et al., 1982; Hallinger and Murphy, 1987). They offer three reasons why one might anticipate that instructional leadership would operate differently in secondary schools – their greater size, their differentiation around specialist subjects, and the age of their students.

Greater size

First, the typical size of secondary schools means it is less likely to be the principal who engages in instructional leadership, in the sense of working with individual teachers on aspect of teaching and the curriculum. The number of teaching staff in a secondary school means that the principal is by necessity removed from the individual teacher and reliant on working through a hierarchy of deputies and middle leaders such as heads of department and deans. The more elaborated hierarchy of secondary schools means that a greater proportion of secondary principals' interactions, relative to those of their primary counterparts, are likely to be with staff who have responsibility for a group of classroom teachers rather than with classroom teachers themselves. It is heads of department who have responsibility for overseeing the work of groups of class teachers in secondary schools, including their planning, assessment and teaching (Siskin, 1991).

These structural differences between secondary and primary schools do not mean that secondary principals do not or should not, visit classrooms, or give feedback to individual teachers. It does mean, however, that since there are middle leaders who have specific responsibilities in these areas, they are less likely to engage in this type of direct instructional leadership than their primary counterparts. Given the delegation of responsibility for teaching and the curriculum to middle leaders, secondary principals' instructional leadership is likely to be exercised more indirectly through oversight of those who have the delegated responsibility for the quality of classroom teaching. Very little is known about how this oversight occurs, including the extent to which principals inquire into what their middle leaders know about the impact of teaching on the students for whom they are responsible.

In addition to such oversight, secondary principals exercise a second form of indirect instructional leadership by creating the norms and routines that ensure quality teaching and learning across the whole school. The principal's instructional leadership is exercised by organizing the school – everything from student management, timetables, resource allocation, staffing allocation and professional development policies. Principals' decisions about these policies and routines set the conditions for what happens in classrooms and hallways between students and teachers (Bossert et al., 1982).

In summary, it may be useful in a secondary school context to distinguish between the direct and indirect instructional leadership of the principal and to recognize that the latter involves overseeing the work of middle leaders and organizing the school in ways that support and require quality teaching and learning.

Departmental organization

The departmentalization of secondary schools is a second major difference between primary and secondary schools. The nature of curriculum delivery by subject areas means that specialist knowledge is needed to provide credible instructional leadership to classroom teachers. Given that such leadership is usually provided by heads of department and not by principals, the question arises as to what specialist knowledge they require to engage credibly with those who have such responsibilities. There is some debate about this in the literature and, while some empirical research has been done on the subject knowledge requirements of primary principalship (Nelson and Sassi, 2005), little work has been done on that of secondary principals. Principal oversight of subject departments is likely to be restricted to monitoring the results of instruction rather than instruction itself. Herriott and Firestone (1984) described the relationship between principals and departments in secondary schools as loosely coupled, and as more tightly coordinated in primary schools. The reason is not just size but a move away from the generalist knowledge base that is shared by primary teachers and their principals.

Quite apart from the knowledge required for secondary principals to usefully engage with their staff about instructional matters, the organization of teachers into departments which are defined by specialist knowledge and disciplinary affiliations means that there are particular challenges for principals in building a whole-school approach to such matters as student management, assessment, reporting and teacher professional learning. This is not only because of the size of the staff but also because departmental differentiation means that departments are likely to develop different subcultures, including different educational, language, values and priorities (Rowan et al., 1991; Siskin, 1991). Scarce resources mean that there will be competition between departments for money, amenities, and teaching time, and this can intensify teachers' identification with their department at the expense of identification with the school (Bolam and Turner, 2003; Little, 2002). The ability of the principal to draw departments and teachers with differing interests together around a common understanding of how to treat students and what they need to learn is a key instructional leadership skill.

Adolescent students

A third difference between primary and secondary schools relates to the nature of adolescence. Secondary schools need to provide a learning environment which engages the diverse interests of adolescents, meets their needs to make choices within clearly defined boundaries, provides multiple pathways for learning and fosters mutually respectful relationships between students, teachers and parents (Bryk and Schneider, 2002; Chenoweth, 2007). While all schools are charged with pursuing multiple educational goals, it is plausible that goal proliferation is greater in secondary schools, for the interests and achievements of students are likely to diversify with age (Blank, 1987; Rutter et al., 1979).

The conclusion might be that these three organizational features – size, specialization and the nature of the student body make instructional leadership, or at least instructional leadership with a whole-school focus, particularly difficult in secondary schools. The forces for differentiation – subject specialization, diverse student populations, competition for resources between separate structural and functional units – foster departmental subcultures, which could be expected to make it difficult for senior leaders to achieve a tight whole-school focus on the quality of instruction. A picture of the effective secondary school principal as the conductor of the orchestra emerges; one who does more coordinating than actually carrying out direct instructional leadership practices.

Instructional leadership in secondary schools: the empirical evidence

It is time to turn now from our theoretical discussion of the organizational differences between primary and secondary schools to the evidence about the nature and impact of principals' instructional leadership in secondary schools. The evidence is discussed in two sections. The first section describes the descriptive data on the extent of instructional leadership in secondary schools and, where possible, compares it with such leadership in primary schools. The second section presents the evidence about the impact of secondary principal leadership on student outcomes.

Descriptions of instructional leadership in secondary schools

In our earlier theoretical discussion of differences between the organization of primary and secondary schools, we discussed the greater diffusion of goals in secondary schools, and hence the challenge for principals in gaining a whole-school focus on such matters as assessment, pedagogy and student management. Our claims about goal diffusion can be checked against the findings of a US study of 111 elementary and high schools (Herriott and Firestone, 1984). The authors measured the degree of goal consensus among a school's teachers about the importance of seven educational goals, and found that it was greater in the elementary than secondary schools.

They also measured the degree of principal influence, relative to that of teachers, over instructional decisions such as selecting required texts and materials, establishing objectives for each course and determining daily lesson plans. A comparison of principals' reported influence over these decisions relative to that of teachers showed that while teachers had far greater influence than principals, primary principals exerted greater influence than their secondary equivalents.

When scores on the two organizational dimensions of centrality (measured by degree of principal influence over instructional decisions) and goal consensus were plotted together, the schools fell into two distinct clusters, with all 22 senior high schools in the sample falling in one cluster and all but one of the elementary schools falling in a second distinct cluster. The results confirm the organizational distinctiveness of secondary and primary schools and the more distant involvement of secondary principals in instructional decisions.

In a study of 32 urban US high schools, Blank (1987) interviewed principals and four teachers in each school about the principal's involvement in six areas of administrative and educational leadership. Less than half of the principals (12/32) received a high score on leading a curriculum or instructional innovation, and considerably fewer (3/32) on making decisions about the curriculum.

The degree of goal consensus was measured by asking the principal and four teachers in each school to name two educational goals and determining the number of respondents who named the same goals. Goal consensus was high in 13 of the 32 schools. When it came to leading staff development, a leadership dimension which has subsequently been shown to have strong impacts on student achievement (Robinson et al., 2008), only nine of the 32 principals were likely to be named as being most involved in making decisions about staff development.

Principals were more likely to be named as leading administrative areas, particularly that of seeking resources from the district office or community agencies. In addition, the principal was highly likely to be named as the person most involved in decisions about rules for student behaviour.

In summary, principal leadership in this US sample was much more likely in areas of student behaviour management and resource acquisition than in areas of curriculum and staff development. What we do not know from this study is how different these results would be in an equivalent study of primary school principals.

A direct comparison between the leadership of primary and secondary school principals is available from a 1989 study of 21 US principals whose staff scored them as at least one standard deviation above average on a measure of instructional leadership (Smith and Andrews, 1989). Eleven of these 'strong' principals led elementary schools and 10 led middle and high schools. Their reports of the amount of time they spent on four different job dimensions showed that while there was considerable similarity in the percentage of time they spent on school community relations and student services, the elementary principals spent a greater percentage of time improving the educational programme and the high school group spent more time on management and district relations. In other words, secondary principals spent more time managing the context for learning than providing the more direct instructional leadership implied by the three activities included in the educational programme improvement category.

Direct comparisons of instructional leadership in primary and secondary schools

All of the descriptive evidence discussed so far comes from studies conducted at least 20 years ago. The most recent comparative evidence we have is from a 1992 study of a sample of 23 Californian elementary and 17 high schools (Heck, 1992). Principals and a random selection of four teachers in each school completed a survey of the extent to which principals implemented 22 instructional leadership behaviours. Instructional leadership was greater in the primary school sample on all of the eight items for which descriptive data were reported. The difference was greatest for the two items 'makes regular classroom visits' and 'promotes discussion of instructional issues'. These results are consistent with the evidence we have already discussed – that secondary principals are less likely than their primary counterparts to lead through direct engagement with teachers about the quality of learning and teaching. Like the research of Smith and Andrews (1989), however, the Heck data show that despite their relatively lower frequency, principals' instructional leadership behaviours are still powerful predictors of the performance of their school. Thus, while the results imply 'some contextual differences in principal leadership that are associated with school level ... these appear to be less important than the differences associated with the performance level of the school' (Heck, 1992: 27).

In summary, secondary school principals tend to have a more distant relationship to the in-class practice of most teachers than their primary level counterparts, and thus they score less highly on many indicators of instructional leadership. At the same time as this descriptive difference must be acknowledged, the degree of secondary principal instructional leadership appears to discriminate, as it does in primary schools, between more and less effective secondary schools. In the next section we look more closely at the impact of principal instructional leadership on student outcomes.

The impact of principal instructional leadership on student outcomes

The state of the research on instructional leadership makes it difficult to draw definitive conclusions about the impact of secondary principals' instructional leadership on student outcomes. First, a search for empirical studies of the relationship between leadership and student outcomes in secondary schools yielded only eight studies (Blank, 1987; Brewer, 1993; Gaziel, 2007; Heck, 1992; 1993; Heck and Marcoulides, 1996; Hofman et al., 2001; Hoy et al., 1990). Second, the study designs varied widely making comparison of their findings quite difficult. In seven of the eight studies, leadership is treated as principalship and in the eighth (Hofman et al., 2001) measures were taken of both school and departmental leadership. The source of data about leadership was typically teachers, though in two studies, self reports from principals were used (Brewer, 1993; Hofman et al., 2001). The student outcome measures were usually drawn from existing data bases comprising standardized external assessments of verbal and numeric ability or of achievement in mathematics and reading.

Third, leadership was conceptualized very differently in these studies. Some measures focused on principal–staff relationships (Hoy et al., 1990), while others were based on transformational leadership theory (for example, Bass and Avolio, 1994; Burns, 1978). Only two studies included measures that could have been associated with instructional leadership (Brewer, 1993; Heck, 1992). These different conceptualizations led to a final difficulty that the relationship between principal leadership and student outcomes was highly variable across the studies.

Given the variation in the studies, it is not surprising that the relationship between principals' leadership and student outcomes was highly variable. The two studies of instructional leadership did suggest, however, that the more instructionally focused the leadership, the greater the impact on student achievement (Brewer, 1993; Heck, 1992).

Conclusion

Our review of the evidence suggests that the instructional leadership of secondary principals differs from that of their primary counterparts. They appear to do less of it, or at least, less of that type of instructional leadership which involves interactions with classroom teachers about the coordination, evaluation and improvement of teaching.

Several of the studies we reviewed suggest that even though it is less prevalent in secondary than in primary schools, the extent of instructional leadership by principals discriminates between high- and low-performing secondary schools. The conclusion seems to be that while instructional leadership is less likely to be exercised by secondary principals than by their primary counterparts, such leadership is nevertheless important in terms of its impact on student achievement.

In the earlier theoretical discussion of the differences between primary and secondary schools we suggested that the greater size and specialization of secondary schools, along with their older student populations, would require principals to exercise instructional leadership through creating the organizational and social conditions that enabled middle leaders to have productive conversations with teachers about instruction. In other words, the instructional leadership of secondary principals was likely to be predominantly indirect, since it was middle leaders such as heads of department who were primarily responsible for the quality of teaching and the curriculum.

Unfortunately, we cannot test our conjectures about these two forms of instructional leadership because this distinction is not made in the studies we reviewed for this chapter. While one might classify instructional leadership indicators about classroom visits and feedback to teachers as clearly of the first direct type, other indicators of instructional leadership are much more difficult to classify as either direct or indirect. An indicator such as 'plans and coordinates the curriculum' allows for a multitude of different practices, some of which might be classified as direct and others as indirect instructional leadership.

The advantage of broad and inclusive indicators of instructional leadership is that they capture the multiple different ways in which curriculum planning and coordination might occur in different school contexts. The disadvantage is that they blur the very considerable difference between creating the social and technical infrastructure for quality teaching and learning and dealing directly with teachers about such quality. If we are to learn more about the leadership of secondary principals and the leadership of principals of large primary schools, we need to make the distinction between the two and investigate how the quality of one effects the quality of the other (Bryk et al., 2009).

Reflective Questions

1 Do you think that increased direct or indirect instructional leadership by secondary principals is an appropriate goal? Why? What do you think the challenges are in achieving such a goal in your educational system?
2 What do secondary principals need to know to be effective leaders of the improvement of teaching and learning?

Reflective Activity

The following readings give rich qualitative accounts of life in secondary schools (Little, 2002; Rutter et al., 1979; Siskin, 1991). Choose one and pay particular attention to the role that the principal and other senior and middle leaders play, or do not play, in monitoring and improving the quality of teaching and learning. Which leadership practices and dispositions seem to be particularly important in being an instructional leader in a secondary school?

Further Reading

Two additional readings provide high quality additional information about how leadership works in secondary schools to improve learning and teaching.

Sammons, P., Thomas, S. and Mortimore, P. (1997) *Forging Links: Effective Schools and Effective Departments*. London: Paul Chapman Publishing.

This book reports a three-year study of the effectiveness of English secondary schools. It shows that there are substantial differences in value-added achievement between different subject departments within secondary schools. Detailed case studies of 30 departments in six of the schools suggest the school and departmental leadership factors that contributed to more and less effective departments.

Little, J.W. (2002) Professional community and the problem of high school reform, *International Journal of Educational Research*, 37(8): 693–714.

This reading provides further insight into the importance of pursuing school improvement in secondary schools through both whole-school and departmental approaches. It is based on a two-year study of two urban comprehensive high schools in the USA, one of which took a whole-school focus on reform the other which focused on departments. Both strategies had important limitations.

Note

1 An effect size is a standardized measure of the strength of the relationship between two variables. The larger the effect size the stronger the relationship between the two variables. Following Hattie (2009) we use the following lower boundaries as a guide when interpreting effect sizes: 0.2, small; 0.4, medium; 0.6, large.

References

Bass, B.M. and Avolio, B.J. (1994) *Improving Organizational Effectiveness through Transformational Leadership*. Thousand Oaks, CA: Sage.

Blank, R.K. (1987) The role of the principal as leader: analysis of variation in leadership of urban high schools, *Journal of Educational Research*, 81(2): 69–80.

Bolam, R. and Turner, C. (2003) Heads of secondary school subject departments and the improvement of teaching and learning, in M. Wallace and L. Poulson (eds), *Educational Leadership and Management*. London: Sage. pp. 133–48.

Bossert, S.T., Dwyer, D.C., Rowan, B. and Lee, G.V. (1982) The instructional management role of the principal, *Educational Administration Quarterly*, 18(3): 34–64.

Brewer, D.J. (1993) Principals and student outcomes: evidence from US high schools, *Economics of Education Review*, 12(4): 281–92.

Bryk, A.S. and Schneider, B.L. (2002) *Trust in Schools: A Core Resource for Improvement*. New York: Russell Sage Foundation Publications.

Bryk, A., Sebring, P.B., Allensworth, E., Luppescu, S. and Easton, J.Q. (2009) *Organizing Schools for Improvement*. Chicago, IL: University of Chicago Press.

Burns, J.M. (1978) *Leadership*. New York: Harper & Row.

Chenoweth, K. (2007) *'It's Being Done': Academic Success in Unexpected Schools*. Cambridge, MA: Harvard Education Press.

Edmonds, R. (1979) Effective schools for the urban poor, *Educational Leadership*, 37: 15–24.

Gaziel, H.H. (2007) Re-examining the relationship between principals' instructional/educational leadership and student achievement, *Journal of Social Science*, 15(1): 17–24.

Hallinger, P. (2005) Instructional leadership and the school principal: a passing fancy that refuses to fade away, *Leadership and Policy in Schools*, 4(3): 221–39.

Hallinger, P. and Heck, R.H. (1998) Exploring the principal's contribution to school effectiveness: 1980–1995, *School Effectiveness and School Improvement*, 9(2): 157–91.

Hallinger, P. and Murphy, J. (1987) Assessing and developing principal instructional leadership, *Educational Leadership*, 45(1): 54–61.

Hattie, J. (2009) *Visible Learning: A Synthesis of over 800 Meta-analyses Relating to Achievement*. London: Routledge.

Heck, R.H. (1992) Principals' instructional leadership and school performance: implications for policy development, *Educational Evaluation and Policy Analysis*, 14(1): 21–34.

Heck, R.H. (1993) School context, principal leadership and achievement: the case of Singapore, *Urban Review*, 25(2): 151–66.

Heck, R.H. and Marcoulides, G.A. (1996) School culture and performance: testing the invariance of an organizational model, *School Effectiveness and School Improvement*, 7(1): 76–95.

Herriott, R.E. and Firestone, W.A. (1984) Two images of schools as organizations: a refinement and elaboration, *Educational Administration Quarterly*, 20(4): 41–57.

Hofman, R.H., Hofman, W.H.A. and Guldemond, H. (2001) The effectiveness of cohesive schools, *International Journal of Leadership Education*, 4(2): 115–35.

Hoy, W.K., Tarter, J.C. and Bliss, J.R. (1990) Organisational climate, school health, and effectiveness: a comparative analysis, *Educational Administration Quarterly*, 26(3): 260–79.

Leithwood, K. and Jantzi, D. (2005) A review of transformational school leadership research 1996–2005, *Leadership and Policy in Schools*, 4(3): 177–99.

Leithwood, K. and Riehl, C. (2005) What do we already know about educational leadership? in W.A. Firestone and C. Riehl (eds), *A New Agenda: Directions for Research on Educational Leadership*. New York: Teachers College Press. pp. 12–28.

Little, J.W. (2002) Professional community and the problem of high school reform, *International Journal of Educational Research*, 37(8): 693–714.

Nelson, B.S. and Sassi, A. (2005) *The Effective Principal: Instructional Leadership for High Quality Learning*. Columbia, NY: Teachers College Press.

Purkey, S.C. and Smith, M.S. (1983) Effective schools: a review, *Elementary School Journal*, 83(4): 427–54.

Robinson, V.M.J., Lloyd, C. and Rowe, K.J. (2008) The impact of leadership on student outcomes: an analysis of the differential effects of leadership type, *Educational Administration Quarterly*, 44(5): 635–74.

Rowan, B., Raudenbush, S.W. and Kang, S. (1991) Organizational design in high schools: a multilevel analysis, *American Journal of Education*, 99: 238–66.

Rutter, M., Mortimer, P. and Maugham, B. (1979) *Fifteen Thousand Hours: Secondary Schools and Their Effects on Children*. Cambridge, MA: Harvard University Press.

Sammons, P., Thomas, S. and Mortimer, P. (1997) *Forging Links: Effective Schools and Effective Departments*. London: Paul Chapman Publishing.

Siskin, L.S. (1991) Departments as different worlds: subject subcultures in secondary schools, *Educational Administration Quarterly*, 27(2): 134–60.

Smith, W.F. and Andrews, R.L. (1989) *Instructional Leadership: How Principals Make a Difference*. Alexandria, VA: Association for Supervision and Curriculum Development.

CHAPTER 11

Instructional Leadership: Teacher Level

Helen Wildy and Simon Clarke

This chapter addresses three questions: What do we mean by instructional leadership? How is instructional leadership practised at the teacher level? What, if any, are its effects?

The focus of this chapter is teacher level instructional leadership. In examining this topic, we focus on three questions: What do we mean by instructional leadership? How is it practised particularly at the teacher level? What are its effects? These questions are explored through three cases: one is a short narrative case of a principal who delegates instructional leadership to two teachers; the second is the case of a system-level school improvement initiative set in Western Australia and built around teacher leadership; and the third is the case of an Australian university initiative adopted by schools in many states of Australia and internationally.

School-initiated instructional leadership

The first case is a narrative account of a principal of a large secondary school, newly arrived, wondering how to begin the process of turning around a school in challenging circumstances.

Taking a risk

Before I came here, a survey of students' feelings about their school indicated that, not only did they find school boring, they also found it threatening. Our community has a reputation for violence, abuse, low employment, single-parent homes and low literacy. I was alarmed that students did not feel safe in their school.

(Continued)

(Continued)

The first change I introduced was to the procedures for managing students' behaviour which looked to me more like managing student punishment. We released four teachers from their classrooms to take on full-time work in a newly formed student services centre. All teachers were given extensive training in conflict resolution, and the four student services staff were given counselling training. We ran regular support sessions for parents to help them learn skills to deal with young adolescents. This initiative has been so effective that after one year we were able to reduce the number of counsellors.

But I knew that all was not well in the lower school. Too frequently I heard teachers complain about the Year 8s and 9s. At first I simply listened. Then I began to ask: So what do you think we could do about the problem? One day I gave a talk in a public forum about my view of schooling. I noticed a couple of our teachers nodding. Afterwards I asked one of them what she thought about what I had said. From then, she and a colleague took an interest in rethinking the programme we offered Year 8 students. Later I asked if they were interested in doing some reading and research. I gave them time and some resources to visit other schools, to attend conferences, to read and plan together. They had six months to plan an alternative programme. Investing resources in planning was a risk for me. I wondered if they would go through with it.

The two teachers agreed to trial teaching English, mathematics, science and social studies to a class of randomly selected students for 16 lessons a week. I had to negotiate with heads of the learning areas. All agreed except the head of mathematics. He would only agree if we left the top mathematics group intact.

We have made the changes to the timetable to accommodate the two classes. The remaining students in Year 8 follow the traditional timetable structure. It is difficult to make even small changes to large tightly structured secondary schools. This initiative, though risky, signals to others that anything is possible given the right amount of support.

We begin with this narrative account to indicate the tentative nature of instructional leadership, or any intervention, and to stress that its intended outcomes, however modest, are not always guaranteed. Learning to be a leader, especially in educational settings, is fraught with challenges, dilemmas and tensions. Wise leaders understand that small steps are needed and at best these will be hesitant.

This narrative can provoke lively debate among school leaders. They talk about the length of time new principals wait before introducing change; they agree that personal safety is a fundamental concern without whose resolution no improvement can be made; and they argue about the process of initiating change. In this case the principal listened and waited. Only after noticing a positive reaction from two teachers did this principal open the conversation about changing the existing programme. Rarely do school leaders acknowledge that their efforts at school improvement might not be successful and so those who read and debate about this narrative are encouraged to reveal that they too sometimes have doubts.

What does this narrative reveal about the nature of instructional leadership? First, the term is not used by the principal in this narrative. Leaders do not use this terminology: the terms such as instructional leadership, educational leadership, curriculum leadership and transformational leadership are debated among academics and researchers. Indeed, instructional leadership is a term that is not used in Australia, where educational leadership is preferred (Gurr et al., 2007). The concept of instructional leadership has its origins in North America and has been a popular topic of writing for more than two decades. However, its definition, like many terms in leadership, is not clear. Nevertheless, a highly effective leader can have dramatic effects on the academic achievements of students, according to Fullan (2005).

The school effectiveness literature is strong in its endorsement of the role of the leader in creating a vision, setting high expectations, creating a supportive environment, working with parents and community, and monitoring performance. This has been agreed for more than a quarter of a century (Mortimore and Sammons, 1987; Renihan and Renihan, 1984). The difficulty lies in describing how leaders practise their instructional leadership. More recent research indicates that leaders make their difference by helping teachers improve their instruction (Odden and Wallace, 2003). For example, school improvement is achieved when teachers engage in frequent, continuous and concrete talk about teaching practices and when they develop norms of collegiality and experimentation (Little, 1982). In her seminal research, Little found in schools that made a difference to student learning, compared with those in schools that made less difference, teachers talked together with greater frequency, with a greater number and diversity of persons and locations, and with a more concrete and precise shared language. Student learning is at the centre of everything that leaders do (Stoll et al., 2003). However, the emphasis is more on the direction and impact of the leader's influence than on the process of the leader's influence, according to Bush and Glover (2003). In the past decade the term instructional leadership has been reconceptualized from a more general school culture focus to a clear and direct focus on students' learning. The term is now enjoying renewed currency in the literature (Robinson, 2007). The link between leadership and learning, however, is more evident in the policy than in the practice, suggest MacBeath and his colleagues (2005). We argue here that the link between leadership and learning is probably even less evident in the outcomes.

Without attempting to define the concept, let us now turn to those actions expected of an instructional leader. According to Smith and Andrews (1989), the instructional leader is the resource provider, instructional resource, communicator and visible presence. Blasé and Blasé (2000) see the instructional leader as one who encourages and facilitates the study of teaching and learning, enables collaborative efforts among teachers, establishes coaching relationships with teachers, and uses research to make instructional decisions. Glickman et al. (2001) portray the instructional leader as one who gives direct assistance to teachers in their day-to-day activities, develops collaborative groups among staff, designs effective staff development, curriculum development and the use of action research.

What does this narrative suggest about the practice of instructional leadership? It is clear that instructional leadership takes place at different levels in the school structure. Here the principal demonstrates such leadership by taking small, cautious steps to engage staff in school improvement. The principal also delegates leadership responsibility to two teachers. The focus is on the teaching programme in four learning areas with two classes in one year group. This required negotiation, timetabling and resourcing. It also involved risk but the principal is willing to take the risk. The principal gives authority and resources to two teachers to visit schools, attend conferences, read and research, and then to design a new programme to meet the needs of the students in this school. The principal and the two teachers know that an appropriate educational programme is necessary if learning is to improve. The principal knows that improving students' learning is a collaborative act that begins with teachers who are motivated to make changes.

What does this narrative suggest about the outcomes of instructional leadership? Clearly we are told only of the process of setting up an intervention whose outcomes are anticipated to be improved learning by a small group of Year 8 students. We assume that the principal's decisions are based on research literature suggesting a high correlation between instructional leadership and student achievement. For example, as early as 1992, Krug studied the instructional leadership of 72 principals and 1,523 teachers and linked this with the achievement results for 9,415 students, taken from the Illinois state-wide student assessment programme, at the third-grade level (56 schools), sixth-grade level (41 schools) and eighth-grade level (15 schools). Krug reports a significantly positive correlation between principals' self-ratings of instructional leadership and student achievement. The correlations were strongest for academic satisfaction, recognition, accomplishment and commitment. However, no significant relationships are reported between teacher ratings of instructional leadership and student achievement.

More recent research focuses on the way in which leaders influence student learning and point to the indirect effect of principals in contrast to the direct effect of teachers. For example, Silins and Mulford (2004) studied leadership effects of 3,700 teachers and their principals in 96 Australian secondary schools. They found the leadership that makes a difference to student outcomes is both positional (the principal) and distributed (administrative team and teachers). However, both kinds of leadership are only indirectly related to student outcomes; their effects are mediated by what these researchers call organizational learning. In this study organizational learning is a sequence of three stages: trusting and collaborative climate, shared and monitored mission, and taking initiatives and risks.

The quality of the teaching makes the most difference to student learning, according to Hattie (2009) and the quality of feedback by teachers is the single factor with the greatest impact. We know that the practice of instructional leadership by both the principal and the teachers has the potential to improve student learning outcomes. We know, too, that if the principal and the two teachers in the narrative 'Taking a risk' pay attention to factors related indirectly to the principal and directly to the teacher, then it is possible they may see changes in the achievements of these Year 8 students.

System-initiated instructional leadership

We turn now to the second case, the system-wide school improvement project known as Raising Achievement in School Education (RAISe). Initiated in 2004 by the Catholic Education Office of Western Australia (CEOWA), the concept draws on national and international research into school improvement and literacy achievement. Longitudinal studies of schools showed improvements in student outcomes related to schools adopting a whole-school approach (Hill and Crevola, 2004). These researchers found that it is difficult, if not impossible, for schools to bring about sustained improvement without both pressure and support from the system.

RAISe

RAISe aims to increase student literacy outcomes by improving teacher effectiveness through a student-centred literacy curriculum, action research and data-informed instruction. Hayes and Noonan (2008: 22) conceptualize four professional development strategies: a focus on time, particularly in the context of the classroom; a focus on support especially through professional learning communities; a focus on leadership, particularly shared leadership; and a focus on students. Professional development both on- and off-site, as well as online, is undertaken by all levels of staff to induct them into the values and goals of RAISe, and the role they play throughout three instructional 'waves' (Hayes and Noonan, 2009).

The first wave of instruction involves establishing excellent classroom routines, teaching practice and learning environments (Hayes and Noonan, 2008). Classroom teachers are supported by a first wave coordinator, who acts as a coach and mentor, facilitating collaboration and communication, and guiding staff as they gather data to identify students needing additional support. These students' needs are targeted during the second wave of instruction. The second wave teacher is trained in the Reading Recovery™ programme to tailor instruction to students' needs. The second wave teacher also provides support to teachers who have second wave students in their classrooms as those students enter, undergo and transition out of the Reading Recovery™ programme. Students who still require additional support access third wave instruction. The third wave coordinator offers continuing support to teachers, families and students, working collaboratively with teachers to develop individual education plans for these students. Data collected throughout all three waves are used to inform decisions about instruction and classroom practice (Noonan and Hayes, 2009).

The project began with 20 primary schools and by 2009, of the 130 CEOWA schools, 83 per cent had opted into the project. Eight literacy consultants work with principals and first and second wave teachers. Schools are encouraged to form networks to induct new teachers into RAISe processes and to stimulate each other's improvement. To assist principals and teachers take responsibility for outcomes of the project, software has been developed showing achievement of students and Year groups over time, and value-added measures of cohort progress. Consultants help principals and teachers interpret these data and to use them in their annual reporting of school achievement (Wildy and Faulkner, 2008).

Let us now examine this case through the three questions posed at the start of the chapter: what do we mean by instructional leadership? How is it practised particularly at the teacher level? What, if any, are its effects?

The case of RAISe was selected to illustrate the concept of instructional leadership for a number of reasons. First, the project was initiated at the system level and so the case is an example of system level instructional leadership. What does the research literature reveal about the role of the system in improving student learning? The Kentucky Cohesive Leadership System (KyCLS), for example, is based on the principle that a system-wide approach to policies and practices improves student learning by strengthening the standards, the training and the performance of leaders as well as the conditions and incentives that affect their success (Kentucky Department of Education, 2009). In the Kentucky Department of Education model, continuing professional development opportunities for leaders are linked to learning goals; leadership is shared rather than resting with single leaders; appropriate data related to learning goals are gathered and leaders are well-trained in their use; and leaders have authority to allocate the people, time and money to meet student learning needs.

Second, although the principal played a key role in the RAISe project in opting into the project and providing symbolic support, the leadership for the project at the school rested with teacher leaders, here called first wave coordinators. The challenge for the principal is to provide support to teacher leaders and to give them the authority to act as leaders of learning. Stoll and Fink (1996) claim that an environment of optimism and care generates energy and creativity which is the outcome of sharing leadership. However, Timperley (2008) warns that sharing leadership with the view to build a critical mass of staff with knowledge and responsibility for improving student learning, what she calls the leadership-plus framework, is a risky business. She argues that such sharing of leadership can simply lead to the greater distribution of incompetence. In the case of RAISe, the system level support in the form of off-site and on-site professional development from centrally provided literacy consultants and leadership consultants is designed to build capacity at the school level.

Third, at the heart of the RAISe project was teachers' practice in relation to the students in their classroom. Professional learning opportunities are centred on the performance and learning needs of current students. Southworth (2009), like Judith Warren-Little (1982) a quarter of a century earlier, claims that increasing the quality of the talk about students and their learning is what makes the difference. A structure to engender talk is the professional learning community (PLC). Emerging in the North American context as a vehicle through which to improve instructional practice and to increase student outcomes (Reichstetter, 2009), the PLC is a group which meets regularly to challenge, question and reflect on teaching practices and learning experiences, and to make group decisions about interventions based on student assessment data. Characteristics of the PLC include a commitment to continuous improvement, a culture of collaboration, collective inquiry, supportive and shared leadership and a results orientation. Professional Learning Communities need a supportive environment including time to meet and talk, physical proximity and explicit communication structures and processes. However, to achieve its full potential the PLC relies on skilled leadership and a culture of trust because teachers are brought together to interrogate their students' learning evidence and to plan for improvement. Hayes and Noonan (2009) stress that, in the RAISe project, the PLC has clear routines and dedicated time so that the collaborative experience becomes professionally enriching for participants. Teachers talk about their students' learning, or its absence, in non-defensive ways, using assessment data to inform and stimulate their discussions.

In the RAISe project, the PLC also incorporates action learning cycles. Teachers are encouraged to experiment with different ways of teaching and they use the PLC as the forum to prompt and support each other. The process of action learning cycles involves thinking systematically about what happens in the classroom, implementing action where improvements are thought possible, and monitoring and evaluating the effects of the action with a view to continuing the improvement. Such a cycle is conceptualized as: initial reflection–planning–acting–observing–reflecting. The literature on such experiential learning (Kolb and Kolb, 2001) indicates that benefits for teachers participating in action learning include a sense of professional empowerment and positive attitude to change.

This discussion of the RAISe project as a case of instructional leadership at the teacher level has illustrated some of its characteristics and practices. First, this is a school improvement process that values people, and gives central place to the role of the teacher as the key to the improvement of student learning. Teacher empowerment is central and the principal's support is essential to empower others to make decisions about pedagogy. 'Stepping back' and 'letting go' are key challenges for principals as has been found elsewhere (Wildy and Louden, 2000). RAISe has its own terminology, which serves to bring together those who are 'in' and exclude those who are not. RAISe develops processes for engaging in professional discussions, particularly for using data to inform instruction and refine teaching practice. However, the question of its effects has not yet been addressed. So, has the centrally supported RAISe project made a difference to student learning in the six years since it was introduced to Western Australian Catholic Education Office primary schools?

At the time of writing, no published outcome data are available. Like other school improvement projects, the RAISe project is based on the expectation that all teachers move steadily through a set of processes, with success. Increase in student assessment scores on national literacy and numeracy tests would count as success and system-level administrators plan to monitor these data for overall growth throughout the six-year period.

Partner-initiated instructional leadership

Finally we turn to the third of the cases through which we explore the concept of teacher level instructional leadership. Led by Crowther at the University of Southern Queensland, the Innovative Designs for Enhancing Achievement in Schools (IDEAS) project was conceptualized in 1997.

IDEAS

IDEAS is premised on teachers as the key to improving student learning, the adoption of processes by teachers committed to improving student learning, and a strong research base. IDEAS derived from research (Kaplan and Norton, 1996; Newmann and Wehlage, 1995) showing positive effects on student achievement when teachers engage as a professional community to construct a philosophy, and then build a shared pedagogy around this vision (Andrews and Lewis, 2002). Four concepts underpin the project.

Organizational alignment, the first concept, links school vision, community input, physical infrastructure, classroom practices and professional development and forms the Research Based Framework for Enhancing School Outcomes (RBF). This alignment is believed to strengthen the identity of the school and increase expectations of student achievement. A diagnostic inventory (DI) is administered to school stakeholders to identify strengths and weakness in the school's current alignment and to set targets (Andrews et al., 2004). Two years later the DI is re-administered to monitor progress towards these targets.

Parallel leadership, the second concept, is defined as mutualism between administrative leaders and teacher-leaders (Andrews and Crowther, 2002). The principal's role changes from a traditional hierarchical leadership model to a shared leadership approach.

The process of IDEAS, the third concept, is represented by the acronym *ideas* and builds capacity to ensure changes are viable and sustainable. The five processes are *initiating, discovery, envisioning, actioning* and *sustaining*. *Initiating* involves commitment from school staff, a crucial element of the change. Once the decision to proceed is made, the IDEAS school management team (ISMT) is established, the DI is administered – the *discovery* phase – and targets are set. The *envisioning* process identifies goals to which the school aspires and a schoolwide pedagogy (SWP) which reflects the school's vision (Andrews and Crowther, 2003). In the *actioning* phase, administrators and teacher leaders collaborate to introduce the vision to the school community. Teachers focus on the SWP, applying it in their practice and exploring it as a professional community. All teachers have a role to play in *sustaining* IDEAS.

The three-dimensional pedagogy (3DP) model, the fourth concept, provides a framework for teachers to refine their practice (Andrews and Crowther, 2003).

IDEAS began in 1998 with five schools in Queensland and by 2005 more than 200, mainly secondary, schools had engaged with the project in five states of Australia as well as in Singapore and Italy.

We end the chapter with the case of IDEAS because in many ways the school improvement process builds on and illustrates much of what we discussed earlier in the chapter. As for the previous two cases, we examine this case through the questions posed at the start of the chapter: what do we mean by instructional leadership? How is it practised particularly at the teacher level? What, if any, are its effects? We begin with a discussion of the ways in which the IDEAS project illustrates instructional leadership at the teacher level.

First, IDEAS builds a culture that is shared, focuses on student learning and aims at school improvement. The IDEAS processes take place over a two-year period which is dedicated to achieving shared understandings about what is to be changed and how the work towards change is to proceed. Its strength lies in culture building, and the processes that foster deep learning about collaborative and empowered ways of working and solving problems. We believe that too often this phase is overlooked, or rushed. Wise change leaders allow at least a year to 'get ready' by creating the vision for change and aligning it with appropriate resources and strategies.

Second, collaborative dialogue is central to IDEAS. The structures of IDEAS become embedded in the routines of the schools. Building a collaborative culture involves spending regular and focused time together, using a shared language, questioning and challenging assumptions and practices. Talking about teaching in concrete terms is well known to make a difference to the quality of teaching (Little, 1982). Using data to trigger inquiry and to inform decisions is similarly powerful in effecting improvement (Hayes and Noonan, 2009). Collaborative ways of working promote teachers' learning by enhancing their sense of self-efficacy (Hargreaves, 1997). Unlike traditional arrangements where teachers worked in a culture of individualism, opportunities for professional learning are more likely to occur when they engage in collaborative activities such as peer interaction, support and feedback (Harris and Muijs, 2005). When conducted on a regular basis, these interactions create teacher communities with potential to deepen knowledge and expertise. In such collaborative settings, information and insights are shared, issues debated, innovative ideas tested and tacit understandings are developed. Collaboration can represent a 'marriage of insufficiencies' (Shulman, 1997) in that professional challenges that are hard for teachers to deal with alone are easily met in the company of others.

However, as with the case of RAISe discussed earlier in this chapter, we note the absence of evidence of improved student learning. The one study of the impact of IDEAS reports that it was too early to measure an impact on academic outcomes for students (Chesterton and Duignan, 2004).

Implications

In our chapter we draw attention to three aspects of instructional leadership that are often overlooked: the changes required of the principal; the time taken to make lasting differences; and the messiness of change. We argue that principals need guidance in sharing leadership with teachers, particularly in treading the path between accountability and responsibility, and between responsibility and dependency (Wildy and Louden, 2000). Learning to share leadership takes time, and support, and this challenges the paradigm of situated power and influence. We argue too that the time required for change is frequently underestimated. There is little doubt that the challenge of improving students' learning is pursued by change theorists and government agencies with a prescriptive tone bolstered by messianic righteousness (Harris and Muijs, 2005). But we believe the key to improvement lies in cultural not structural change, with investment in professional learning and collaborative communities of practice. At the heart of such cultural shifts lies the teacher as instructional leader.

In concluding we add two points of caution. First, teachers as instructional leaders know, as we as researchers know, that change is hard work, especially changing teaching practice built over years. Teachers experience disappointment, frustration, even resistance, all of which are common features of school improvement processes. Despite this knowledge there is pressure on teachers to make dramatic changes in short time lines. However, change takes time and emotional work. Giving teachers permission to view their progression beyond the horizon of the school term or the school year can, we believe, provide a realistic set of expectations for teachers both for themselves and for those who press for school improvement. Developing a culture of collaboration and enquiry is one necessary step towards school improvement. In this step the culture shifts from one of acceptance that the performance of students is all that can be expected to a culture of inquiry that asks: is this all we can expect of our students? Unless all teachers are skilled and willing to address this question, student learning outcomes are unlikely to improve.

Second, working towards improvements in student learning is aided by continuous monitoring, assessment and reporting of the outcomes of actions that are implemented. Without sound evaluation, it is hard to determine both what works and whether improvement is being made. Furthermore, without robust evaluation designs, it is simply impossible to know whether the intervention is the source of change, in other words, whether the intervention, such as RAISe or IDEAS, has caused the student performance to improve.

We suggest that there are three different kinds of reporting. The most prevalent is reporting of the use of funds, that is, financial accountability. Less frequent, but still common, is the reporting of actions, that is, accounting that resources are expended on the actions for which they are intended which we call process accountability. What is absent from the literature about the projects described in this chapter is the third and most important kind of reporting: accountability for outcomes. Without robust evaluations, claims of the programme remain as merely claims and wide implementation by policy-makers is seriously compromised.

We argue, too, that building a culture of routine and systematic evaluation of interventions such as those we describe in this chapter can foster a sense of shared accountability. The processes of designing evaluations and collecting, collating and interpreting outcomes data is a collaborative act and one that builds community. Generating outcomes data is a strategy for enriching school communities. The relationships through which such evaluations are conducted are likely to develop confidence, risk taking and openness among participants.

Reflective Questions

1 What are some preconditions for teacher leadership?
2 To what extent is teacher leadership a collective activity?
3 What kinds of support and pressure are helpful in promoting improvements in student outcomes and what kinds of support and pressure are unhelpful?

Reflective Activities

1 Consider your own workplace. To what extent are teachers given authority to take on leadership responsibilities? To what extent are they held accountable for the outcomes of their efforts to improve student learning? Draw up a list of four or five leadership tasks teachers are given and then rate the level of discretion they have to do these tasks (from low 1 to high 5) for each of the tasks. Using a similar rating process, indicate the extent to which teacher leaders are supported to carry out these leadership tasks. Finally, rate the extent to which these teacher leaders are held accountable for the outcomes of the tasks they are delegated. Comment on the alignment of discretion, support and accountability in the work of teacher leaders in your workplace.

2 If you were given free rein to make changes in your workplace, describe three aspects that you would alter, explaining why you would make these changes and what differences you would anticipate as a result of your changes.

Further Reading

Hayes, P. and Noonan, P. (2009) From knowledge of action to knowledge in action, *The Australian Educational Leader*, 31(1): 16–20.

The authors conceptualize three domains of knowledge: subject content, pedagogy and student learning. Teachers' impact on student achievement is maximized when teachers are confident of the subject matter of their teaching, are skilled in the best ways to teach that subject matter and understand how to support every student in their class.

Little, J.W. (1982) Norms of collegiality and experimentation: workplace conditions of school success, *American Educational Research Journal*, 19(3): 325–40.

This is a seminal piece of research that has endured for more 25 years and should be read closely by all who care about schooling. Four relatively successful and two relatively unsuccessful schools were studied. More successful schools were differentiated from less successful schools by patterned norms of interaction among staff.

References

Andrews, D. and Crowther, F. (2002) Parallel leadership: a clue to the contents of the 'black box' of school reform, *International Journal of Educational Management*, 16(4): 152–9.

Andrews, D. and Crowther, F. (2003) 3-dimensional pedagogy: the image of 21st century teacher professionalism, in F. Crowther (ed.), *Teachers as Leaders in a Knowledge Society*. Deakin West: Australian College of Educators. pp. 95–111.

Andrews, D. and Lewis, M. (2002) The experiences of a professional community: teachers developing a new image of themselves and their workplace, *Educational Research*, 44(3): 237–54.

Andrews, D., Conway, J., Dawson, M., Lewis, M., McMaster, J., Morgan, A. and Starr, H. (2004) *School Revitalization the IDEAS Way*, ACEL Monograph Series, 34.

Blasé, J. and Blasé, J. (2000) Effective instructional leadership: teachers' perspectives on how principals promote teaching and learning in schools, *Journal of Educational Administration*, 38(2): 130–41.

Bush, T. and Glover, D. (2003) *School Leadership: Concepts of Evidence.* Nottingham: National College for School Leadership.

Chesterton, P. and Duignan, P. (2004) Evaluation of the national trial of the IDEAS project, report to the Department of Education, Science and Training, Australian Catholic University, Melbourne.

Fullan, M. (2005) *Leadership and Sustainability: Systems Thinkers in Action.* Thousand Oaks, CA: Corwin Press.

Glickman, C.D., Gordon, S.P. and Ross-Gordon, J.M. (2001) *SuperVision and Instructional Leadership: A Developmental Approach.* 6th edn. Needham Heights, MA: Allyn & Bacon/Longman.

Gurr, D., Drysdale, L. and Mulford, B. (2007) Instructional leadership in three Australian schools, *International Studies in Educational Administration,* 35(3): 20–9.

Hargreaves, A. (1997) Cultures of teaching and educational change, in M. Fullan (ed.), *The Challenge of School Change.* Arlington Heights, IL: IRI/Skylight.

Harris, A. and Muijs, D. (2005) *Improving Schools Through Teacher Leadership.* London: Open University Press.

Hattie, J. (2009) *Visible Learning: A Synthesis of over 800 Meta-analyses Relating to Achievement.* Abingdon: Routledge.

Hayes, P. and Noonan, P. (2008) Best practice or better practice: challenging the paradigm of teacher professional development, *The Australian Educational Leader,* 30(2): 19–24.

Hayes, P. and Noonan, P. (2009) From knowledge of action to knowledge in action, *The Australian Educational Leader,* 31(1): 16–20.

Hill, P.W. and Crevola, C.A. (2004) Key features of a whole-school, design approach to literacy teaching in schools. Available at: www.eduweb.vic.gov.au/edulibrary/public/teachlearn/student/hillcrev.pdf (accessed 12 June 2008).

Kaplan, R.S. and Norton, D.P. (1996) *The Balanced Scorecard: Translating Strategy into Action.* Boston, MA: Harvard Business School Press.

Kentucky Department of Education (2009) Kentucky cohesive leadership system. Available at: www.education.ky.gov/KDE/Administrative+Resources/School+Improvement/Leadership+and+Evaluation/Kentucky+Cohesive+Leadership+System+(KyCLS)/ (accessed 17 December 2009).

Kolb, A. and Kolb D.A. (2001) *Experiential Learning Theory Bibliography 1971–2001,* Boston, MA: McBer and Co. Available at: www.trgmcber.haygroup.com/Products/learning/bibliography.htm

Krug, S.E. (1992) *Instructional Leadership, School Instructional Climate, and Student Learning Outcomes.* Project report. Urbana, IL: National Centre for School Leadership, University of Illinois at Urbana-Champaign.

Little, J.W. (1982) Norms of collegiality and experimentation: workplace conditions of school success, *American Educational Research Journal,* 19(3): 325–40.

MacBeath, J., Frost, F.D. and Swaffield, S. (2005) Researching leadership for learning in seven countries, *Educational Research and Perspectives,* 32(2): 24–42.

Mortimore, P. and Sammons, P. (1987) New evidence on effective elementary schools, *Educational Leadership,* 45(1): 4–8.

Newmann, F. and Wehlage, G. (1995) *Successful School Restructuring: A Report to the Public and Educator.* Madison, WI: Centre of Organization and Restructuring of Schools, University of Wisconsin-Madison.

Noonan, P. and Hayes, P. (2009) Find your voice: real professional renewal, *Professional Educator,* 8(2): 28–31.

Odden, A. and Wallace, M.J. (2003) Leveraging teacher pay, *Education Week,* 22(43): 64.

Reichstetter, R. (2009) Defining a professional learning community: a literature review, E&R Research Alert. Available at: www.wcpss.net/evaluation-research/reports/.../0605plc (accessed 19 December 2009).

Renihan, F.I. and Renihan, P.J. (1984) Effective school, effective administration and institutional image, *The Canadian Administrator*, 24(3): 1–6.

Robinson, V.M.J. (2007) *The Effective Principal: Instructional Leadership for High Quality Learning*. Columbia, NY: Teachers College Press.

Shulman, L. (1997) Professional development learning from experience, in L.S Shulman (ed.), *The Wisdom of Practice: Essays on Teaching, Learning and Learning to Teach*. San Francisco, CA: Jossey-Bass. pp. 503–20.

Silins, H. and Mulford, B. (2004) Schools as learning organisations: effects on teacher leadership and student outcomes, *School Effectiveness and School Improvement*, 15(3–4): 443–6.

Smith, W.F. and Andrews, R.L. (1989) *Instructional leadership: How Principals Make a Difference*. Alexandria, VA: Publications, Association for Supervision and Curriculum Development.

Southworth, G. (2009) Learning-centred leadership, in B. Davies (ed.), *The Essentials of School Leadership*. 2nd edn. London: Sage.

Stoll, L. and Fink, D. (1996) *Changing our Schools*. Buckingham: Open University Press.

Stoll, L., Fink, D. and Earl, L. (2003) *It's About Learning*. London: RoutledgeFalmer.

Timperley, H.S. (2008) A distributed perspective on leadership and enhancing valued outcomes for students, *Journal of Curriculum Studies*, 40(6): 821–33.

Wildy, H. and Faulkner, J. (2008) Whole school improvement Australian-style: What do IDEAS and RAISe offer?, *Leading & Managing*, 14(2): 83–96.

Wildy, H. and Louden, W. (2000) School restructuring and the dilemmas of principals' work, *Educational Management and Administration*, 28(3): 173–84.

Section III

Broadening Ideas of Learning and Knowledge Development

CHAPTER 12

A Distributed Perspective on Learning Leadership

James P. Spillane, Kaleen Healey, Leigh Mesler Parise and Allison Kenney

In this chapter, we detail the implications of applying a distributed perspective to the relationship between school leadership and management and professional learning, including the entailments of the leader plus aspect, the practice aspect and the central role of the situation. Suggestions for policy and future research are also addressed.

Over the past decade, distributed leadership has garnered a great deal of attention and, seemingly effortlessly, entered the conversation about school leadership and management. Both scholars and practitioners have invoked distributed leadership as an improvement strategy for schools, often with simplistic and unwarranted mantras such as 'everyone is a leader' or 'the more leaders, the better'. For some researchers, distributed leadership is a conceptual lens for studying or diagnosing the phenomena of leadership and management. While some scholars have not gone beyond armchair theorizing – a popular pursuit – many have combined their theorizing with the application of a distributed perspective in empirical investigations of school leadership and management. We take a distributed perspective in this chapter to examine relations between school leadership and management and professional learning. Specifically, we consider the entailments of taking a distributed perspective in studying relations between school leadership and professional learning.

Professional learning is a popular strategy for improving classroom teaching and student learning. The theory of action is straightforward; through learning, school staff acquire new knowledge and skills that enable them to practise in new, hopefully improved, ways that in turn contribute to improvements in student learning. Most work on professional learning in education focuses on classroom teachers (Desimone et al., 2002; Goddard et al., 2007) with less attention to school leaders. With the exception of a few recent works (for example, Knapp et al., 2003;

Leithwood et al., 2004), the knowledge and expertise that school leaders need to perform well has received short shrift in the scholarly literature. Further, investigations of school leaders' opportunities to learn rarely venture beyond the school principal. By taking a distributed perspective, we argue for casting a wider net in efforts to understand relations between school leadership and professional learning.

We attend to *both* formal professional learning and on-the-job professional learning (Parise and Spillane, 2010). By formal professional learning, we mean workshops and coursework *intentionally designed* to enable school leaders' learning, commonly referred to by researchers and policy-makers as professional development. We typically distinguish formal pre-service preparation programmes from formal in-service professional development programmes. While much of the literature focuses on formal professional learning opportunities, in part because these are more accessible to researchers, scholars are increasingly paying attention to on-the-job learning. We define on-the-job professional learning as those opportunities to learn that arise from the social interactions among school staff in their work, such as conversations in the hallway or planning sessions or meetings with colleagues. Work in various traditions argues for attention to learning on the job; that is, learning in and from daily work practice (Bryk et al., 1999; Horn, 2005; Seibert, 1999). We use the phrase 'on-the-job' to denote that the *primary* intent of these social interactions is not necessarily to enable leader learning; learning is more likely to be secondary or *incidental* rather than intentional in these situations, at least relative to formal professional learning. We acknowledge that these two sorts of professional learning can be related and at times confused. For example, some professional development workshops occur during the work day, but as the primary design intention is to influence learning we consider these formal professional learning.

Our chapter is organized as follows: we begin by outlining our understanding of a distributed perspective on school leadership and management. In the remainder of the chapter, we examine the entailments of this framework for thinking about relations between professional learning and school leadership and management. First, we consider the entailments of the *leader plus aspect* of a distributed perspective for examining relations between school leadership and professional learning. We not only argue for attention to the professional learning of multiple formally designated schools leaders, but also to informal leaders as well as the implications for teacher learning. Second, we consider the entailments of the *practice aspect* of a distributed perspective for school leadership and professional learning by attending to what we know about relations between social interactions and professional learning. Third, we focus on the situation in which social interactions are nested to consider how aspects of the social situation enable and constrain professional learning.

A distributed perspective

We take a distributed perspective on school leadership and management (Spillane, 2006; Spillane and Diamond, 2007). Usage of the terms 'distributed perspective' and 'distributed leadership' vary widely, and even those who use distributed leadership as a conceptual lens do not do so uniformly. Some scholars focus exclusively on *who* takes responsibility for key organizational functions, whereas others add to this a consideration of the *practice* of leading and managing. Yet even when scholars take the practice aspect into account, some equate leading and managing practice with the actions or behaviours of individuals (Leithwood et al., 2007) whereas others see this practice as a web of interactions (Spillane, 2006; Spillane and Diamond, 2007).

As a conceptual framework for studying school leadership and management, a distributed perspective involves two aspects – the *leader plus aspect* and the *practice aspect* (Spillane, 2006). To begin, the leader plus aspect of a distributed perspective acknowledges that the work of leading and managing schools extends beyond the school principal to include other formally designated leaders (for example, assistant principals, mentor teachers). Numerous studies document how responsibility for leadership and management in schools involves multiple actors (Copland, 2003; Frost, 2005; Harris, 2002; Portin et al., 2003; Spillane and Diamond, 2007). Further, school staff without any formal leadership designation can and do take responsibility for leading and managing the school (Burch, 2007; Hallett, 2007). So while allowing for heroes and heroines, a distributed perspective moves us beyond the 'heroics of leadership paradigm' (MacBeath and McGlynn, 2002; Spillane, 2006; Yukl, 1999: 292). In doing so, the leader plus aspect acknowledges something that organizational scholars have recognized for decades: investigations of leadership and management must move beyond those at the top of the organization and pay attention to other formal and informal leaders (Barnard, 1938; Cyert and March, 1963).

The practice aspect of a distributed perspective brings the practice of leading and managing to the foreground. The *practice* of leadership and management has not been a major focus of researchers. But, a distributed perspective frames practice in a particular way, not simply as individual actions but rather as a product of the interactions among school leaders and followers as mediated by aspects of their situation (Gronn, 2002; Spillane, 2006; Spillane et al., 2004). Drawing on various theoretical traditions including sociocultural activity theory, distributed cognition and situated cognition, a distributed perspective frames practice as a product of the interactions among school *leaders*, *followers* and aspects of their *situation*. This framing departs from the rather narrow psychological view that primarily equates practice with individual actions. In this framing, the practice of leading and managing is stretched over the work of two or more leaders and followers. Interactions, not just actions, are central to investigating practice.

Further, aspects of the situation, including tools, artefacts, organizational routines and language (among others), define practice by enabling and constraining interactions among people. We do not interact directly with one another in the world; rather our interactions are mediated by a host of features of our situation, from language to the organizational routines that structure our professional work. While education scholars have long recognized that the situation matters with respect to leadership and management (Murphy, 1991), from a distributed perspective, aspects of the situation do not simply affect what school leaders do or moderate their impact; instead, the situation is a core constituting element of practice (Spillane, 2006; Spillane and Diamond, 2007).

Professional learning reconsidered from a distributed perspective

As detailed above, professional learning includes both formal professional learning and on-the-job professional learning. Applying a distributed perspective to
frame relations among professional learning and school leadership and management, we focus on three core areas. First, we argue that a distributed perspective
presses us to broaden our scope in investigations of the professional learning of
school leaders by going beyond the school principal to consider other formally
designated school leaders and informal leaders. In doing so, we also argue for
attention to how formal and informal leaders figure in the professional learning
of teachers. Second, a distributed perspective on school leadership and management draws our attention to not just the actions of individual leaders, but to
interactions. Third, taking a distributed perspective focuses our attention as scholars
on the central role of the situation in constituting school leadership and management. We organize our discussion around these three issues.

It's not just the school principal: the professional learning of other leaders

School principals matter with respect to school improvement. Several lines of
enquiry, from the 'effective schools' research (Purkey and Smith, 1985) to research
on the school as a professional community (Louis and Kruse, 1995; McLaughlin
and Talbert, 2001), have repeatedly noted the importance of the school principal,
particularly in influencing those in-school conditions that enable instructional
improvement (Hallinger and Murphy, 1985; Waters et al., 2003). A distributed
perspective does not undermine the role of the school principal (Spillane and
Diamond, 2007) nor the importance of the expertise necessary for school principals to perform well (Brenninkmeyer and Spillane, 2008; Goldring et al., 2009;
Spillane et al., 2009).

   A distributed perspective, however, presses us to consider more than the school
principal by drawing our attention to the professional learning opportunities of
other formally designated school leaders such as assistant principals, curriculum
coordinators, mentor teachers, literacy and mathematics coaches, among others.
This is no small task because the available empirical evidence in the USA suggests
that schools have at least two or three other formally designated school leaders in
addition to the school principal (Camburn et al., 2003; Spillane and Healey,
2010). Whereas some of these formally designated leadership positions were full-
time in a single position, most were part-time or even zero-time leadership positions, with staff often reporting holding multiple positions in addition to their
full-time teaching responsibilities. Even if we only take *full-time* formally designated school leaders into account, these studies suggest that research on the professional learning of school leaders that focuses exclusively on the school principal
misses the majority of school leaders in a building.

   Factoring in all of the formally designated leaders in a school, and even including the informal leaders, is an important step for scholars, but we also have to
consider how these leaders might work and learn as a collective. Leadership 'team'

composition might matter to the professional learning of team members. There is a considerable, if inconclusive, literature on team diversity, indicating that diversity in areas such as gender, race, experience and beliefs, hinders some aspects of group performance but promotes others. A study of Chicago schools, for example, illustrates the motivation losses that can be associated with leadership team homogeneity: in several schools in the study, a core group of senior faculty created obstacles to school reform, because they had come to accept the dysfunctional conditions in the school and were not inclined to make changes (Bryk et al., 1993). In this way, leadership team homogeneity can serve as an obstacle to professional learning. Diversity can enhance the performance of school leadership teams if it increases the innovation and openness to learning and change that are necessary for school improvement (McLeod and Lobel, 1992; Watson et al., 1993). However, it can also contribute to conflict and lower levels of trust among group members (Brewer, 1979; De Dreu and Weingart, 2003).

Taking the professional learning of other formally designated school leaders (and potentially informal leaders) into account also has implications for how we think about the professional learning of teachers. After all, school leaders primarily influence student achievement indirectly through teachers and their classroom teaching (Heck and Hallinger, 2009). Though much of the work on the relationship between school leadership and teacher learning centres on the school principal, our account to date suggests that in doing so we miss many of those who take responsibility for leading and managing schools. One recent study, for example, found that the ratio of formally designated leaders to teachers in one mid-sized urban school district in the USA ranged from 1:6.4 to 1:1.4. So, while one school had roughly one formally designated leader for nearly every other staff member, another had one formally designated leader for every six staff members. This suggests substantial differences between schools in terms of the number of formally designated leaders available to classroom teachers to support their professional learning. Indeed, aside from the principal, the vast majority of formally designated leaders (89 per cent) reported engaging in activities that support classroom instruction, including modelling instructional practices, discussing student work and standardized test results, and monitoring classroom instruction, as part of their leadership role (Spillane and Healey, 2010).

For research on school leaders' professional learning, a distributed perspective suggests at least two factors that must be taken into account. First, in studying professional learning we must also consider the professional learning opportunities of other formally designated leaders in addition to the school principal. The second and more challenging factor is the need to investigate not simply the learning of individual formally designated leaders within a school, but also to examine how the team of formally designated leaders as a collective enable and constrain professional learning. We will turn our attention to this again in the next section on social interactions.

For policy and practice, our argument presses us to reconsider our approach to school leader preparation and professional development. An individual-centric approach – typically focused on the school principal – continues to dominate. An alternative approach would centre on the preparation and development of teams of school leaders rather than preparing or developing individuals for particular school leadership positions. Some recent work offers examples of how school leader team development might be accomplished. For example, the Penn Center for Educational Leadership (University of Pennsylvania) designed and implemented a leadership development programme for teams of leaders from schools in the School District of Philadelphia that takes a distributed perspective to the work of leading and managing schools.[1] In addition to the school principal, members of these distributed leadership teams included other formally designated leaders and teachers. Similarly, the University of Chicago in cooperation with Chicago Public Schools has designed a new programme for preparing school leaders for Chicago high schools that also centres on preparing teams of leaders rather than just school principals (www.ssa.uchicago.edu/programs/slpp.shtml).

It's not just other school leaders: professional learning in and through social interaction

As described earlier, a distributed perspective is not simply about recognizing the multiple formally designated school leaders and acknowledging the informal leaders who are involved in leading and managing the schoolhouse; it is also fundamentally about the practice of leading and managing. Moreover, a distributed perspective frames this practice in terms of the interactions among leaders and followers. Thus, taking a distributed perspective to investigating relations between professional learning and school leadership and management foregrounds social interactions.

Various lines of research in education and other fields suggest that social interactions are important with respect to professional learning in organizations. The construct of social capital has figured prominently in some of this work. Though scholars focus on different aspects of social capital, the construct denotes real or potential resources for action that are attained *through relationships*. Social relations can be a source of various resources including trust (Bryk and Schneider, 2002; Louis et al., 1996), expertise (Frank et al., 2004; Spillane, 2004), opportunities for joint sense-making (Coburn, 2001; Spillane, 2004), and incentives for innovation through peer pressure or sense of obligation (Spillane, 2004). These resources are critical for professional learning; for example, trust is essential so that individuals feel comfortable discussing their shortcomings or challenges with their colleagues, whereas expertise is a key ingredient for knowledge development. A distributed perspective then focuses our attention on the nature of the social relations among school leaders and school staff writ large. Through discussion and argumentation, social interactions can surface new insights and understandings on an instructional issue among school leaders and other staff (Coburn, 2001; Spillane, 2004). Indeed, we can think about new knowledge or expertise as emerging in social interactions, as different people offer new insights or knowledge depending on the task (Sawyer, 2004; Spillane, 2006).

Research on social networks also offers suggestions into how social interactions might influence professional learning among school leaders (Coburn and Russell, 2008; Daly and Finnigan, 2010). Tie strength and tie span are especially salient with respect to professional learning. Tie strength refers to the salience or intensity of a relationship (Marsden and Campbell, 1984). While *weak ties* are sufficient for transferring explicit or simple information (Hansen, 1999), *strong ties* are necessary for the transfer of tacit, complex and sensitive knowledge (Reagans and McEvily, 2003), the sort of knowledge that is often critical for school reform. Strong ties also support joint problem-solving among organizational members. While acknowledging the importance of strong ties for professional learning, we should not ignore the potency of weak ties to enable the transfer of explicit procedural knowledge (Hansen, 1999). Such knowledge is a critical component of what school leaders need to know and learn in order to lead and manage their schools successfully.

Tie span indicates the extent to which an individual's relationships cross organizational or group boundaries, potentially providing access to resources not available in their immediate surroundings. Interactions that span 'multiple knowledge pools' (Reagans and McEvily, 2003: 242) enable school staff to access new information. External ties – ties that span organizational boundaries to other organizations and people – are important in the development of new knowledge because they can provide access to fresh ideas and practices that may be unavailable within the organization (Hansen, 1999; Reagans and McEvily, 2003). Further, these ties potentially minimize conformity and group think among organizational members by exposing them to 'outsider' views that may challenge the dominant orthodoxy within the organization (Hansen, 1999; Leana and Pil, 2006; Reagans and McEvily, 2003). Hence, we might expect that school leaders who have connections that extend beyond their immediate school building increase their likelihood of accessing new information, and/or encountering ideas that challenge their thinking about instruction and its improvement, both critical ingredients in learning. There is evidence that the internal and external ties of school staff are related to student achievement. A study of 88 urban schools in the USA, for example, concludes that a school's internal and external ties predict student achievement (Leana and Pil, 2006).

By focusing our attention on social interactions among school leaders and school staff writ large, a distributed perspective shifts our investigations of professional learning away from an exclusive focus on the learning of individual school leaders to consider whether and how their interactions enable and constrain their learning. Research on social capital and social networks offers suggestions as to how school leaders' social interactions might influence their professional learning. This work also offers insights into how school leaders might think about the professional learning of teachers in their school. If teachers' social interactions about work, for example, are confined to their subject area, department or grade level, it might undermine their access to new information that is essential for developing new knowledge. Similarly, the absence of social trust among teachers may undermine their professional learning, leaving school leaders to figure out how to build trust in order to promote professional learning among staff.

It's not just social interactions: the situation matters

Applying a distributed perspective to relations between school leadership and professional learning also draws our attention to the situation, another core constituting element of practice. Work in distributed cognition and symbolic interactionism focuses on interactive systems that *extend beyond the individual*. These interactive systems are *distributed* across a web of actors, artefacts, and situations (Hutchins, 1995) and the configuration of these systems can influence professional learning in schools. Cognition is distributed through a situation's material and cultural artifacts (Pea, 1996). From a distributed perspective, then, social interactions are not just a function of mental schemas and models alone. Language (for example, referring to grades as 'feedback'), rules (for example, 'all curriculum changes must be approved by the principal'), norms (for example, do not interrupt another teacher's class), tools (observation protocols, computer programs) and organizational routines (for example, teacher evaluations, grade level meetings, faculty meetings) serve as 'mediational means' that enable and constrain social interactions, and comprise work practice (Leont'ev, 1981; Vygotsky, 1978).

School staff *notice* and *interpret* with and through material and cultural artifacts such as language, protocols and organizational routines (Anagnostopoulos and Rutledge, 2007; Spillane et al., under review). These 'things' involve particular representations of learning, teaching and school improvement – key aspects of school work. School staff notice and interpret their surroundings not just with their mental scripts and schemas but also *with* material and cultural artefacts such as classroom observation protocols and the organizational routines in which they participated. What is noticed and how what is noticed is interpreted influences what and how school leaders learn on the job. Over the past several decades, for example, through various local district, state and federal policy initiatives, standardized test data has become a central feature of work in America's schools. These shifts in the policy environment are not just new pressures on schools to improve, they also involve a shift in how learning – and by extension teaching – becomes represented in the work of school staff members.

Consider organizational routines, a staple organizational feature of schools. Organizational routines more or less structure interactions among school leaders and teachers, influencing who talks to whom about what. Organizational routines figure prominently in school leaders' efforts to transform school leadership and improve classroom instruction and students' learning (Spillane and Diamond, 2007; Spillane et al., 2007). An example from a recent case study of instructional leadership is illustrative here. In the study of Hillside Elementary, Principal Nelson created a writing folder review routine, where she reviewed monthly writing folders from students in grades two through eight, including one composition written by each student and their teachers' grading of the composition (Coldren and Spillane, 2007). Mrs Nelson read students' work and provided both students and teachers with written feedback in an effort to improve both student writing and writing instruction. The writing folder review routine provided an opportunity for Principal Nelson to learn about Hillside students' writing abilities and how teachers grade their students' writing. The routine focused interactions among the school principal, teachers, and students on actual student work: it was based on what students were learning (or not learning), rather than on teachers' claims about what they were teaching, as would have been the case if Principal Nelson had introduced a different organizational routine. For example, if Principal Nelson had designed a routine in which she regularly reviewed teachers' written lesson plans, her focus and the focus of her staff's professional learning would have been on what content teachers planned to teach, rather than on what students were learning. This case demonstrates how an organizational routine enabled (and constrained) practice in general, and professional learning practice in particular, around writing instruction. Organizational routines and other aspects of the situation such as tools (for example, classroom observation protocols, LearningWalk® protocols) are not simply containers in which school leaders' and teachers' learning occurs. Rather, as a defining component of school practice, these aspects of the situation enable and constrain professional learning by framing and focusing the interactions among school staff.

When framed from a distributed perspective, aspects of the situation are not simply accessories for professional learning but central defining elements of professional learning practice. We need much more research on how the situation enables and constrains the professional learning of both school leaders and teachers. From a leadership development perspective, a focus on the situation also offers alternative ways of thinking about the professional learning of school leaders. For example, we can think about the introduction and scaffolded implementation of 'kernel' organizational routines in a school as an approach to professional learning that centres on developing a team of school leaders *in situ* (Resnick and Spillane, 2006). Moreover, this approach focuses on developing the *practice* of leadership rather than starting with developing the knowledge and skill of individual leaders. It also potentially contributes to reducing the knowledge transfer problems associated with more conventional approaches to leadership development.

Conclusion

In this chapter we took a distributed perspective to reframe relations between school leadership and management and professional learning. We conceptualized professional learning in terms of both formal and on-the-job learning, and focused primarily on school leaders' learning, though we also touched on classroom teachers' learning as enabled by school leaders. We argued that an exclusive focus on the school principal substantially underestimates the professional learning challenge vis-à-vis school leadership and management. Our account suggests that investigations of professional learning for school leadership and management need to work at identifying other formally designated leaders (in addition to the principal) and gather data on these leaders' learning in order to estimate the investment in professional learning and its effects on valued school outcomes. We hope to encourage other researchers to adopt a broader perspective when thinking about which school personnel should be included in studies of professional learning related to school leadership and management. Future work might also attend to informal leaders, those school staff members without a formally designated leadership position but who exercise influence over their colleagues' work.

Moving on to attend to social interactions among school leaders and school staff writ large, as dictated by the practice aspect of a distributed perspective, we argued for attention to how social interactions might enable and constrain professional learning of school leaders. Moreover, we considered the entailments of a focus on social interaction or practice for relations between school leadership and management and teacher learning. Finally, working from a distributed perspective, we took into account the situation not simply as a site for professional learning but a constituting element of professional learning. Specifically, we argue that aspects of the situation such as organizational routines and tools embody representations of core aspects of school work that enable and constrain professional learning in schools.

Reflective Questions

1 In your school, identify four organizational routines. For each routine, identify the function it is meant to serve. Specify the theory of action for each routine. Does the routine work? How do you know?
2 Who are the informal leaders in your school? How do you know? What roles do they serve? Do formal and informal leaders work together?

Further Reading

Spillane, J.P. and Healey, K. (2010) Conceptualizing school leadership and management from a distributed perspective, *The Elementary School Journal*, 111(2).

This article addresses the question: how are leadership and management related to school and classroom conditions and school outcomes? Using a distributed perspective to answer this question, the authors argue for attention to research fundamentals in the form of study operations and measures in school leadership and management research.

Spillane, J.P., Parise, L.M. and Sherer J.Z. (in press) Coupling administrative practice with the technical core and external regulation: the role of organizational routines, *American Educational Research Journal*.

This article explores the school administrative response to the changing institutional environment of America's schools. The authors describe how government regulation becomes embodied in the formal structure of four schools through organizational routines. Analysing the performance of these routines, the authors show how both government regulation and the technical core featured prominently and explore how routines enabled recoupling.

Note

1 This initiative is funded by the Annenberg Foundation.

References

Anagnostopoulos, D. and Rutledge, S.A. (2007) Making sense of school sanctioning policies in urban high schools: charting the depth and drift of school and classroom change, *Teachers College Record*, 109(5): 1261–302.

Barnard, C.I. (1938) *The Functions of the Executive*. Cambridge, MA: Harvard University Press.

Brenninkmeyer, L. and Spillane, J.P. (2008) Problem-solving processes of expert and typical school principals: a quantitative look, *School Leadership & Management*, 28(5): 435–68.

Brewer, M.B. (1979) In-group bias in the minimal intergroup situation: a cognitive-motivational analysis, *Psychological Bulletin*, 86(2): 307–24.

Bryk, A.S. and Schneider, B. (2002) *Trust in Schools: A Core Resource for Improvement*. New York: Russell Sage Foundation.

Bryk, A.S., Camburn, E.M. and Louis, K.S. (1999) Professional community in Chicago elementary schools: facilitating factors and organizational consequences, *Educational Administration Quarterly*, 35(5): 751.

Bryk, A.S., Easton, J.Q., Kerbow, D., Rollow, S. and Sebring, P. (1993) *A View from the Elementary Schools. The State of Reform in Chicago: A Report of the Steering Committee, Consortium on Chicago School Research*. Chicago, IL: Consortium on Chicago School Research.

Burch, P. (2007) School leadership practice and the school subject: the Baxter case, in J.P. Spillane and J.B. Diamond (eds), *Distributed Leadership in Practice*. New York: Teachers College Press. pp. 129–45.

Camburn, E., Rowan, B. and Taylor, J.E. (2003) Distributed leadership in schools: the case of elementary schools adopting comprehensive school reform models, *Educational Evaulation and Policy Analysis*, 25(4): 347–73.

Coburn, C.E. (2001) Collective sensemaking about reading: how teachers mediate reading policy in their professional communities, *Educational Evaluation and Policy Analysis*, 23(2): 145–70.

Coburn, C.E. and Russell, J.L. (2008) District policy and teachers' social networks, *Educational Evaluation and Policy Analysis*, 30(3): 203–35.

Coldren, A.F. and Spillane, J.P. (2007) Making connections to teaching practice: the role of boundary practices in instructional leadership, *Educational Policy*, 21(2): 369–96.

Copland, M.A. (2003) Leadership of inquiry: building and sustaining capacity for school improvement, *Educational Evaluation and Policy Analysis*, 25(4): 375–95.

Cyert, R.M. and March, J.G. (1963) *A Behavioral Theory of the Firm*. Englewood Cliffs, NJ: Prentice-Hall.

Daly, A.J. and Finnigan, K.S. (2010) A bridge between worlds: understanding network structure to understand change strategy, *Journal of Educational Change*, 11(2): 111–38.

De Dreu, C.K.W. and Weingart, L.R. (2003) Task versus relationship conflict: a meta-analysis, *Journal of Applied Psychology*, 88: 741–9.

Desimone, L.M., Porter, A.C., Garet, M.S., Yoon, K.S. and Birman, B.F. (2002) Effects of professional development on teachers' instruction: results from a three-year longitudinal study, *Educational Evaluation and Policy Analysis*, 24(2): 81–112.

Frank, K.A., Zhao, Y. and Borman, K. (2004) Social capital and the diffusion of innovations within organizations: the case of computer technology in schools, *Sociology of Education*, 77(2): 148–71.

Frost, D. (2005) Resisting the juggernaut: building capacity through teacher leadership in spite of it all, *Leading and Managing*, 10(2): 83.

Goddard, Y.L., Goddard, R.D. and Tschannen-Moran, M. (2007) A theoretical and empirical investigation of teacher collaboration for school improvement and student achievement in public elementary schools, *Teachers College Record*, 109(4): 877–96.

Goldring, E., Huff, J., Spillane, J.P. and Barnes, C.A. (2009) Measuring the learning-centered leadership expertise of school principals, *Leadership and Policy in Schools*, 8(2): 197–228.

Gronn, P. (2002) Distributed leadership as a unit of analysis, *The Leadership Quarterly*, 13(4): 423–51.

Hallett, T. (2007) The leadership struggle: the case of Costen elementary school, in J.P. Spillane and J.B. Diamond (eds), *Distributed Leadership in Practice*. New York: Teachers College Press. pp. 85–105.

Hallinger, P. and Murphy, J. (1985) Assessing the instructional management behavior of principals, *The Elementary School Journal*, 86(2): 217–47.

Hansen, M.T. (1999) The search-transfer problem: the role of weak ties in sharing knowledge across organization subunits, *Administrative Science Quarterly*, 44: 82–111.

Harris, A. (2002) Effective leadership in schools facing challenging contexts, *School Leadership & Management*, 22(1): 15–26.

Heck, R.H. and Hallinger, P. (2009) Assessing the contribution of distributed leadership to school improvement and growth in math achievement, *American Educational Research Journal*, 46(3): 659–89.

Horn, I.S. (2005) Learning on the job: a situated account of teacher learning in high school mathematics departments, *Cognition and Instruction*, 23(2): 207–36.

Hutchins, E. (1995) *Cognition in the Wild*, Cambridge, MA: MIT Press.

Knapp, M.S., Copland, M.A. and Talbert, J. (2003) *Leading for Learning: Reflective Tools for School and District Leaders*. Seattle, WA: Center for the Study of Teaching and Policy, University of Washington.

Leana, C.R. and Pil, F.K. (2006) Social capital and organizational performance: evidence from urban public schools, *Organization Science*, 17(3): 353–66.

Leithwood, K., Louis, K.S., Anderson, S. and Wahlstrom, K. (2004) *How Leadership Influences Student Learning: A Review of Research for the Learning from Leadership Project*, New York: The Wallace Foundation.

Leithwood, K., Mascall, B., Strauss, T., Sacks, R., Memon, N. and Yashkina, A. (2007) Distributing leadership to make schools smarter: taking the ego out of the system, *Leadership and Policy in Schools*, 6(1): 37–67.

Leont'ev, A.N. (1981) *Problems of the Development of the Mind*. Moscow: Progress.

Louis, K.S. and Kruse, S.D. (1995) *Professionalism and Community: Perspectives on Reforming Urban Schools*. Newbury Park, CA: Corwin Press.

Louis, K.S., Marks, H.M. and Kruse, S.D. (1996) Teachers' professional community in restructuring schools, *American Educational Research Journal*, 33(4): 757–98.

MacBeath, J. and McGlynn, A. (2002) *Self Evaluation: What's in It for Schools?* London: RoutledgeFalmer.

Marsden, P.V. and Campbell, K.E. (1984) Measuring tie strength, *Social Forces*, 63: 482–501.

McLaughlin, M.W. and Talbert, J.E. (2001) *Professional Communities and the Work of High School Teaching*. Chicago, IL: University of Chicago Press.

McLeod, P.L. and Lobel, S.A. (1992) 'The effects of ethnic diversity on idea generation in small groups', paper presented at the Academy of Management Annual Meeting.

Murphy, J. (1991) *Restructuring Schools: Capturing and Assessing the Phenomena*. New York: Teachers College Press.

Parise, L.M. and Spillane, J.P. (2010) Teacher learning and instructional change: how formal and on-the-job learning opportunities predict changes in elementary school teachers, instructional practice, *Elementary School Journal*, 110(3): 323–46.

Pea, R.D. (1996) Seeing what we build together: distributed multimedia learning environments for transformative communications, in T. Koschmann (ed.), *CSCL: Theory and Practice of an Emerging Paradigm*. Mahwah, NJ: Lawrence Erlbaum.

Portin, B., Schneider, P., DeArmond, M. and Gundlach, L. (2003) *Making Sense of Leading Schools: A Study of the School Principalship*. Seattle, WA: Center on Reinventing Public Education, Washington University.

Purkey, S.C. and Smith, M.S. (1985) School reform: the district policy implications of the effective schools literature, *The Elementary School Journal*, 85(3): 353–89.

Reagans, R. and McEvily, B. (2003) Network structure and knowledge transfer: The effects of cohesion and range, *Administrative Science Quarterly*, 48(2): 240–67.

Resnick, L.B. and Spillane, J.P. (2006) From individual learning to organizational designs for learning, in L. Verschaffel, F. Dochy, M. Boekaerts and S. Vosniadou (eds), *Instructional Psychology: Past, Present and Future Trends: Sixteen Essays in Honour of Erik de Corte*. Amsterdam: Elsevier. pp. 259–76.

Sawyer, R.K. (2004) Creative teaching: collaborative discussion as disciplined improvisation, *Educational Researcher*, 33(2): 12–20.

Seibert, K.W. (1999) Reflection-in-action: tools for cultivating on-the-job learning conditions, *Organizational Dynamics*, 27(3): 54–65.

Spillane, J.P. (2004) *Standards Deviation: How Local Schools Misunderstand Policy*, Cambridge, MA: Harvard University Press.

Spillane, J.P. (2006) *Distributed Leadership*. San Francisco, CA: Jossey-Bass.

Spillane, J.P. and Diamond, J.B. (2007) *Distributed Leadership in Practice*. New York: Teachers College Press.

Spillane, J.P. and Healey, K. (2010) Conceptualizing school leadership and management from a distributed perspective, *The Elementary School Journal*, 111(2).

Spillane, J.P., Camburn, E.M. and Pareja, A.S. (2007) Taking a distributed perspective to the school principal's workday, *Leadership and Policy in Schools*, 6(1): 103–25.

Spillane, J.P., Halverson, R. and Diamond, J.B. (2004) Towards a theory of leadership practice: a distributed perspective, *Journal of Curriculum Studies*, 36(1): 3–34.

Spillane, J.P., Parise, L.M. and Sherer J.Z. (in press) Coupling administrative practice with the techinical core and external regulation: the role of organizational routines, *American Educational Research Journal*.

Spillane, J.P., White, K.W. and Stephan, J. (2009) School principal expertise: putting expert-aspiring principal differences in problem-solving processes to the test, *Leadership and Policy in Schools*, 8(2): 128–51.

Vygotsky, L.S. (1978) *Mind in Society: The Development of High Psychological Processes*. Cambridge, MA: Harvard University Press.

Waters, T., Marzano, R.J. and McNulty, B. (2003) *Balanced Leadership: What 30 Years of Research Tells Us about the Effect of Leadership on Student Achievement*, Auna, CO: Mid-continent Research for Education and Learning.

Watson, W.E., Kumar, K. and Michaelsen, L.K. (1993) Cultural diversity's impact on interaction process and performance: comparing homogeneous and diverse task groups, *The Academy of Management Journal*, 36(3): 590–602.

Yukl, G. (1999) An evaluation of conceptual weaknesses in transformational and charistmatic leadership theories, *The Leadership Quarterly*, 10(2): 285–305.

CHAPTER 13

Leadership and Diversity

Marianne Coleman

After offering a definition of diversity in the context of education, the chapter focuses on the implications of diversity for leadership theory and practice and for the appointment of educational leaders.

Defining diversity

In this chapter diversity refers to the range of differences found in people, both students and staff, working in the field of education. In this context, diversity generally refers to the more visible differences between individuals such as: gender, ethnicity, age or physical disabilities. Other differences may be less obvious, for example, religion, sexuality or class. However, perceptions of difference are not value free and we unconsciously use stereotypes relating to differences to categorize people. Stereotyping provides an easy and quick way to make judgements about people who we locate within a category and they also generally work to preserve the status quo (Fiske and Lee, 2008). On the whole the qualities that are stereotyped positively and valued are being male, white, able, middle class, heterosexual and probably without visible religious affiliations. Those who are not in these categories might experience negative stereotyping and overt or covert discrimination and feel like an outsider in work and/or social situations. So diversity is not just about difference but also the ways in which differences are perceived and valued. Those concepts that are called on to counter discrimination on the basis of diversity include: equity, social justice and inclusion.

Changing attitudes

Social change has brought about a greater realization of the ways in which people may be labelled to their disadvantage. For example, attitudes of casual racism and sexism and derogatory remarks about other aspects of diversity that were common as recently as the mid to late twentieth century are now mainly seen as anachronistic and embarrassing. Despite this change and the legislation that is in place to protect individuals from discrimination on the basis of most of the types of difference listed above, there are still unthinking prejudices and covert discrimination on the basis of difference. Therefore there is still a need to examine current practice if we aim to achieve greater levels of social justice where social justice is defined as: 'the formal expression that the world does not treat all people fairly and that society should be made to be fairer' (Light and Luckin, 2008: 3). This standpoint on social justice implies developing interventions to bring about change. The nature of the intervention might be personal, at the level of an institution, such as a school where an anti-bullying policy is adopted or it might be at national level where the policy depends on the political stance. For example, a liberal intervention would be equal opportunities legislation. A more radical programme would be of affirmative or positive action. An example of this would be the now abandoned femocrat policy that ensured the appointment of women to senior positions in the public sector in Australia.

The case for valuing diversity largely rests on a social justice argument. However, there is also an important 'business case' for valuing diversity. This idea is based on meeting the demands of the market. The argument goes that if customers are diverse then it is important to meet diverse needs. In order to best meet these needs, the workforce, including the management and the board of directors should be diverse. As one example of this, research in the USA has shown that having three rather than the token one or two women on a corporate board improves the quality of decision-making and, ultimately, profit levels (Kramer et al., 2006). Recognizing the business case for diversity has given weight to campaigns such as the FTSE-100 Cross-Company Mentoring Programme which aims to increase the proportion of women on the boards of top companies in the UK (Thomson and Graham, 2005).

Before moving on to consider the importance of diversity for leadership it is worth noting that the term 'diversity' has also been used rather differently in England and Wales to refer to the large range of types of state schools that are available. The government emphasis has been on providing a diversity of school types ostensibly to increase parental choice within a quasi-market (Whitty, 2002). However, Millar (2009) points out that this type of choice and diversity has not actually brought about social justice outcomes, for example, a narrowing of the gap in attainment at GCSE level of socio-economic groups, with 'poorer children … still clustered in particular schools' with a 57 per cent gap between the top and bottom socio-economic groups.

In this chapter I am not directly concerned with diversity as it applies to government policy on choice of schools, but am using the term 'diversity' to apply to categories of difference in individuals, to which value judgement stereotypes are consciously or unconsciously applied, bringing advantage to dominant groups and disadvantage to others.

The implications of diversity for leadership theory and practice

Most of the research and literature about leadership in education does not mention diversity, although there is now a growing body of work that focuses specifically on it (for example, Lumby with Coleman, 2007). In general there seems to be an underlying assumption that educational leaders and the schools and colleges that they lead are homogenous in make-up. Also the focus tends to be on barriers and problems, with little consideration of the positives and added value that diversity can bring. However, in reference to black and minority ethnic (BME) school leaders, Campbell-Stephens (2009) points out that they bring 'additionality' to their work and that the process of assimilation is not beneficial to them or their pupils as it 'dilutes their essence and robs ... their students of the permission to be all that they can be as young people with multiple identities' (Campbell-Stephens, 2009: 18). The idea of diversity bringing additional value to leadership has not yet been fully absorbed into the area of leadership theorizing.

Diversity and leadership theory

The literature on leadership continues to develop as we seek to keep abreast of new thinking and to make a more comprehensive and relevant theory or set of theories about leadership. There are categorizations and typologies of leadership (Bush, 2003; Gunter and Ribbins, 2002; Ribbins and Gunter, 2002). There are new explorations of types of leadership, such as democratic leadership (Woods, 2005) and new designations of leadership such as 'ecological' (Bottery, 2004) or 'creative' (Stoll and Temperley, 2009). Leadership theory is a dynamic field, and may be growing towards 'leadership for diversity' through a number of theories and styles of leadership approaches. Perhaps those that are the most relevant to diversity are:

- values-led and moral leadership
- servant leadership
- authentic leadership.

Values-led and moral leadership

All leaders hold values that underpin the ways in which they lead. As Haydon (2007: 6) states: '"values" is not a technical term. In talking about values, we are talking about something that is part of the experience of everyone' (Haydon, 2007: 6). What is important is to revisit, examine and articulate these values. There is not one moral purpose in leadership. In conversation with John Portelli (Portelli and Campbell-Stephens, 2009: 19), Rosemary Campbell-Stephens draws on the conception of moral leadership to examine her own value stance:

> When I think about it for myself what I'm talking about is a moral purpose that meets the needs and the aspirations of those who have traditionally been failed by the education system ... I think the way that you judge which kind of moral purpose underpins most systems is to view who benefits and who does not, what they choose to measure, what they choose to reward

and affirm and what the outcomes are for the masses who go through that process, which research is done and when completed acknowledged and informs practice.

Servant leadership

Servant leadership (Greenleaf, 2002) is relevant to issues of diversity, inclusion and social justice as the emphasis is on serving the individual or follower rather than the needs of the organization or the leader. As the focus is on service to the followers, this type of leadership would take account of each individual irrespective of their origins and attributes.

Authentic leadership

Similarly authentic leadership focuses on the needs of others. Bhindi and Duignan (1997: 130) link authenticity in leadership with ethics and spirituality: 'Authentic leadership is intrinsically ethical. It involves an authentic view of self mediated by significant values (ethical standards) and meaningful relationships. It is also imbued with a sense of spirituality and a sensibility to the feelings, aspirations and needs of others.' Their conception of leadership is rare in the literature, in drawing on traditions outside the Western world. Theories about leadership and styles of leadership discussed in books on leadership are generally Western and are thus not necessarily appropriate to non-Western cultures, and also tend to exclude individuals who are in the UK but who can draw on different heritages and cultures. As migration between countries increases and the work force becomes culturally more diverse it is relevant to take cross-cultural theories (for example, Hofstede, 1991) into account in our leadership and management thinking.

The implications of theories including authentic and servant leadership and cross-cultural theories are far-reaching and lead us on to consideration of the more practical issues of the relationship between educational leadership and diversity. As Portelli and Campbell-Stephens (2009: 58) state: 'What we must create is a space for different leaders to practice leadership in a range of ways'.

Leadership and reflection on diversity

It is important to be aware of the values that underpin day-by-day leadership and leaders should revisit or audit their own views as they model leadership to others (Begley, 2003). This process of reflection can bring about critical consciousness (Capper et al., 2006) enabling issues relating to diversity to be seen differently. Another way of expressing this is that one might look through a different lens, exercising empathy to experience the reality of someone with different life chances. It is easy for us to assume that our way of being is the norm and everyone else is deviating from it. Most examples from research relate to gender or ethnicity, but reflection and critical consciousness are equally appropriate to all aspects of diversity.

In an Australian study of teacher training there is clear evidence that white Australians see themselves as having 'no' ethnicity and:

> Thus culturally diverse students can be seen as 'problems' that need to be 'managed' so they fit in with the beliefs and values of the dominant ethnic majority. Alternatively, their cultural differences might render them novel, exotic and 'colourful'. In either case, these constructions can simply affirm and reinforce stereotypes. (Santoro, 2009: 41)

Another Australian study focused on an attempt to bring about critical consciousness in pre-service teachers and this involved them spending some time in: 'an array of community organizations that catered for the needs of a diverse population of children and adults' (Ryan et al., 2009: 162). Their reflections on their experiences changed their views and understandings of the society in which they lived and were about to work. For example, one observed: 'These people are functioning in society with absolutely minimal English skills, and to see them on the street, and to interact with them on a lot of levels ... you wouldn't be aware of how little English they have. For me that's a real eye opener' (2009: 162).

Research designed to investigate the experiences of black and minority ethnic beginning teachers emphasized the importance of reflection on the part of both students and tutors: 'Reflection not only helps the retention of black and minority ethnic students, but is vital to the success of the course as a whole in developing a new generation of diverse and well rounded teachers' (CEHRE, 2008: 8). There will be parallels to these experiences and insights from beginner teachers for leaders in education, who must find their own ways of reflecting on the complexities of society. Begley (2003: 11) sums up how educational leaders (he refers to them as administrators) should proceed from their own self-reflection: 'Administrators must then take the next step towards authentic leadership. That is, they must strive to develop sensitivity to the values orientations of others in order to give meaning to the actions of the students, teachers, parents and community members with whom they interact.'

Cultural awareness

Increasing international mobility including movements of refugees, whether political or economic, creates opportunities and challenges both for the migrant and the society into which they move. Ethnocentrism, the belief that one's own culture is the 'correct' and normal one, is a natural tendency that includes: 'beliefs that the way business is conducted in one's own country is the only way to be effective, that people of one's own culture are naturally better suited to almost any management job, and the role of women in management is correct only as it exists at home' (Thomas, 2008: 45). Although most leaders in education would be aware of the flaws in this thinking, cross-cultural theory (Hofstede, 1991) is useful in showing how cultures differ in custom and practice related to work. The theory was developed from research carried out for a major international company operating in many countries, where despite an apparently uniform institutional culture, there were many differences in the ways that employees saw the world. Through the establishment of a number of dimensions it was possible to see how cultures differed and how therefore work practice might differ. This in turn indicated how difficult and inappropriate it might be to expect people from different cultures to work or respond to a new initiative in the same way. Insights of this kind are extremely useful to inform leaders who are working with people from different cultural backgrounds. To take one example, the dimension of power/distance refers to the relative deference of employee to employer. Whereas in the USA for example, there is very little apparent social distance in the relationship, in Confucian cultures the norm is for there to be a considerable distance between them.

The other dimensions include:

- Individualism/collectivism: the degree to which people value the individual or the group. In Western cultures like the USA and UK the individual and individualism is greatly valued. In China for example, there has traditionally been greater value placed on the group or the family than the individual.
- Uncertainty avoidance: this dimension relates to the extent that people feel threatened by unknown or uncertain situations.
- Masculinity/femininity: this dimension refers to the stereotypical idea of masculine values of achievement and feminine values which are more people-oriented, valuing good relationships.
- Long-term versus short-term orientation.

Other insights into different cultures may be equally helpful, and recommendations for further reading are made at the end of the chapter. One further example of cultural insights is the different ways in which time is perceived in different cultures. On the whole, in the Western world, time is seen as sequential with one event following another in an orderly sequence, where critical path analysis is valid and where punctuality is important. In other cultures, time is seen as synchronic where people may commonly be doing more than one thing at once, where queuing may be less important and there are worse things than being late.

Meeting times may be approximate in synchronic cultures. The range is from 15 minutes in Latin Europe, to part or all of a day in the Middle East and Africa. Given the fact that most of those with appointments to meet are running other activities in parallel, any waiting involved is not onerous and later arrival may often even be a convenience, allowing some time for unplanned activities. (Trompenaars and Hampden-Turner, 1997: 125)

This is just one example of cultural differences which may not be fully recognized when working with a multicultural team.

Leadership and organizational culture

Those who are responsible for leadership within an educational institution are responsible for setting the culture and modelling behaviour. As we have seen, the starting place for leaders and led is with an examination and understanding of the values that underpin the ethos. If valuing the diversity of individual students and staff is a key part of the ethos this should feed through to every aspect of their leadership. The importance of the way that the leaders act can be seen from one of the major findings of an independent study into school leadership (PriceWaterhouseCoopers, 2007: 1). This was that: 'The *behaviours* of school leaders have a greater impact on pupil performance than school *structures* or leadership models' (original italics).

Policies

Although structures may be less important than behaviours, it is nevertheless important to have structures to support equity and diversity, including policies to that effect. Deem and Morley (2006) in a study of such policies in higher education institutions in the UK found that although they might be in place for students they were much less likely to exist in relation to staff. Where structures do not exist there is less likelihood of good practice. In a study of diversity in 10 further education (FE) colleges (Lumby et al., 2005) only one was found to be working whole-heartedly towards inclusion and this college had structures in place including action plans, a race equality action group, a diversity and equality coordinator as well as codes of practice, relevant development events, a black managers network and a commitment to staff development for all. The college was situated in a multicultural area, and it was the leadership of the college, which was described by respondents as 'empowering' that set the standards by which it operated.

Targets and monitoring

Policies may also involve setting official or unofficial targets and monitoring how well they are met. Official policies might mainstream diversity, for example the strategy adopted by the Cabinet Office (2008: 9) has key themes that include creating an inclusive culture 'confident in its own diversity', leadership that is accountable for 'delivering diversity', and managing potential in a way that they 'bring on people from different backgrounds' and finally achieving:

> A diverse workforce at all levels: measured against workforce targets to reach over the next few years, for women in the Senior Civil Service, women in top management posts and people from minority ethnic backgrounds and disabled people in the Senior Civil Service, that drive progress towards our aspiration to reflect the society we serve by 2020. (2008: 9)

A much more informal but nevertheless values based approach is exemplified in the stance of a headteacher of a secondary school:

When I took over the headship you had to go down the rankings 15 places to find a senior woman in the school … It was about 50/50 men and women, but all the promoted posts were male and all the teaching staff and support staff except for technicians were women. Now we have a balance on every-thing … In a position of leadership where I can influence, I think it is right to develop female alongside male with equal opportunities. (Coleman and Glover, 2010: 19)

Professional development: example of 'Investing in Diversity'

One way in which leadership can set standards is to ensure, as in the college men-tioned above, that professional development is an entitlement for all staff. In this section I am drawing on qualitative research concerning a year-long professional development course developed specifically for black and minority ethnic (BME) senior staff in schools in London (see Coleman and Campbell-Stephens, 2010). Among the respondents, there was a perception that opportunities were not always open to them: 'We are not given opportunities and initiatives. We tend to be stuck in the same job. People recruit you for what they want. BME candidates tend to be in schools that are in some sort of difficulties. You might get temporary opportunities. It's a challenge' (2010: 42–3). Professional development may include being given a particular responsibility or project to manage, induction into a new role and career mentoring and coaching to bring out the best in individuals. Awareness of diversity issues may mean that particular attention is given to the career mentoring of women for example, and that care is taken to ensure that individuals are not stereotyped by their ethnicity or any other aspect of diversity.

The programme 'Investing in Diversity' achieves wonderful evaluations from staff because it specifically helps to break down negative stereotypes and enables partici-pants to aspire to senior leadership. One Asian woman commented:

The course prepared me for a bigger wider picture of what headship was about. I completed the course and came to the realization that I needed a change. I had been in the school for too long. I decided I did have the skill sets, training and understanding necessary. The course de-mystified what headship was about. It wasn't that I did not have skills, but that I had low expectations, aspirations. It was a cycle of deprivation. How could I possibly achieve that [a headship]? It is the messages you acquire, they are subtle both from the outside community and your own. (Coleman and Campbell-Stephens, 2010: 47)

In the same way simply seeing other black men or women in prestigious roles is powerful in setting aspirations:

It was common for successful BME individuals to be mentioned as role mod-els. One respondent, now a head teacher, saw that the deputy head at her daughter's school was Black and thought: 'If she can do it, I would love to do it too; she was a positive role model and this led me into teaching. Another was inspired by seeing an Ofsted inspector who was a 'Black lady'. (2010: 46)

Professional development for all leaders

Programmes like Investing in Diversity that are specifically for BME staff are relatively rare and evaluation shows they have an important role to play. However, it is equally important that professional development for *all* staff, not just BME, includes the opportunities to address issues of diversity and equity. Brundrett and Anderson de Cuevas (2008: 258) draw on knowledge of school leadership development programmes over the previous 10 years to make a recommendation of: 're-examination of the curriculum content of leadership preparation programmes to ensure that key topics are included that assist school leaders in developing the reflective consciousness, knowledge and skill sets required to lead on issues of social justice'.

Future educational leaders need to be prepared for a changing world where individuals are valued for all that they can bring to a role, although it is important to recognize and prepare for sensitivity in discussing emotive issues such as ethnicity:

> When the conversations go sour, people's feelings get hurt. People are often misheard, misunderstood, and misread. There is usually a group that finds the conversation unnecessary while at the same time, another group that finds the conversation insufficient. And, somehow, everyone involved ends up feeling falsely accused of something. (Chugh and Brief, 2008: 5)

In a work situation where mentoring was between pairs of different ethnicities Ragins (2002) found that there was considerable discomfort unless the pair at the outset had clarified exactly how they were going to deal with issues connected to ethnicity. The concept of reverse mentoring (Lumby with Coleman, 2007) was originally applied to younger staff mentoring older and more senior staff in the adoption of information technology (Bnet.com) but has also been used to coach senior staff reach greater understanding in implementing diversity policies where they are mentored by someone who is from a group who might have experienced discrimination linked to diversity (Ian Dodds Consulting).

The discussion of leadership and culture has so far concentrated on the impact on staff. However, the culture set through leadership as mentioned at the start of this section (PriceWaterhouseCoopers, 2007), is extremely important in relation to teaching and learning and the achievement of pupils.

Leadership, diversity and learning

It is accepted that a culture of high academic expectations is important in raising students' levels of achievement, and educational leaders have a particular role to play in bringing such a culture about. In relation to issues of diversity it is therefore particularly important that stereotypes are identified and questioned. There is wide-ranging evidence (listed in Gillborn, 2008) that: 'whenever teachers are asked to assess their students' "potential" against some academic or behavioural norm, Black students are typically under-represented in the highest ranked groups … and over-represented in the low-ranked groups' (Gillborn, 2008: 240). Deep-seated stereotypes can cloud the way in which teachers and school leaders perceive their students. In the wake of 9/11 and 7/7, Shah (2009: 535) identifies the growing problems faced by Muslim students in English schools and calls for leaders to be 'sensitive to ethnic and faith difference', noting that 'A pride and confidence in their heritage contributes to the learners' enhanced performance, and it is the teachers' and leaders' task to facilitate that goal by respecting diversity, by enhancing the students' confidence in identity and by strengthening the notion of equality relationships' (2009: 535).

Leaders' sensitivity to diversity is vital, but procedures also contribute to leadership for diversity, for example, the careful management and interpretation of data on pupil achievement are important issues for school leaders. Gillborn (2008: 245) points out how statistics can be interpreted in a simplistic or even misleading way. For example, he points out how the measure of who has free school meals (13.2 per cent of school pupils) is subject to 'discursive slippage' to apply to the whole working class, a much larger proportion of the school population than those who have free meals. He also shows how the government and the media: 'construct[s] the view that race inequality is narrowing and, therefore, that policy is moving us inexorably towards equity', something that a nationally representative sample and a longer time period show is not the case (2008: 245).

Although generally girls now outperform boys in schools and in higher education, gender is still an issue in education. While understandably, there has been a focus on underachieving boys, there are still issues around career choices for girls and boys, which in some cases remain stubbornly gendered. The analysis of empirical data from a European project on gender and qualifications led to the development of the concept of 'gender autonomy' (Evans, 2006) to describe those exceptional people who made career choices that were atypical, and crossed gendered lines, for example women who became engineers and men who became nursery workers. Although gendered career choices are often seen to disadvantage young women, young men also meet gendered expectations where early childhood teaching is seen as 'women's work' (Anliak and Beyazkurk, 2008). Awareness of gendered choices and expectations may be particularly important for women in education where leadership and management are still generally associated with males (Schein, 2001).

Diversity and choice of leaders

Leadership roles in education, particularly in the secondary and tertiary sectors are mainly held by white, middle-class men, although the proportion of women who gain leadership roles is slowly increasing. However, data indicate regional variations. For example, Fuller's (2009) analysis of local authority figures in England shows that in London and Birmingham around 40 per cent of the secondary headteachers are women, but that in the regions, particularly the north, the proportion is very much lower, in some cases 20 per cent or less. In Wales the proportion of women secondary headteachers overall is just over 17 per cent. It is difficult to get detailed figures on other aspects of diversity of leaders in education but the tendency is to stick to what may be seen as a 'safe' option. In a national survey of headteachers of primary, secondary and special schools (Coleman, 2005), 96 per cent of the heads indicated that they were white and only 1 per cent stated that they had any disability. Of this very small percentage, most stated their disability as deafness, one as diabetes and one that they were a wheelchair user. Issues of sexuality are sensitive and difficult to research and religious factors are rarely considered, so it is impossible to obtain figures and proportions relating to some aspects of diversity among leaders. However, the large-scale survey on teachers' careers (Powney et al., 2003) indicated that ethnicity and gender have a big impact on promotion. They found that over a third of white males and 20 per cent of white females held a promoted post, but only 9 per cent of BME males and 5 per cent of BME females held the higher-status positions.

Earlier in the chapter I considered how it might be useful for individuals to reflect on their beliefs and values and how that might be carried through into institutional policies and practice. It may be equally necessary for local authorities and others responsible for the appointment of educational leaders to consider and reflect on issues of equality, diversity and social justice.

Conclusion

In a context of change where economic and political factors underlie population movement and the trend towards globalization, there is a need to enlarge horizons and value ethnic and linguistic diversity, and this need has profound implications for leadership theory and practice. Social justice and business arguments both lead to the same conclusion, that there are benefits, where differences of all kinds are seen positively and not as reasons for exclusion. It is particularly important that leaders in education are persuaded of this and are themselves drawn from a field that is equally open to all.

Reflective Questions

1 As a leader in education what do you consider to be the key values relating to leadership and diversity in education?
2 In what ways might your institution ensure that diversity is fully considered in policies and practice?

Reflective Activity

Combining individuals from several different cultures in a work team may be problematic if no account is taken of the differences. How would you set about coaching such a team to enable success? Remember that successful team leadership involves three aims: achieving the targets set, ensuring that the team works together well and that each individual feels valued (Adair, 1988).

Further Reading

For more about the theory and practice of leadership and diversity take a look at:
Lumby, J. with Coleman, M. (2007) *Leadership and Diversity: Challenging Theory and Practice in Education*. London: Sage.

For further fascinating details about culture see Trompenaars, F. and Hampden-Turner, C. (1997) *Riding the Waves of Culture*. London: Nicholas Brealey.

A special 2010 edition of *School Leadership and Management*, 30(1) is devoted to leadership and diversity and includes articles that focus on religion, sexuality, gender and ethnicity, and the implications of diversity for theory and research.

References

Adair, J. (1988) *Effective Leadership*. London: Pan Books.

Anliak, S. and Bayazkurk, D.S. (2008) Career perspectives of male students in early childhood education, *Educational Studies*, 34(4): 309–17.

Begley, P. (2003) In pursuit of authentic school leadership practices, in P. Begley and O. Johansson (eds), *The Ethical Dimensions of School Leadership*. London: Kluwer Academic.

Bhindi, N. and Duignan, P. (1997) Leadership for a new century: authenticity, intentionality, spirituality and sensibility, *Educational Management and Administration*, 25(2): 117–32.

Bnet.com. Available at: www.dictionary.bnet.com/definition/reverse+mentoring.html (accessed 10 December 2009).

Bottery, M. (2004) *The Challenges of Educational Leadership*. London: Paul Chapman Publishing.

Brundrett, M. and Anderson de Cuevas, R. (2008) Setting an agenda for the development of the next generation of school leaders: a commitment to social justice or simply making up the numbers?, *School Leadership and Management*, 28(3): 247–60.

Bush, T. (2003) *Theories of Educational Leadership and Management*. 3rd edn. London: Sage.

Cabinet Office (2008) *Promoting Equality, Valuing Diversity: A Strategy for the Civil Service*. London: Cabinet Office. Available at: www.civilservice.gov.uk/Assets/diversity_strategy_tcm6-2258.pdf (accessed 10 December 2009).

Campbell-Stephens, R. (2009) Investing in diversity: changing the face (and the heart) of educational leadership, *School Leadership and Management*, 29(3): 15–25.

Capper, C., Theoharis, G. and Sebastian, J. (2006) Toward a framework for preparing leaders for social justice, *Journal of Educational Administration*, 44(3): 209–24.

Centre for Equalities and Human Rights in Education (CEHRE) (2008) *Respecting Difference: Good Practice Guide for PGCE Tutors in Issues of Race, Faith and Culture*. London: Institute of Education, University of London.

Chugh, D. and Brief, A.P. (2008) Introduction: Where the sweet spot is: Studying diversity in organizations, in A.P. Brief (ed.), *Diversity at Work*. Cambridge: Cambridge University Press.

Coleman, M. (2005) *Gender and Headship in the Twenty-First Century*. Nottingham: NCSL. Available at: www.ncsl.org.uk/mediastore/image2/twlf-gender-full.pdf

Coleman, M. and Campbell-Stephens, R. (2010) Perceptions of career progress: the experience of black and minority ethnic school leaders, *School Leadership and Management*, 30(1): 35–49.

Coleman, M. and Glover, D. (2010) *Educational Leadership and Management: Developing Insights and Skills*. Maidenhead: McGraw-Hill.

Deem, R. and Morley, L. (2006) Diversity in the academy? Staff perceptions of equality policies in six contemporary higher education institutions, *Policy Futures in Education*, 4(2): 185–202.

Evans, K. (2006) Achieving equity through 'gender autonomy': the challenges for VET policy and practice, *Journal of Vocational Education and Training*, 58(4): 393–408.

Fiske, S.T. and Lee, T.L. (2008) Stereotypes and prejudice create workplace discrimination, in A.P. Brief (ed.), *Diversity at Work*. Cambridge: Cambridge University Press.

Fuller, K. (2009) Women secondary head teachers: alive and well in Birmingham at the beginning of the twenty-first century, *Management in Education*, 23(1): 19–31.

Gillborn, D. (2008) Coincidence or conspiracy? Whiteness, policy and the persistence of the Black/White achievement gap, *Educational Review*, 60(3): 229–48.

Greenleaf, R.K. (2002) *Servant Leadership: A Journey into the Nature of Legitimate Power and Greatness*, Mahwah, NJ: Paulist Press.

Gunter, H. and Ribbins, P. (2002) Leadership studies in education: towards a map of the field, *Educational Management, Administration and Leadership*, 30(4): 387–416.

Haydon, G. (2007) *Values for Educational Leadership*. London: Sage.

Hofstede, G. (1991) *Cultures and Organizations*. London: HarperCollins.

Ian Dodds Consulting. Available at: www.iandoddsconsulting.com/index.php?link name_sub=reverse-mentoring (accessed 10 December 2009).

Kramer, V.W., Konrad, A.M. and Erkut, S. (2006) *Critical Mass on Corporate Boards: Why Three or More Women Enhance Governance. Executive Summary*. Wellesley, MA: Wellesley Centers for Women's Publication Office.

Light, A. and Luckin, R. (2008) *Designing for Social Justice: People, Technology, Learning*. Bristol: Futurelab.

Lumby, J., Harris, A., Morrison, M., Muijs, D., Sood, K., Glover, D. and Wilson, M., with Briggs A.R.J. and Middlewood, D. (2005) *Leadership, Development and Diversity in the Learning and Skills Sector*, London: LSDA.

Lumby, J. with Coleman, M. (2007) *Leadership and Diversity: Challenging Theory and Practice in Education*. London: Sage.

Millar, F. (2009) Ten years: for richer or poorer? *Education Guardian*, 8 December.

Portelli, J.P. and Campbell-Stephens, R. (2009) *Leading for Equity: The Investing in Diversity Approach*, Toronto: Edphil Books.

Powney, J., Wilson, V. and Hall, S. (2003) *Teachers' Careers: the Impact of Age, Disability, Ethnicity, Gender and Sexual Orientation*. London: DfES.

PriceWaterhouseCoopers (2007) *Independent Study into School Leadership*. RB818. Nottingham: DfES.

Ragins, B.R. (2002) Understanding diversified mentoring relationships: challenges in diversified mentoring programmes, in D. Clutterbuck and B.R. Ragins (eds), *Mentoring and Diversity*. Oxford: Butterworth-Heinemann.

Ribbins, P. and Gunter, H. (2002) Mapping leadership studies in education: towards a typology of knowledge domains, *Educational Management, Administration and Leadership*, 30(4): 359–85.

Ryan, M., Carrington, S., Selva, G. and Healy, A. (2009) Taking a 'reality' check: expanding pre-service teachers' views on pedagogy and diversity, *Asia-Pacific Journal of Teacher Education*, 37(2): 155–73.

Santoro, N. (2009) Teaching in culturally diverse contexts: what knowledge about 'self' and 'others' do teachers need?, *Journal of Education for Teaching*, 35(1): 33–45.

Shah, S. (2009) Muslim learners in English schools: a challenge for school leaders, *Oxford Review of Education*, 35(4): 523–40.

Schein, V.E. (2001) A global look at psychological barriers to women's progress in management, *Journal of Social Issues*, 67: 675–88.

Stoll, L. and Temperley, J. (2009) Creative leadership teams: capacity building and succession planning, *Management in Education*, 23(1): 12–18.

Thomas, D.C. (2008) *Cross-Cultural Management*. London: Sage.

Thomson, P. and Graham, J. (2005) *A Woman's Place is in the Boardroom*. Basingstoke: Palgrave Macmillan.

Trompenaars, F. and Hampden-Turner, C. (1997) *Riding the Waves of Culture*. London: Nicholas Brealey.

Whitty, G. (2002) *Making Sense of Education Policy*. London: Paul Chapman Publishing.

Woods, P.A. (2005) *Democratic Leadership in Education*. London: Paul Chapman Publishing.

CHAPTER 14

Educators as Knowledge Leaders

Lorna Earl and Lynne Hannay

> Knowledge work must become the core business of school leaders if innovation is to move beyond tinkering with the status quo. To do so it must be innovative and disciplined at the same time, with all in the organization needing to know and being willing to share new learning.

Education in a knowledge society

The explosion of knowledge is revolutionizing our society and escalating the pace of change. Increasingly, managing and distributing knowledge is critical for successful societies. Indeed, in 1996 the Organization for Economic Co-operation and Development (OECD) reported that: 'OECD countries continue to evidence a shift from industrial to post-industrial knowledge-based economies. Here, productivity and growth are largely determined by the rate of technical progress and the accumulation of knowledge. Of key importance are networks or systems which can efficiently distribute knowledge and information' (1996: 18). Having knowledge as the *raison d'être* of an organization is a massive paradigm shift in all sectors. Rifkin (2000) suggested that while the industrial age emphasized the exchange of goods and services, knowledge-based societies engage in the exchange of concepts. In such paradigm shifts, the products of the past are still required: in the industrial age people still needed agriculture to provide food, and in the new knowledge-based economy people need the physical products provided through industry (Stewart, 1997). Yet these paradigm shifts transformed both the agricultural society and the industrial society. In the same way, the shift to a knowledge society is changing the current conceptual landscape (Hannay, 2009).

Schools and school districts around the world are caught in this paradigm shift, with one foot in the industrial age where individuals need to learn basic skills that prepare them to work in an industrialized economy, and the other foot moving into a knowledge-based society focusing on creativity and innovation. This is not a comfortable position. Innovation in education is deeply problematic. Education is a foundational societal institution that is responsible, in part, for maintaining the status quo and protecting societal norms. At the same time, it is the primary contributor to the preparation of young people to cope throughout their lives. For the most part, educators are cautious and move forward through incremental changes to current systems and processes. Public organizations like schools and school systems do not typically foster innovative thinking that could challenge or question the 'black box' that frames their world views. However, too frequently this can lead to the continuation of status quo practices through a static view of knowledge (Hoban, 2002). Forward thinking is imperative as leaders in public organizations are being bombarded with technological and social change. Idiosyncratic adjustments to practice are no longer adequate to the task of transforming schools, which will now need to create and sustain an explicit climate of experimentation and planned innovation (Hargreaves, 2003).

The need for change means that schools and school systems must move quickly, but carefully and thoughtfully, into the knowledge era to hasten innovation. Educational leaders are morally obligated to bring a disciplined process to the creative and divergent activities inherent in innovation, that allow it to flourish, to be shown to work and to spread through the profession.

Knowledge work (the power source for innovation and change)

In the knowledge-based society, there is a recognition that knowledge is multifaceted and can be a tool, a process and a product, all at the same time. Knowledge is information that is available for investigation and use (a tool) during knowledge creation (a process) that results in new understanding and action (a product). Knowledge can be viewed as static and immutable information that can be transferred from one person to another with explicit knowledge that was codified as the collective wisdom of the culture and passed on being the most important. When knowledge is conceived as a dynamic and ever-changing commodity that is constructed and tested by individuals as they seek solutions to new problems (Hakkarainen et al., 2004; Hoban, 2002), tacit knowledge that is acquired through practical experience (Lam, 2000) becomes a critical element in the definition of knowledge as well.

Knowledge work is the process of intentionally combining tacit and explicit knowledge to come to new insights that are distributed across and beyond the organization. When people engage in knowledge work they are actively participating in a cyclical process of new learning and sharing of ideas to stimulate and foster innovative solutions to real problems. This process provides the forum for generation of ideas, challenging assumptions, testing hypotheses, formulating plans and routinely monitoring progress and making adjustments.

The creation of knowledge is not the job of any one individual. It is a social process (Scardamalia and Bereiter, 2003) that requires collective responsibility for accomplishments. Knowledge leaders share responsibility for the interrelated

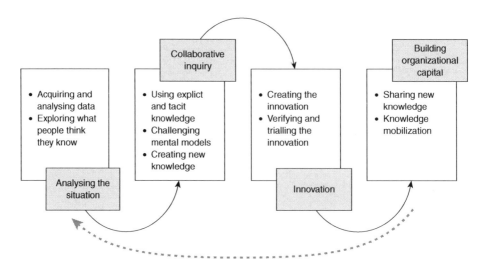

Figure 14.1 The cycle of knowledge work

network of ideas, sub-goals, and designs, with success dependent on all members rather than concentrated in the leader. As issues emerge, the group works collectively to shape next steps, build on each other's strengths, and improve their ideas and designs. Members create the cultural capital of their organization as they refine the 'knowledge space' and share the learning from their collective work.

Engaging in knowledge work is a complex cyclical process of acquisition, creation, representation, dissemination, distribution, validation, utilization and renewal of purposeful knowledge (Lin et al., 2006; Moteleb and Woodman, 2007). Figure 14.1 provides a simplified graphic of the various elements that contribute to this cycle.

Becoming knowledge leaders

Educational systems represent an interesting paradox in this transition to knowledge work. On the one hand, education is the primary purveyor of explicit knowledge to future generations, with the discipline-based knowledge that is shared through education systems being largely explicit. On the other hand, education has a long history of individuality and private work, and it is not culturally or structurally organized to allow for sustained collective collaboration. Educators have relied almost exclusively on their tacit knowledge (prior knowledge, beliefs and experiences) in conceptualizing and doing their work (Coburn, 2003; Earl and Katz, 2000; Spillane, 2000).

If deep change comes from creating new knowledge, the challenge for educational leaders is to operate as 'knowledge leaders' who work together to engage in a productive interchange between tacit and explicit knowledge to generate new collective knowledge that can be explicitly codified so that it is accessible throughout the organization and beyond (Hakkarainen et al., 2004).

But what does this mean in practice? What does being a knowledge leader mean for educational leaders? In this section, we address the major tasks involved in knowledge work by describing seven activities of knowledge leaders. Knowledge leaders:

- are learners
- use data and evidence to frame their discussions
- make tacit knowledge visible
- use both explicit and tacit knowledge to create new knowledge
- challenge their own mental models
- learn collaboratively through cycles of inquiry
- use their new knowledge for innovation
- validate their new knowledge in action
- share their learning with others in the organization.

Knowledge leaders are learners

Knowledge leaders engage in continual new learning, in a collaborative context, using both explicit and tacit knowledge to routinely challenge their existing beliefs and create new collective knowledge. Knowledge work is about learning – new learning that challenges and changes people's existing mental models in ways that result in new knowledge and in disciplined innovation.

As Fullan states, the core of improving schools rests with professionals at all levels continuously improving learning so that their collective efficacy enables them to 'raise the bar and close the gap of student learning for all students' (Fullan, 2006: 28). New learning, however, is not passive and it is not easy. 'Knowledge leaders live in a continual learning mode. They never "arrive" ... It is a process. It is a lifelong discipline' (Senge, 1990: 142).

One of us has written elsewhere about developing an inquiry habit of mind – a habit of using inquiry and reflection to think about where you are, where you are going and how you will get there, and then turning around to rethink the whole process to see how well it is working and make adjustments (Earl and Katz, 2006). Leaders with an 'inquiry habit of mind' consider a range of evidence and keep searching for increased understanding and clarity by engaging in a spiral of systematic analysis of the situation, professional reflection, action and re-analysis. This inquiry cycle of wanting to know, appealing to evidence and making changes to practice is fundamentally a process of new learning, of knowledge creation through a process of questioning past assumptions, past tacit knowledge and past mental models.

The principals of seven primary schools have decided to work together to improve the learning conditions for all their students. The schools in the network are situated geographically in three towns that have grown together into one large municipality. They have typically

(Continued)

(Continued)

competed with one another for students but as enrolment is declining, they are thinking that they need to work together. Several of them are also new to the role or to the region and they were keen to have a community to share ideas with and to learn from. Although they had agreed to working together, they did not yet trust one another completely.

At their first meeting they shared stories about their schools and agreed that it was time for something to be done, especially because some students (especially those from low income families) do not achieve well in any of their schools. They agreed that they would continue to meet and explore their mutual concerns.

Knowledge leaders learn collaboratively through cycles of inquiry

Learning in a knowledge-based society is social (Boder, 2006), with collaboration between knowledge leaders. Recent research suggests that collaboration is almost a prerequisite for sustained educational change and for teachers to reconstruct their mental models. Without such collaboration, it is more difficult for individuals to engage in the kind of rethinking or experiential practices which are essential for the reconstruction of professional knowledge and mental models (Hannay, 2003; Putnam and Borko, 2002). Learning in collaborative communities provides the cognitive tools – ideas, theories and concepts – to make sense of their experiences (Putnam and Borko, 2000). Working collaboratively requires that participants 'dwell in the experiences, perspectives, and concepts of other participants – to shift from a commitment to one's own interest to that of the group' (Von Krogh et al., 2000: 58).

Learning together is not a linear or mechanistic process, but an iterative one of 'thinking in circles' (O'Connor and McDermott, 1997) that is dynamic, creatively chaotic, transformative, and evolves through the interaction within groups. The whole community works in public 'knowledge spaces' in order to advance the state of the community knowledge. In collaborative inquiry, a group works together in repeated episodes of reflection and action to examine and learn about an issue that is of importance to them. Engaging in collaborative inquiry allows educators to work together searching for and considering various sources of knowledge (both explicit and tacit) in order to investigate practices and ideas through a number of lenses, to put forward hypotheses, to challenge beliefs, and to pose more questions and to embark on a course of action to address authentic problems (Earl and Timperley, 2008; Katz et al., 2009).

The network of principals had agreed to meet once a month for the school term to explore what working together might mean. They agreed that they needed to look at the data about their schools and, because this was a relatively new experience for most of them, they decided to employ a facilitator.

Knowledge leaders use data and evidence to frame their discussions

Knowledge work involves gathering, organizing and using data or evidence for new learning and innovation. Knowledge leaders are routinely locating and accessing data from multiple sources and using all kinds of evidence in a continuous and iterative process of problem identification and problem resolution. When leaders have an 'inquiry habit of mind', they rely on rigorous data collection and interpretation as the foundation for decisions and actions (Earl and Katz, 2006). Most school districts have lots of data available in their district information systems, although they may not be easily accessible or organized in a way that they can be used by individual schools. Schools are also likely to have various kinds of other formal and informal data that tend not to be electronically stored – data like classroom records, classroom assessments and programme descriptions. Educators can draw on many different forms of evidence – research studies, test results, surveys, observations, testimonies and witnesses all qualify as data. If school leaders are going to be active in interpreting and using data, as well as challenging and disputing interpretations or uses that they believe are contestable, they must become 'data-literate' (Earl and Katz, 2006), that is:

- identify what data they need for specific purposes, not just use data that are available.
- ascertain the quality of the data that they intend to use.
- understand the principles that underlie the statistics and analyses being used.
- recognize that statistics are not the only kinds of data that they can utilize. Opinions, anecdotes and observations are all acceptable as data if they are collected in some systematic way and organized and analysed to allow various views to be expressed and incorporated into the interpretation.
- realize that data do not provide right answers or quick fixes. Instead, they offer decision-makers an opportunity to view a phenomenon through a number of different lenses, to put forward hypotheses, to challenge beliefs and to pose more questions. Interpretation requires time, thoughtfulness, reservation of judgements and open challenge of, as well as support for, ideas.
- consider the various audiences and present the data to explain and justify their decisions to those who care to know.

Knowledge leaders use data to engage in reflection and inquiry and learn from continually collecting relevant evidence, reflecting on that evidence, and revising their actions to reflect their learning. The data or evidence that leaders draw on is a form of explicit knowledge that has been codified and can be easily communicated to others. They may also refer to research and literature in the area to ascertain what has been learned about this area elsewhere.

The principals each brought data to their next meeting: achievement data analysed in rela-tion to school-level census data about family income; teachers' descriptions of classroom practices; and school self-evaluation reports. They confirmed that many low-income students were not doing well in all their schools but some were actually doing very well. They also found that teachers seemed to be using similar classroom practices; students were generally engaged and the self-evaluation reports indicated that most students in all the schools felt safe, teaching practices were rated good, and formative assessment was being used as a mechanism for improving student learning.

The discussion was wide-ranging. They wondered what was different for the low-income students who were doing well. They were not sure if the students who were not engaged were the same students who were struggling. The conversation created more questions than answers.

Several members of the group thought that they were not being bold enough and wanted to explore more radical ideas. Others were not so sure. At the end of the session, the group decided that they wanted to really investigate how to enhance learning in all their schools in a way that would be viable well into the future.

Their homework was to go back to their schools and go deeper to find out more about their students, about how teachers were addressing the needs of low-income students and what seemed to be working.

Knowledge leaders make tacit knowledge visible

Tacit knowledge is knowledge based on experience and observation. It is what individuals have come to believe to be 'true' based on their personal history. It is 'intuitive and unarticulated', 'personal and contextual' and acquired through practical experience (Lam, 2000: 490).

Tacit knowledge is important in knowledge work for a number of reasons. Knowledge leaders need to find ways to tap into the tacit knowledge of people who are involved because it will shape their contribution to any discussion. Without understanding the beliefs and views that people bring, misunderstand-ings and confusion are likely. In addition, the creativity necessary for innovation derives not only from obvious and visible expertise, but from invisible reservoirs of experience, which need to get vitalized and stimulated. When a group of diverse individuals, all with knowledge of the context, addresses a common prob-lem, each person frames both the problem and its solution by applying their mental schemata and patterns.

Because tacit knowledge resides in the thoughts and beliefs of people and is woven into the very fabric of an organization, it is not publicly available and cannot fully be transferred into formal language. It is made visible through conversations about the nature of situations and possible solutions, where it comes into play in framing the situation and through its application in proposing possible solutions. Sharing tacit knowledge requires time devoted to per-sonal contact in a working environment which supports respect for different thinking styles without penalties for failure and encouragement of creative thinking.

At their next meeting, the facilitator started with the unique background that each principal brought to the conversation and emphasised the value of the diversity of their experiences in thinking about possibilities. She wanted them to generate a wide pool of ideas about the schools and the students in them and posed the following questions: What have you learned about your target students since the last meeting? What have you learned about teachers' approaches with these students? What are your hypotheses about why the situation is as it is? What else do you need to know? She audio-taped the conversation.

During the next hour, the conversation was wide-ranging and sometimes challenging. There was discussion about the nature of the homes that the children came from, about the quality of instruction, about lack of time and the 'crowded curriculum', and much more. It became clear that, even when they had similar data, the seven principals saw the situations in their community in very different ways and had differing views about what the future might look like.

The facilitator collected all the hypotheses that they generated for them to return to at the next meeting.

Knowledge leaders use explicit and tacit knowledge for new learning

Both explicit and tacit knowledge need to be managed to realize their potential in creating new knowledge. There are pitfalls associated with operating using one or the other. Tacit knowledge can reflect past know-how as opposed to innovative practices and explicit knowledge can come from a limited pool of information that thwarts innovative thinking. Innovative knowledge is created when individuals intentionally draw on both explicit and tacit knowledge to deliberate on authentic problems and co-construct solutions (Lam, 2000; Seidler-de Alwis et al., 2004; Von Krogh et al., 2000). They consider the evidence and share the disparate views within the group to question and possibly adapt their respective tacit knowledge and create new collective explicit knowledge. This is an iterative process. One idea leads to another. Some ideas lose credibility in the process. Others become clearer. New information, additional evidence and different perspectives lead the work in a different direction. Figure 14.2 shows the relationship between tacit knowledge, explicit knowledge and the new knowledge that evolves from blending them in context.

Before the next meeting, the facilitator had taken the hypotheses that they had generated and she had listened to the audio-tape and identified more hypotheses that had been talked about but not written down. She wrote all of these hypotheses on cards. When the principals met again, the facilitator had them compile the hypotheses into an unduplicated list of possibilities. They ended up with a very long list of things they thought were true that they could now revisit to look for evidence. This session was spent largely reconsidering the hypotheses, debating them again, asking for clarification and adding details, determining how they would find evidence to support or challenge the claim and adding new hypotheses that emerged during the discussion. The discussion continued over several more meetings, as they came back with data associated with their hypotheses and talked about what they were finding out.

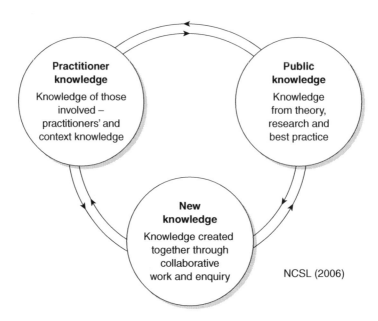

Figure 14.2 Three fields of knowledge (Jackson and Temperley, 2006)

Knowledge leaders challenge their own individual mental models

Tacit knowledge is held as individual mental models, acquired and honed over a lifetime of experience. Making tacit knowledge visible and open for discussion means exposing and examining mental models. As Senge described it: 'The discipline of mental models starts with turning the mirror inwards; learning to unearth our internal pictures of the world, to bring them to the surface and hold them rigorously to scrutiny' (1990: 9).

Cognitive psychologists have written for decades about the two 'A's – two ways that people respond when they are confronted with new knowledge – assimilation and accommodation. Assimilation happens when new information is largely consistent with an individual's prior ideas and beliefs, combines easily with existing knowledge and reinforces existing views. If new information conflicts with existing ideas, the learner may be required to transform his or her beliefs. This process is called accommodation. We would like to add a third 'A' to this model – avoidance. Human beings also need to preserve and conserve their existing belief systems and ignore or dismiss the new information to avoid incorporating it into existing beliefs and values.

This means that new ideas are accepted as 'more of the same' or 'what I do already'. This can be a direct assimilation of ideas that are actually not new. Sometimes there is 'over-assimilation' when the new ideas are reframed to become something familiar and can be accepted as already in place. Avoidance of new ideas can occur when the considering of them is too big a change or if ideas just do not fit. As Duffy (2003: 31) argued: 'If the individual cannot link the new information to an existing mental model, he or she may construct a mental model to understand the new information or discard the information as irrelevant, unimportant, or wrong.'

It is critical that school leaders understand that over-assimilation and avoidance are not likely to contribute to innovation. The new learning that fosters innovation comes from active episodes of accommodation. Accommodation is hard work that is essential for conceptual change and, therefore, for new learning (Olsen and Bruner, 1996). Accommodation creates dissonance and disorder, and it requires sustained attention and energy. This is not just a cognitive process; it is also emotional because every piece of information gets evaluated for its bearing on the self and the potential effect on the learner's environment.

Leaders who are knowledge leaders are prepared to open their own mental models (that is, 'deeply ingrained assumptions, generalizations, and images that influence how we understand the world and how we take action' – Senge, 1990) to investigation and to challenge. Coming to genuinely new professional knowledge involves linking new ideas, information, or strategies to current mental models and being prepared to rethink the mental models, even when they are deeply cherished and long-standing (Duffy, 2003).

> Over many meetings, the principals examined their situation from many different angles. The facilitator kept pushing them to express their ideas and then to test their ideas with each other and with data or research. After several more meetings, she asked them to draw a concept map of (1) things they now know and can support with evidence (2) things they think they know but there is less certainly about and (3) the issues that have emerged as a priority for them as a group. They were not allowed to present solutions. As they worked on the concept map, it became obvious that they had moved closer together in their thinking and that they were willing to leave some of their deeply felt convictions as areas of less certainty. And priorities were beginning to emerge.

Knowledge leaders use their new knowledge for innovation

Innovation can be best understood as a process in which the organization creates and defines problems and then actively develops new knowledge to solve them. David Hargreaves (2003) has suggested that innovation in education is a matter of learning to do things differently in order to do them better. Most innovation in education is the creation of new professional knowledge about educators' work, although it can also extend to relationships, governance and technologies. Sometimes innovation is incremental, where there's a bit-by-bit evolution of a practice into something better and sometimes it can be radical where there is a discontinuity between the new practice and the one it displaces.

The challenge for educators is to use their collaborative inquiry process to investigate their situation, set priorities, determine what kind of innovation is required, imagine the possibilities and then create the processes necessary to bring it to life. This process cannot be haphazard. If educators are launching a new era of innovation, it is absolutely essential that it be undertaken in a disciplined way (Hargreaves, 2003).

It is important that educators are confident about managing innovation by blending ideas that have merit with disciplined inquiry to situate the ideas in new ways, maintaining a stance of investigation and curiosity that is receptive and flexible; generating energy and harnessing it with enough regulation to discipline it, but not smother it, all the while continuing to operate in the traditional context of schooling.

With clearer understanding of the priorities and the possibilities, the principals were ready to think about directions. They had decided that that they wanted to go beyond tinkering and change their working relationship drastically. Since they served the same community, they would work as a federation of schools to serve all of the children, rather than stand-alone competitors. They also agreed that no child or group of children would be placed at a disadvantage by their organizational decisions. Facilities and equipment would be shared by all of them. They had some ideas about organizational structure but the most important priority was one of providing all of their students with high-quality teaching, They wanted teams of teachers to pay attention to individual students – watching their progress on a regular basis through shared consideration of formative assessment and joint planning for targeted teaching.

They realized that there was more to learn before they could proceed in making this a reality and that they could not operate as lone rangers. Although they had been briefing the local council and had been discussing their deliberations with teachers in their schools, it was time to really bring the community and the teachers more fully into the discussion, as well as continuing their own investigation and learning.

Knowledge leaders validate their new knowledge in action

Before innovations are unleashed on others, knowledge leaders need to check on how they work in practice, by validating the emerging knowledge through the action/evidence/revision spiral (Earl and Hannay, 2009) to assess its usefulness. Especially in educational contexts, it is important to ascertain the outcomes of innovations, not only to gauge the extent to which they accomplish the expected aims but also to identify unanticipated consequences and consider whether alternative approaches would work as well.

Validation involves an ongoing process of trials and pilots of the ideas and collecting evidence about how things are going, in order to determine the value and power of the innovation. Before knowledge leaders can validate their ideas, there is a critical stage of working collaboratively to determine what they will count as evident so that they can track progress against a set of pragmatic and project-specific goals that are agreed upon and explicit. Actual experience with the innovation allows the knowledge leader to reflect once again and to readjust goals in light of the successes and any unanticipated setbacks.

During the next term, the group met with all of their staff members as a group and they paired up to have conversations within and across schools about their plans. They agreed that they would trial offering technical activities for the senior students in one of the better equipped schools and the teachers of these programmes agreed that they would plan and teach together so that the classes could be mixed. A group of teachers in each school agreed to work in teams to focus intensively on learning more about how to differentiate instruction for individual students.

The council agreed to work support the principals to plan their shared leadership approach and to revisit the concept when they had it more fully developed.

Knowledge leaders share their learning with others in the organization

It is not enough for knowledge leaders to learn for themselves or in small groups. Instead, knowledge work involves continual learning for everyone within the organization (OECD, 1996), to ensure that all individuals within the organization share the resulting learning. This means that the ultimate goal for educational leaders is to have teachers participate as knowledge leaders as well. Although it might be appealing to package the new learning that leaders have created and give it to others, the actuality of knowledge transfer and 'scaling up' is more complex. As Cordingley and Bell indicate:

> The actual transfer of learning – resulting in embedded and sustainable change – depends on a combination of measures to encourage take up and to facilitate the development of ownership and control of new practices. Going to scale involves combining both the take up of practices developed elsewhere and the transfer of learning. Going to scale in effect means the transfer of practice by the many – easy to set as a goal but hard to achieve. (Cordingley and Bell, 2007: 3)

Coburn (2003: 3) argues that 'definitions of scale must include attention to the nature of change required; issues of sustainability; spread of norms, principles, and beliefs; and a shift in ownership such that a reform can become self-generative' and results in new learning and new practices that are deep, sustainable, and that spread across many people who have ownership in the changes. Knowledge leaders have the responsibility for creating the conditions for other members of the community to engage in knowledge work as well, through real encounters or face-to-face relationships that allow best practices to be demonstrated, not just explained, practised through trial and error, and creatively adapted to capture the spirit of the innovation that is being transferred (Hargreaves, 2003).

Stoll (2009) describes 'knowledge animation' as a social process of helping people to learn and use ideas generated elsewhere in real encounters, and through this process create their own knowledge. Knowledge animation is concerned with finding ways of making knowledge accessible and mobile so that it stimulates dialogue that challenges thinking, promotes new understanding and helps them generate new knowledge that will enhance their practice and policy. Knowledge leaders need to develop a range of strategies to make their own new learning visible (move it from tacit to explicit) and facilitate opportunities for others to share, ask questions, add other knowledge, process ideas and think together, also in the context of real problems and issues.

Fast forward several years – all of the schools in the municipality operate as a single entity, with responsibility for all of the students. The principals work as a cabinet and they assume primary responsibility for some aspect of the federation, as well as overseeing the daily operations of an individual school. Timetables are developed across the schools and students are often mixed for their classes.

Changes to teaching have been slower in implementation. The principals realized after their trial of the process with the technical programme that this work would only proceed with teachers who were committed and who felt ownership for the changes. Creating a culture of sharing and working together meant working alongside teachers as they themselves learned about what differentiated teaching means, how it works, why it matters and how to do it. The way they went about the change was very different from the imaginings of the principals when they set the priority, but the outcome has been true to the principles of success for every student, with ongoing adjustments and refinements, and sometimes even dramatic changes, as the teachers revisit what they are doing and how it is working.

Conclusion

Knowledge work is ultimately a cycle of learning and sharing, running endlessly and driven by the constantly changing context and the new knowledge that pervades the culture. It is both innovative and disciplined at the same time. And, finally, it is a moral imperative for all in the organization – needing to know, acquiring new knowledge (both tacit and explicit), challenging mental models, growing and learning through collaborative inquiry, validating new ideas, using newly developed knowledge for innovation, and sharing this learning with others through communities of practice that pervade the system.

Further Reading

Katz, S. Earl, L. and Ben Jaafar, S. (2009) *Building and Connecting Learning Communities: The Power of Networks for School Improvement.* Thousand Oaks, CA: Corwin Press.

Ideal for school leaders and superintendents leading change efforts, this book describes how separate professional learning communities can be linked across schools by common instructional and learning issues to create dynamic networked learning communities (NLCs). Drawing on their work with schools throughout North America and England, Steven Katz, Lorna M. Earl and Sonia Ben Jaafar show how participants in NLCs can share professional knowledge that ultimately improves performance at the school and district level.

Through a sample school narrative, the book illustrates how NLCs can significantly enhance instruction, increase student performance, and empower local professional learning communities. This resource examines:

- collaborative inquiry as a process that challenges teachers' thinking, generates new learning, and fosters trusting relationships
- the development of formal and informal leadership roles in NLCs
- how NLCs support systematic data analysis and accountability.

Demonstrating how NLCs – small or large, local or state-wide–can promote critical reforms while strengthening the work of individual professional learning communities, this book reveals how educators can join forces across school and district boundaries to generate deep, meaningful and sustainable change.

Earl, L. and Timperley, H.S. (eds) (2008) *Professional Learning Conversations: Challenges in Using Evidence for Improvement.* Amsterdam: Springer.

This edited volume, in which researchers 'listen in' on learning conversations about data provides informed arguments, theory and practical examples based on what it looks like when educators, policy-makers, and even students, try to rethink and change their practices by engaging in evidence-based conversations to challenge and inform their work. It allows the reader to experience these conversations. Each story reveals the depth of thinking that change requires and gives important insights into the challenge associated with changing thinking and practice. Some of the stories are encouraging and others are frustrating. Taken together, they give tremendous insight into 'what it takes' for conceptual change that will fundamentally shift educational practice. 'This book moves beyond just promoting the use of evidence to examining just what is known and how it occurs in a range of settings, especially in interaction with others. This type of book will be key in a desired move to where professional educators reestablish their knowledge and responsibility base in educational policy and practice.'

Reflective Activity

Rate your school or district as knowledge workers:

	Most of the time	Sometimes	Rarely
We are learners			
We learn collaboratively through cycles of inquiry			
We use data and evidence to frame our discussions			
We make tacit knowledge visible			
We use explicit and tacit knowledge for new learning			
We use our new learning for innovation			
We validate our new learning in action			
We share our learning with others in the organization			

References

Boder, A. (2006) Collective intelligence: a keystone in knowledge management, *Journal of Knowledge Management*, 10(1): 81.

Coburn, C. (2003) Rethinking scale: moving beyond numbers to deep and lasting change, *Educational Researcher*, 32: 3–12.

Cordingley, P. and Bell, M. (2007) *Transferring Learning and Taking Innovation to Scale*. London: The Innovation Unit.

Duffy, F.M. (2003). I think, therefore I am resistant to change, *Journal of Staff Development*, 24(1): 30–6.

Earl, L. and Hannay, L. (2009) Evidence based inquiry in support of a knowledge creating school district, paper presented at the International Congress for School Effectiveness and School Improvement, Vancouver, January.

Earl, L. and Katz, S. (2000) Changing classroom assessment: teachers' struggles, in N. Bascia and A. Hargreaves (eds), *The Sharp Edge of Educational Change*. London: Falmer Press.

Earl, L. and Katz, S. (2006) *Leading in a Data Rich World*. Thousand Oaks, CA: Corwin Press.

Earl, L. and Timperley, H.S. (eds) (2008) *Professional Learning Conversations: Challenges in Using Evidence for Improvement*. Amsterdam: Springer.

Fullan, M. (2005) *Systems Thinkers in Action: Moving Beyond the Standards Plateau*. London: DfES, Innovation Unit/NCSL.

Hakkarainen, K., Palonen, T., Paavola, S. and Lehtinen, E. (2004) *Communities of Networked Expertise: Professional and Educational Perspectives*. Amsterdam: Elsevier.

Hannay, L. (2003) Developing alternative conceptions of leadership and organisations through restructuring, in N. Bennett and L. Anderson (eds), *Rethinking Educational Leadership: Challenging the Conventions*. London: Paul Chapman Publishing. pp. 100–12.

Hannay, L (2009) Structures and practices for knowledge-managing organizations, paper presented at International Conference on Primary Education, Hong Kong, November.

Hargreaves, D. (2003) *Education Epidemic: Transforming Secondary Schools Through Innovation Networks*, London: Demos.

Hoban, G.F. (2002) *Teacher Learning for Educational Change*. Philadelphia, PA: Open University Press.

Jackson, D. and Temperley, J. (2006) *From Professional Learning Community to Networked Learning Community*. Nottingham: National College of School Leadership.

Katz, S., Earl, L. and Ben Jaafar, S. (2009) *Building and Connecting Learning Communities: The Power of Networks for School Improvement*. Thousand Oaks, CA: Corwin Press.

Lam, A. (2000) Tacit knowledge, organizational learning and societal institutions: an integrated framework, *Organizational Studies*, 21(3): 487–513.

Lin, Y., Wang, L. and Tserng, H.P. (2006) Enhancing knowledge exchange through web map-based knowledge management systems in construction: lessons learned in Taiwan, *Automation in Construction*, 15: 693–705.

Moteleb, A. A. and Woodman, M. (2007) Notions of knowledge management systems: a gap analysis, *The Electronic Journal of Knowledge Management*, 5(1): 55–62.

O'Connor, J. and McDermott, I. (1997) *The Art of Systems Thinking*. London: Thorsons.

OECD (1996) *The Knowledge-based Economy*. OCDE/GD(96)102. Paris: OECD.

Olson, D.R. and Bruner, J.S. (1996) Folk psychology and folk pedagogy, in D.R. Olson and N. Torrance (eds), *The Handbook of Education and Human Development*. Cambridge: Blackwell. pp. 9–27.

Putnam, R. and Borko, H. (2000) What do new views of knowledge and thinking have to say about research on teacher learning? *Educational Researcher*, 29(1): 4–15.

Rifkin, J. (2000) *The Age of Access*. New York: Penguin Putnam.

Scardamalia, M. and Bereiter, C. (2003) Knowledge building, in *Encyclopedia of Education*. 2nd edn. New York: Macmillan Reference. pp. 1370–3.

Senge, P. (1990) *The Fifth Discipline: The Art and Practice of the Learning Organization*. Toronto: Doubleday.

Seidler-de Alwis, R., Hartmann, E. and Gemunden, H. (2004) The role of tacit knowledge in innovation management, competitive paper submitted to the 20th Annual IMP Conference, Copenhagen, September.

Spillane, J.P. (2000) Cognition and policy implementation: district policymakers and the reform of mathematics education, *Cognition and Instruction*, 18(2): 141–79.

Stewart, T.A. (1997) *Intellectual Capital*. New York: Bantam Doubleday Dell.

Stoll, L. (2009) Connecting learning communities: capacity building for systemic change, in A. Hargreaves, A. Lieberman, M. Fullan and D. Hopkins (eds), *Second International Handbook of Educational Change*. Dordrecht: Springer.

Von Krogh, G., Ichijo, K. and Nonaka, I. (2000) *Enabling Knowledge Creation*. New York: Oxford University Press.

CHAPTER 15

Why the Study of Emotion Matters in School Leadership

Megan Crawford

This chapter asks whether affect in leadership is important, and if so, what the essential aspects of emotion and leadership are for those who lead in schools. It considers some of the theoretical underpinnings of emotion and relates them to the leadership role. It asks whether more research would reveal more aspects particular to leadership in schools.

Affect is the overarching term for emotion, and encompasses many aspects of study and research. In this chapter, I refer more generally to emotion. The study of affect in organizations is a developing one, and continues to shed insight into not only how people relate to each other, but how those relationships drive the organization's strategic purposes. This chapter is aimed at those in schools who wish to understand more about how emotion influences their leadership role in school. It is for both new and experienced leaders, and charts the interplay between two particular affective concepts – emotional intelligence and emotional regulation. I examine how leadership shapes the social context through talk, and the meaning derived from it within the organization, through examples drawn from my own research. Finally I will suggest areas for further discussion of emotion and leadership in schools and ask what future research might fruitfully consider.

The title I have used is a deliberate allusion to Barsade and Gibson's article (2007: 36) in which they argue that: 'affect permeates organizations. It is present in the interdependent relationships we hold with bosses, team members and subordinates ... affective processes (more commonly known as emotions) create and sustain work motivation. They lurk behind political behaviour; they animate our decisions; they are essential to leadership'. This chapter takes emotion as essential to leadership as its starting point, and unpacks what an increasing knowledge of emotion and its processes might mean to a developing or established leader in our schools. Those experiences are ones that we commonly call emotion, and are parts of every leader's everyday experience in schools.

Aspects of affect

In this chapter, emotion is viewed as a key part of the work that leaders do with staff, governors, students and the wider school community. I draw mainly on the social constructivist approach to emotion, which views the social context of emotion to be crucial to how people create meanings, as well as draw the readers' attention to some recent research in psychology. Taking the social context of a school as a place where emotion is deeply involved in daily life, I discuss how, and in what ways, leadership and emotion relate to each other.

Davel and Vier Machado consider that leadership is a mutual process of attachment between leader and follower. It involves the leader being able 'to significantly order social reality and its resonance in the collective imaginary' (2002: 5). The contention of this chapter is that emotion is a key part of that social reality in which leadership is exercised.

This chapter does not attempt to look at the more unconscious processes of emotion, nor in detail at people's own affective traits, although their importance should not be underestimated (James and Crawford, 2006). They are also a fruitful area for leaders in schools to further their knowledge. I start with probably the most popular concept in emotion and leadership, emotional intelligence (EI).

Emotional intelligence

Daniel Goleman's (1995; 1998). work has made a huge impact upon the leadership area, in business particularly, but also in education. School leaders are often unaware of the debates in the discussion of EI, and how, in fact, EI is a much more complex idea than one might at first realise. Salovey and Mayer are often called the architects of emotional intelligence. They define EI as, 'the ability to monitor one's own and other's feelings and emotions, to discriminate among them, and to use this information to guide one's thinking and actions' (1990: 189). Salovey and Mayer developed this into a model that divides EI into four key factors. These are:

- perceiving emotion
- using emotion
- understanding emotion
- managing emotions.

I return to these below. It is worth noting that much of the discussion of EI, especially in schools has been carried out within a competency framework, stressing that many aspects can be learned by leaders to improve their overall performance. While this may have some merits in helping individuals find areas for development, it does mean that the more complex or difficult aspects of EI have been overlooked, and the competency aspect focused upon. Salovey et al. (2000: 504) make an important point about the intrapersonal aspects of EI which are more than just competency bases. They state:

We believe that emotional competencies are fundamental to social intelligence. This is because social problems and situations are laden with affective information. Moreover, emotional competences apply not only to social experiences but to experiences within the individual. Indeed, some investigators have argued that self-knowledge and the individual's inner life are characterized most saliently by emotional experiences. Thus, emotional intelligence is more focused than social intelligence, in that it pertains specifically to emotional phenomena and yet can be applied directly to a broad range of emotional problems embedded in both interpersonal and intrapersonal experience.

Thus for a school leader, knowledge of the interpersonal is crucial, but the intrapersonal must not be neglected. In terms of EI, Ornstein and Nelson (2006: 44) note that 'The bedrock competency (of EI) is self-awareness. People adept at self-awareness recognise their emotions, their genesis and the potential outcome of their state of feeling'. This is understanding and using emotions in practice.

Perceiving emotions may also be seen as a vital part of leadership. This aspect of EI was something that headteachers in the UK that I have interviewed have drawn upon in their leadership roles. Francesca, a primary (5–11 years) principal, noted the importance of the emotional dimension in making decisions about staff and their competence:

All manner of informal situations contribute to views of people as teachers – conversations, things you know and hear about people's lives outside school. You form a quite secure view on whether a person is committed to the job and want to develop, etc. All these are things that are difficult to quantify, but useful as a means of supporting more formal views. It is the intuitive side and it can be used to back up perceptions, but people can surprise you so it is not an exact science!

Another headteacher, also from the primary sector, noted that caring as a head was important to her:

On a basic level it is that you can see that the whole community knows that you care about the whole school and then even more at a more detailed level about specific people (mum in hospital, etc.). These are the things that are important and delightful. I try to encourage caring as a staff as it is good for individual self-esteem and teams. I always send each child a Christmas card.

These two school leaders are articulating aspects of emotional intelligence. Salovey and Mayer's four factors are a helpful way to think of EI as a leader in schools. I have argued elsewhere (Crawford, 2009) that the reality of organizational life in schools means that there is much more to the study of emotion and leadership than just having this working knowledge of EI, although this is important. The term itself can be used in many different ways, and some have even asked whether a theoretically sound concept can be identified from the works written on EI (Locke, 2005). Barsade and Gibson point out that work on EI is still in its infancy but there is growing research evidence to show that these four factors will be crucial to future understandings of organizational life.

The term emotional intelligence can also be used to suggest that cognition and rational processes have a lesser place in the school leadership literature. Mayer et al. (2008: 507) note that EI works in tandem with the rational/cognitive side of interpersonal life. They suggest that, 'Emotional Intelligence involves the ability to carry out accurate reasoning about emotions and the ability to use emotions and emotional knowledge to enhance thought.' This definition recognizes the links between emotion and rationality (Crawford, 2010).

The dangers with this 'emotional intelligence' approach have been noted by several writers (Beatty, 2002; Fineman, 2000). Fineman (2000: 108) calls it the 'seduction of emotional intelligence'. Fineman's argument is that Goleman conceptualizes emotional management as just another workplace competence, and so Goleman promises a form of rationality that is at best illusory, and perhaps even counterfeit, and that as an approach it is aimed at managerial behaviours. Therefore, Beatty argues (2002: 29–30), EI emphasizes working smoothly together, and 'pursuing goals', which means that in fact your perspective may narrow, not widen, and avoid any more deeper and problematic emotional meaning. The wider literature (Bolman and Deal, 1995; Fineman, 2000; Ogawa and Bossert, 1997; Sergiovanni, 2003) seems to suggest a far stronger meaning for emotional intelligence, not aimed at managerial behaviours, but at the whole culture of the organization, and the values of its stakeholders. In other words, it is aimed at leadership. One of the four factors is managing emotions. Managing emotions is to do with regulation, which has its own conceptual background.

Emotional labour and emotional regulation

Emotion is part of the social reality we create through what has been described by many writers as a kind of performance. This is because if emotion creates part of the social reality of life, then social encounters can be regarded as some sort of performance. Goffman (1961) proposed that every kind of social interaction is just like a game, in which we take on roles. We can become more or less strongly engaged in a role, and fulfilment is more likely to occur when we are fully engaged in a role. This can of course lead to tensions both interpersonal and intrapersonally. Organizations such as schools have their own well-defined roles that people choose to play, and a leader may find themselves moving rapidly from one role to another – from teacher to counsellor, from head of department to mentor. All of these roles involve not only different skill sets, but also different aspects of our affective sides. In addition to this, schools also demand on many occasions that both teachers and those in leadership positions do not show their emotion outwardly as it would be seen as unprofessional to do so. This can lead to dilemmas, but it is also a crucial part, in particular, of the leader's life.

When we show emotions that are very different to what we are actually feeling inside, we subject ourselves to emotional regulation. As we saw above, this is linked to emotional intelligence. People differ in the amount of emotional regulation they are able to sustain, and organizations demand different types of regulation from their employees. Organizational emotional regulation can be conceptualized as emotional labour. Emotional labour is the public face of emotion in leadership. The concept of emotional labour arose from the work of Arlie Hochschild who originally studied the role of emotion management in the life of flight attendants. Hochschild (1979) explored the tensions that build up when an individual has to give a particular performance as part of their job role. So, airline hostesses for Delta had to make passengers feel welcome on board, and were constantly exhorted to smile. From this study, she coined the phrase 'emotional labour', where workers may be required to simulate or suppress feeling in order to maintain a specific outward appearance in order to produce the required emotional state in others as part of their job role. Hochschild stated that this labour/work operates through 'feeling rules'. Feeling rules are those that are deemed to be appropriate to the social settings that people work in. So, a person's expression of emotion is socially shaped.

Organizational feeling rules can also determine how people publicly express emotion. Although not discussing schools, Hochschild contended that these rules can have a high personal cost (Hochschild, 1979). Positional expectations amid the hierarchy of schools can define the boundaries within which leaders function in terms of emotional display. It could also be suggested that there are different boundaries for such display both in different phases of school, that is, primary and secondary, and in the differing social contexts that leaders create in schools. More recent research has suggested that such surface acting does not cause strain if individuals feel that the acting they are doing is part of their work role and is enhancing their job. This may also be to do with both the individual and their different personalities and the organisational context (Barsade and Gibson, 2007: 41). I would argue that a key part of that organizational context is the leadership. Regulation of emotion is a significant part of the educational leader's work. Barsade and Gibson's article notes that the research in this area seems to be suggesting that regulating emotion by anticipating when emotions might occur and reframing them in advance to be objective in a potentially difficult situation may cause less personal strain than suppressing anger over a longer time frame.

We know (Argyris 1996; 1999) that organizations that function well are psychologically safe, even though it is common for organizations to be places where relationships are superficial and wary. One of the ways that leaders might help with the overall regulation of emotion within a school is by realizing the importance of talk to emotion. Oatley and Jenkins put this succinctly (1996: 99); 'In talk, we cultivate, define, and redefine, ourselves and our relationships by presenting out experiences to others – we elaborate our emotional bonds and antipathies with specific people we know.' Thus talk can be seen as both an aspect of emotional regulation and as a way of perceiving the emotions of others more clearly. Leadership is a meaning-making process and Fineman (2000: 49) notes, 'what people want for meaning is more modest and mundane. It is a connection to others'. Emotion can define work relationships, and one of the ways that we can understand this is through the medium of stories, both informally as a leader and in research.

Life-history researchers in education often use stories, and this can provide a useful starting point. Through story we can look at affect in schools and the meanings leaders take from encounters and events. Goodley et al. (2004: 195) tell us that: 'Storyteller still smacks of the last period of primary school, still lacks seriousness in the adult world … Stories are more than individual tales. They are the products of complicated research relationships. They are imbued with theory, with practice and policy implications, and with humanity.'

Sarbin (1989), notes when people are asked to give a descriptor of a particular emotion, they almost always tell a story. Sandelands and Boudens (2000: 60) put this very simply:

'We note that stories have a unique epistemological significance. They can tell a truth about feeling even while they tell many lies about fact. This is because a story states facts, but exemplifies feelings … the emotional truth of a story is evident.'

You may want to bear this in mind when reading the example below.

Emotional regulation for the school leader concerns their own emotions and the emotions the organization needs its workers to display to be effective at the tasks allotted to them. Leaders may want to control this latter aspect of organizational life through the social norms or what Hochschild (1979) would call the feelings rule of the organization. This is not quite the same as what Fineman (2000: 7) would call the 'formal techniques of control', for example, performance management, appraisal, and so on. In a study (Fineman and Sturdy, 1999) he carried out looking at the dynamics of control in organizations, he notes that status and professional competence are shaped emotionally in a variety of situations. The leader's role in shaping this is, I would argue, pivotal. It could be argued, for example, that feelings of being controlled or controlling others are very much to the surface in schools in many countries that are controlled or constrained by a performativity agenda driven by government. These 'emotional scripts' (Fineman, 1999) that the leader uses, may well influence outcomes in a variety of ways that have not yet been fully explored in the school context. Read the following example, which concerns an experienced educational leader, and see which of the concepts discussed so far is particularly relevant.

Example

Gill was an experienced headteacher of a medium-sized (200 pupils) junior school in a market town in the Midlands. The school was her third headship in the church section of education, and she had been in post for just over 18 months when she was interviewed. I had originally met her on a training course, where she had been vocal in her opinions about current difficulties in primary schools due to staff shortages. It is significant, I think, that I interviewed her at a time of great personal tension when it had become obvious that her school was to close in a local merger with the infant school to become an all-through primary school. In effect, the affective side of her leadership role overwhelmed her. Despite manifest success in her two previous headships, she confided to me that this time she did not seem able to manage everything. Her whole language was coloured by that of emotion. She had decided to apply for the new headship, but expressed the view that she would not be the favoured candidate as the infant head was 'better liked' by the governors, and would get the post. This in fact turned out to be the case, and Gill later took early retirement.

The research interview itself was carried out under difficult circumstances. Staff and children with queries constantly interrupted us. Gill seemed unwilling, or unable to stop this happening, despite requests from myself. There was tension in the school that day because one of the younger pupils had been the victim of an attempted abduction by a non-custodial parent the day before. She talked about why she had gone into headship – it seemed to be the expected thing in teaching to do that. She enjoyed being a head because she valued 'seeing plans come to fruition with children', but found that tasks such as having to deal with staff redundancies alongside the merger 'ripped me apart'. She told me of the situation regarding the merger, and the governors' meeting that dealt with how staff would have to be made redundant, and that she would have to apply for the merger headship. She felt that it had been made very clear that her job was to 'clear up' the staff before the merger, but that there would be no place for her afterwards. The language she used to describe her feelings as she came out of this meeting was very evocative: 'I was wearing a beige jacket, and when I came out my skin was the same colour as the jacket! ... I felt wrung out like a wet lettuce.'

The appearance of competence at leadership in a work setting is underpinned by emotional labour. This labour is apparently far greater for some people than others, and relates to both the past and the present context of their lives, within an educational climate that does not often allow the personal to become visible. Visibility can open up a headteacher to criticism, of 'being emotional' and also not being able to cope. Ironically, this labour means that by the time that the headteacher has admitted their inability to keep up the labour under pressure, it may be too late for their physical and mental well-being (Ashforth and Tomiuk, 2000; Carlyle and Woods, 2002; West-Burnham and Ireson, 2006). This seemed to be the case for Gill. Somehow she had lost the ability to play the professional role. Unable to regulate her emotions, she could no longer grasp the emotional labour, or what Fineman (2000: 12) calls 'emotional hypocrisy': 'The public smile, the pretence of concern and the professional demeanour, lubricate and reinforce social relationships. Emotional hypocrisy helps to fix a social order as well as to strain it; this is the heart of emotional work.'

Barsade and Gibson put it this way, ' If there are two managers who are both high in ability to read each other's emotions, but one is better than the other in regulating her own emotions or those of others the latter manager may well be more successful at her job' (2007: 45). For many leaders, the concept of emotional hypocrisy will be value laden and perhaps contrasted with notions of authenticity. However, emotional work requires the leader to think beyond themselves and to the social context of the organization as a whole. This might involve the kind of emotional hypocrisy that lubricates social life. Another way to look at influencing social order is through emotional contagion.

Emotional contagion

So far, this chapter has looked at two key concepts for school leaders – emotional intelligence and emotional regulation (individual and in the form of emotional labour). School leadership could also find much of use in the psychological construct of emotional contagion. Emotional contagion is a process by which emotions are shared across a group in a social context. Barsade and Gibson note that emotional contagion can occur without conscious knowledge, but can also be consciously induced (2007: 42). Some people are also more likely to be more influenced because of either their own emotional disposition or the particular group was functioning well as a team. As one leader in school told me:

> Overall, I aim to be positive and control the raw stuff. I sort of move out of that particular feeling if it's bad, and try to orchestrate myself and others towards something positive. I believe that if you talk up, you feel up, and can talk yourself and others into becoming positive and buoyant.

Barsade and Gibson also propose that there are a significant number of research studies, which show clear links between emotional contagion and performance outcomes. This is for both individuals and groups. As the quote above suggests, leaders in particular could influence the nature of the group contagion in school performance settings, especially if they are more aware of the nature of its effects overall. Barsade and Gibson relate it to leadership (2007: 51): 'leader effectiveness is at least partially defined by the satisfaction and emotional liking of followers'. There is also evidence that followers are influenced by leaders' displays of emotion. This sense of balancing the public and the private is key for leaders in school and highlights the fact that all organisational emotion is relational (Waldron, 2000).

It may be that emotional contagion also links to the capacity of a school for trust (Bottery, 2002; Seashore, 2003) as trust has both emotional and social components, but this is not yet clearly researched in schools.

Conclusion

So where does this leave current and potential school leaders in terms of emotion? Barsade and Gibson suggest that leaders have to be able to regulate their own emotions so as not to demotivate their followers. Some potential leaders will find this more of a challenge than others. Transformational leaders also have to work with managing difficult emotions about change that may mean that the emotional labour involved is greater than anything they have experienced before. Positive emotion is an enhancer of performance at individual and organisational levels, and Barsade and Gibson cite several studies that show that the leaders' positive moods are associated with better performance in the group that they are leading as is the ability to read others' emotions. Intriguingly, they also note that extraversion enhances this relationship which could be an interesting further research area in schools. Extraversion and leadership in schools might sound an odd area to consider, but it might be a fruitful one.

This chapter took as its base the contention that workplaces are full of emotion, and that part of the leaders understanding of leadership is bound up in emotion. However, the relationship between leadership and emotion in the organization is a complex one. It relates to the interpersonal and intrapersonal parts of the leader's role. The school context in many countries may require leaders to emotionally labour at greater and greater levels in order to present the accepted rational front to stakeholders. Fineman puts it this way 'Some are more than content to "fake in good faith" in the service drama' (Fineman, 2000: 5). How the boundaries between 'faking in good faith' and excessive emotional labour, are managed is one of the key dilemmas for school leaders.

Emotion in schools deserves to have more focused research. Some key concepts (EI, emotion regulation and emotional labour) all have a bearing on the practice of school leadership. In order to define these constructs further in the school context with which we work as practitioners and researchers further focus on the connections to leadership are needed. To sum up, educational leadership is about people, and people necessarily work in an emotional context, intra-personally and inter-personally. As Glatter (2006: 82) states:

> We should consciously seek to contribute to … the broader field of organization and management studies, in which … schools and universities can be viewed – along for example with churches, counselling agencies, hospitals and prisons – as *human service organizations* whose core task is transforming humans. That is not the core task of (for example), either H.M. Revenue and Customs, in the public sector, or of Tesco in the private sector.

To date, aspects of affective research have influenced the educational leadership field, primarily by its emphasis on emotional intelligence. While this has had its advantages, it means that the educational leadership field has only begun to discover how emotion can enrich educational leadership. More emphasis on the richness of affect, perhaps through the stories of leaders and aspiring leaders, and the emotional interactions that occur within the school context, could be one way of facilitating this.

Reflective Questions

1 Having read this chapter, note down two recent occasions in your work setting where you have needed to regulate your emotions. Were you conscious of this at the time? What were the triggers that made you realize regulation was necessary?
2 Looking at EI, which of its components do you find most difficult to see as useful to your daily practice. Examine with a trusted colleague why this might be so.
3 Reflect on a recent difficult situation you have been involved with. What were its emotional aspects? If you can, ask a trusted colleague who was there to talk you through your responses at the time, and afterwards.

Further Reading 📖

Fineman, S. (2003) *Understanding Emotion at Work*. London: Sage.

This excellent book draws on psychology, sociology and organizational theory, to explore a number of familiar and not so familiar work arenas. In this book you can find out how emotion penetrates leadership, decision-making and organizational change. It's a book that leaves you thinking about the importance of emotions to the design and management of organizations.

Loader, D. (1997) *The Inner Principal*. London: Falmer.

This is a really easy to read account of how a principal combines the rational and emotional components of leadership to lead the transformation of a school. David Loader's highly personal account of how principals develop into sensitive, thoughtful, proactive leaders can easily be related to emotion and leadership. His use of metaphor can also stimulate the reader to original ways of considering leadership.

References

Argyris, C. (1996) *Organisational Learning*. Reading, MA: Addison Wesley.

Argyris, C. (1999) *On Organizational Learning*. Oxford: Blackwell.

Ashforth, B. and Tomiuk, M.A. (2000) Emotional labour and authenticity: views from service agents, in S. Fineman (ed.) *Emotion in Organizations*. London: Sage.

Barsade, S.G. and Gibson, D.E. (2007) Why does affect matter in organizations?, *Academy of Management Perspectives*, 59 (Feb.): 36–59.

Beatty, B.R. (2002) *Emotion Matters in Educational Leadership: Examining the Unexamined*. Graduate Department of Theory and Policy Studies in Education, Ontario Institute for Studies in Education. Toronto: University of Toronto.

Bolman, L. and Deal, T. (1995) *Leading with Soul – an Uncommon Journey of Spirit*. San Francisco, CA: Jossey-Bass.

Bottery, M. (2002) *The Use and Misuse of Trust*. Birmingham: BELMAS, Aston University.

Carlyle, D. and Woods, P. (2002) *Emotions of Teacher Stress*. Stoke-on-Trent. Trentham Books.

Crawford, M. (2009) *Getting to the Heart of Leadership*. London: Sage.

Crawford, M. (2010) Emotion and the leader, in Coleman M. and Glover D. (eds) McGraw-Hill: *Educational Leadership and Management: Developing Skills and Insights*, Open University Press.

Davel, E. and Vier Machado, H. (2002) *Leadership and Identification Dynamic*. Montreal: Graduate School of Commercial Studies of Montreal.

Fineman S. (1999) Emotion and organizing, in S. Clegg and C. Hardy (eds), *Studying Organization: Theory and Method*. London: Sage.

Fineman, S. (ed.) (2000) *Emotion in Organizations*. London: Sage.

Fineman, S. (2003) *Understanding Emotion at Work*. London: Sage.

Fineman, S. and Sturdy, A. (1999) The emotions of control: a qualitative study of environmental regulation, *Human Relations*, 52(5): 631–63.

Glatter, R. (2006) Leadership and organization in education: time for a re-orientation?, *School Leadership and Management*, 26(1): 69–84.

Goffman, E. (1961) *Encounters: Two studies in the Sociology of Interaction*. Indianapolis, IN: Bobbs-Merrill.

Goleman, D. (1995) *Emotional Intelligence*. New York: Bantam.

Goleman, D. (1998) *Working with Emotional Intelligence*. London: Bloomsbury.

Goodley, D., Lawthom, R. et al. (2004) *Researching Life Stories*. London: Routledge-Falmer.

Hochschild, A. (1979) Emotion work, feeling rules, and social structure, *American Journal of Sociology*, 85(3): 551–75.

James, C. and Crawford, M. (2006) *A New Emotional Paradigm for Educational Leadership and Management*. Direct: BERA, Warwick University.

Loader, D. (1997) *The Inner Principal*. London: Falmer.

Locke, E.A. (2005) *Why emotional intelligence is an invalid concept*, Journal of Organizational Behaviour, 26: 425–31.

Mayer, J.D., Roberts, R.D. and Barsade, S.G. (2008) Human abilities: emotional intelligence, *Annual Review of Psychology*, 59: 507–36.

Oatley, K. and Jenkins, J.M. (1996) *Understanding Emotions*. Oxford: Blackwell.

Ogawa, R.T. and Bossert, S.T. (1997) Leadership as an organisational quality, in M. Crawford, L. Kydd and C. Riches (eds), *Leadership and Teams in Educational Management*. Buckingham: Open University Press.

Ornstein, S. and Nelson, T. (2006) Incorporating emotional intelligence competency building into the preparation and delivery of international travel courses, *Innovations in Education and Teaching International*, 43(1): 41–55.

Salovey, P., Bedwell, T.B. Detweiler, J.P. and Mayer, J.R. (2000) Current directions in emotional intelligence research, in M. Lewis and J. Haviland-Jones (eds), *The Handbook of Emotions*. New York and London: Guilford Press.

Salovey, P. and P. Mayer (1990) Emotional intelligence, *Imagination, Cognition and Personality*, 9: 185–211.

Sandelands, L.E. and C.J. Boudens (2000) Feeling at work, in S. Fineman (ed.), *Emotion in Organizations*. London: Sage.

Sarbin, T.R. (1989) Emotions as narrative employments of in M.J. Packer and R.B. Addison (eds), *Entering the Circle: Hermeneutic Investigations in Psychology*. Albany, NY: State University of New York Press.

Seashore, K. (2003) Trust, BELMAS keynote lecture, Milton Keynes.

Sergiovanni, T.J. (2003) *The Lifeworld at the Center: Values and Action in Educational Leadership*, in N. Bennett, M. Crawford and M. Cartwright, *Effective Educational Leadership*. London: Paul Chapman Publishing. pp. 14–24.

Waldron, V. (2000) Relational experiences and emotion at work, in S. Fineman (ed.), *Emotion in Organizations*. London: Sage. pp. 64–82.

West-Burnham, J. and Ireson, J. (2006) *Leadership Development and Personal Effectiveness*. Nottingham: NCSL.

CHAPTER 16

Partnership in Leadership and Learning

Jan Robertson

Coaching partnerships create formal and informal opportunities for educational leaders to co-construct new ways of being and of knowing about learning and leadership. The concept of partnership changes leadership and learning from that of transmission of advice or information to a complex process of jointly creating new knowledge.

In many countries throughout the world decentralizing education services and blurring the public–private divide has created competition between schools in local communities, and supported a general policy shift to user-pays, market-driven education based on discourses of excellence, effectiveness and quality (Ball, 2006). Alongside these new policies underpinned by principles of choice and competition is a rhetoric of collaboration, system leadership, the lateral sharing of knowledge through coaching, networking and professional learning communities, as well as calls to keep the child and the family at the centre of practice across public services. This complex environment challenges schools to continually adapt and change to keep pace with new and increasing demands. It also brings opportunities for innovation and development and makes the work of school leadership more complex. To successfully transform current practice and create future practice in this challenging educational context, school communities will need high levels of capability, high levels of trust, and leadership practice that creates and maintains such cultures. Caldwell (2002) believed that leaders must have the capability to work with others to create a design for the learning conditions for their schools. He and his colleague (Caldwell and Spinks, 1998) offered a design to guide efforts to create schools for the knowledge society, which they believed was a whole that was greater than the individual parts. The model of self-management they presented challenged leaders to completely rethink their ways of working within education. Leithwood (1996) also stated that the restructuring movements in many countries to self-managing schools has created a shift in power and responsibility to the school level, which requires new ways of thinking about work. But new ways of working and current paradigms of thinking about work in schools are not easily changed (Muijs, 2009). Over the past five decades in particular, researchers and theorists have searched for the answers to successfully create and sustain teacher, school and system-wide change. Despite the extensive body of research and interventions, schools and the practices in them are very similar to those that were established to meet the needs of the industrial age, not a knowledge society. In this information-rich age, over a decade ago, Choy and Fatt (1998) advised that students needed smart learning environments where they are surrounded by innovation, creativity and problem-solving in experiential learning. We may well ask, have schools transformed paradigms of learning sufficiently to reflect these trends in either adult learning or student learning?

The need for transformational leadership learning experiences

Leithwood (1996: xii) observed that from the decentralization of decision-making to the local level, there 'has emerged a decidedly different image of the ideal educational organization ... This is an organization less in need of control and more in need of both support and capacity development'. Schools today present a complex context for professional practice and, therefore, professional learning. 'Leadership must be conceptualised as a mutual influence process, rather than as a one-way process in which leaders influence others' (Hallinger, 2003: 346). The New Zealand Māori people have only one word for this mutual influence process – *ako* – teacher as learner, learner as teacher. So often in education teachers are told what to do and then come to expect that someone else will evaluate them, and again, tell them what they need to do. This is not the type of problem-solving, problem-posing, critical thinking environment that Choy and Fatt (1998) called for over a decade ago. As Kohn (1993: 4) states, 'The way a child learns how to make decisions is by making decisions, not by following directions.' Teachers also need to work with leaders who challenge them to think and make decisions and reflect upon their professional practice. But leaders need experiences of leadership learning based on mutuality rather than control, and reflection and critical thinking rather than advice and the transmission of knowledge if they are to get comfortable with these ways of working. A new type of learning organization, then, requires a new view of school leadership and its development and a new type of teacher who will be willing to take up the responsibility for educational leadership and to demonstrate an intellectual independence for continued professional learning. This is learned behaviour.

A sociocultural theory of leadership does not distinguish leadership *practice* from leadership *learning* (after Vygotsky, 1978). It acknowledges that the everyday experiences and the dialogue of educators play an important part in their new learning. It is also founded on a withholding of assumptions and willingness to develop reciprocal relationships for the construction of new knowledge. Lim and Renshaw (2001: 19) state that:

Socio-cultural theory's relevance to culturally inclusive communities is that its tenets support a pedagogy for difference which can be used to guide not only the formation of culturally reciprocal relationships and partnerships but also to enhance the social usefulness of research to informing and (re)inventing practice in the lives of people who face the reality of communities that are inherently diverse.

The social and cultural interactions that leaders have with others can be opportunities for developing self-awareness, for new ideas to develop and therefore, for new learning about leadership. A sociocultural construction of knowledge upholds the principle that these interactions create the interstices at which new knowledge can be co-constructed. New learning then becomes an active process to which people *contribute*, not simply receive. This process needs two or more people to generate the opportunities for reflection, dialogue and development of shared meaning in cycles of inquiry. In this chapter, I argue that engagement in mutually supportive coaching relationships can help leaders become self-aware and develop the capacity to challenge, support, reflect on, and change their professional practice.

The Certificate for School Management and Leadership (CSML) programme for aspiring principals, based at the University of Victoria, British Columbia between 2005 and 2009 was a unique and innovative model for university undergraduate study. One component of the programme was the allocation of a credible, successful practising educator to mentor the aspiring leaders throughout their year of academic study. Some of these mentors had previously been participants in the programme, some became returning mentors on later programmes, and yet others decided to participate in the year of academic study after mentoring a participant. The mentors were carefully selected by the programme lecturers. They needed to be demonstrating the mindsets (Kaser and Halbert, 2009) and making genuine gains for learners in their own settings on a twenty-first century model of learning. Optimal cognitive and personal style match/mismatch and geographical proximity were also considered.

The programme participants had chosen this programme for many reasons but all of them had one important quality in common – they were all seeking further challenge and support for greater reflection on their professional practice and thus improvement of their educational leadership.

Troy, an aspiring principal, said:

This particular programme provides the means to grow, the CSML and particularly the mentorship piece. The mentorship programme has provided me with a springboard as far as my leadership goes ... it has opened the door to a lot of different relationships and the relationships that I am able to have with my colleagues.

Thelma described it in this way:

(Continued)

(Continued)

Our relationship could have ended after the first year but we've continued our coaching sessions because they have become quite valuable for both of us ... I know that the coach that I have now is going to be with me throughout my career. I feel very confident and very happy about that ... I look forward to one day hopefully being able to provide that same opportunity for someone else as they are going through their learning.

Shared construction of meaning and co-learning

If teachers are to be challenged to examine their professional practice, they will need to be working with leaders who lead through mutual influence. At a Hechinger Institute seminar Schlechty told journalists:

> Innovation requires change. Teachers have to see themselves differently and principals have to act differently. Not just to be better at what they've always done, but do things they've never done ... If we're going to get the kind of improvement we need, we have to be prepared to change the system to create new systems, new rules, new roles and new relationships. (Colvin, 2008: 6)

New roles, new relationships mean examining current uses of power and thus control. The current notion of power-over in learning relationships in schools is the nemesis of co-construction of new knowledge. Research on coaching has shown that peer partnership provides a new avenue for learning about leadership and developing mutuality within relationships (Robertson, 2008). These new spaces for leadership learning and practice are more collaborative and less hierarchical. Power is the silent indicator of how relationships will develop. If people are given the power – the space to think, to speak, to justify and articulate ideas – the more likely it is that they will gain in confidence, efficacy and engagement in the process (Bishop and Glynn, 1999). Many teachers are nervous as to the uncertainty of outcome that a power-sharing relationship with students and their colleagues might bring. Experiencing the power of reciprocal processes necessary to constructivist leadership practice (Lambert et al., 1996) is essential to the process of gaining understanding and confidence.

I worked with the participants and their mentors for two days within their two-week summer school programme of study. During the two days the participants studied the principles and theory of coaching and mentoring leadership, they learned the skills of active listening, reflective questioning, self-assessment and goal-setting, and they practised these skills in context with their mentor as they focused on their leadership and their goals and outcomes for their school-based inquiry. The participants and their mentors explored their values, beliefs and assumptions on the leadership of learning, they listened to each other's stories of challenge and success, and through the critique and reflection on their current reality, established clear direction and outcomes for their leadership of change. I asked them to enter the professional relationship as a learner, asking: 'What am I thinking and learning as I hear this leader describe their professional practice, their challenges, their successes? What might extend the reflection and dialogue?'

An important part of the professional partnership was understanding the meaning of partnership and reciprocal processes and challenging the usual top-down, hierarchical models of the transmission of advice and knowledge, and entering into a more facilitative relationship. Adelle described it in this way:

> The mentorship experience influenced my practice in a couple of ways. In the first part, being the learner, I was able to distance myself from my own district and school. It influenced my practice later when I turned around the next year and became a mentor for another participant in the programme ... and for us it became a very natural and organic way for that whole process to evolve. Over time I could see myself actually doing the same thing within my own school even though it was not deliberate and there was no intention on my part to go in that direction I found myself listening more and more and helping to serve that mentorship role on my staff even though it wasn't part of the normal exercise.

Meta-cognition in leadership learning

If teachers are told what to do within a school culture, students are also invariably 'told what to do' within that same culture. Kohn (1993: 5) sums it up in this way:

> Every teacher who is told what material to cover, when to cover it, and how to evaluate children's performance is a teacher who knows that enthusiasm for one's work quickly evaporates in the face of being controlled. Not every teacher, however, realizes that exactly the same thing holds true for students: deprive them of self-determination and you have likely deprived them of motivation.

Self-determination and self-regulation are important capabilities to enhance students' engagement in the learning process (Butler and Schnellert, 2008). Teachers who are self-regulatory are more likely to be able to develop this in others. To experience a reciprocal and self-regulating process within their own professional learning relationship and reflect on it and their thinking, is perhaps the most effective way to challenge leaders to emulate partnership in the learning relationships they then develop with others. The experience and subsequent self-awareness can have an almost immediate effect on the way they then approach their leadership. Understanding their own learning processes, through meta-cognition and the resulting powerful experience of responsibility for and ownership of one's own learning, effectively highlights for leaders the culture of dependency that they had previously been creating through hierarchical, 'one-way' interactions in the classroom or staffroom or community meeting (Robertson, 2008). Effective leadership influence is through relationships and leadership and learning are relational care processes (Noddings, 2005). Reciprocity – the give and take of information, the levelling of power relations, the sharing of vulnerability – allows and enables professionals to enter a deeper place of learning and being. This 'reciprocal acceptance of the relevance of the experiences and concerns of others' (Lim and Renshaw, 2001: 17) offers a validation of personal practice (Robertson and Webber, 2002), which enables people to feel their practice is relevant to the whole professional community. High levels of capability and high levels of trust are then formed through the ongoing dialogic interactions between the people within such communities.

> Although coaching leadership is a meta-cognitive process in itself, an important aspect of the development of this model of coaching through professional partnership was the meta-cognition of the process of coaching. After each coaching activity the whole group reflected on their role as mentor or partner – describing their thoughts and reflections, and the impact of the activity on their thinking about their own practice. The participants became increasingly aware of their changed beliefs and assumptions and changing paradigms of learning and leadership through this in-depth reflection on their own thinking and the thinking of others and the vicarious reflective opportunities thus initiated. As they thought about their relationships with the coaching process, they began to think about their own relationships in their leadership practice. The coaching partners described how after the meta-cognition on the earlier concrete experience of coaching, the next experience of the coaching was enhanced and deepened. They became increasingly self-aware of their learning processes.
>
> Thelma said:
>
> The most powerful learning experience that has come from my coaching sessions is that the answers are inside of me. I know that sounds funny but with the gifted questioning that my coach does I am always taken to the answers that are already within me. She always guides me with her questions to all my options and what foreseeable things could get in the way and every time I come up with the solution that I will try the next day on my own.

Inquiry-mindedness

As principals and other leaders of learning create the conditions and habits of mind for professional learning through reflection on their own everyday practice, those engaged with them are then also involved in different types of practice, and they move into a paradigm of inquiry-mindedness (Earl and Timperley, 2008) and what Kaser and Halbert (2009) describe as an inquiry leadership mindset. Principals and other senior formal leaders in schools can create learning opportunities through their dialogic interactions with teachers on a daily basis. This encourages teachers to approach their relationships in similar ways. If teachers are encouraged to move beyond the boundary of their own practice, to observe and reflect on the practice of a trusted colleague, they can move beyond self to a place where new learning can take place. This vicarious learning, through the observation of others in similar role positions, can provide opportunities not only for the affirmation of current practice, but also challenges to current practice, and access to new ways of knowing and being. We know that dialogic encounter is an essential element in the learning process and yet the majority of educators' 'conversation' is not a deep articulation and justification of values, beliefs, assumptions and practices. While professional learning requires a context that fosters dialogue about the learning experience and the learning of others, it is also important to again highlight that spaces for effective adult learning *do not just happen*. Such spaces need to be creatively designed, practised and then modelled by those facilitating learning opportunities. New professional learning needs to be generative and responsive to the context and requires inquiry, critical reflection on practice and on the process of change.

The coaching element was designed to support the inquiry-minded focus of the academic course of study. The coach became the critical friend, the challenger, questioner, guide and conscience. The aspiring principals worked on their leadership inquiry over the next year of their study with the additional support of their mentor. More often than not, because of the vast geographical distances in British Columbia, this support was 'virtual' throughout the year – provided through phone calls, emails, skype – supported at times perhaps with the occasional meeting at professional events.

The participants talked about how they listened more, questioned often, and developed an inquiry mindset in their approach to the change process. Thelma said:

> I absolutely believe that my coaching experience has changed the informal leader and hopefully the formal leader I will be one day. I am no longer, when someone is speaking, thinking about what my response is going to be. I sit there and listen to them and without value or judgement I just try to hear what they are talking about and work with them through questions and suggestions in a subtle way and let them come to that solution on their own because what I have found is that everyone, at the end of the day, knows deep down maybe what they ought to try – sometimes it is just hard to go about with that without any reassurance or talking it through.

Partnership learning relationships

Approaching leadership and learning relationships through partnership is a new way of knowing and being for many leaders in education who have developed their leadership practice through experiences of control rather than mutuality (Robertson, 2005). Incremental change is usually not immediately transformational but changes to school culture from control to mutual influence do happen through the myriad of interactions over time. Such cultures are built of respect and trust, and hence provide a strong basis for innovation to occur (Bryk and Schneider, 2002). Principals and teachers need both support and challenge in their new learning processes to achieve changes to their existing practice, including being able to work effectively with colleagues.

As they explore the notion of being a learning partner, leaders begin to see changes in their relationships. They find that when colleagues share similar and different challenges and issues, as participants in deep professional dialogue, they are then willing to approach a stage of vulnerability – a movement out of their comfort zones and beyond the known – to a place of new learning and potentially new leadership. Earlier research (Robertson, 1998) had revealed that school principals knew they established a 'whited sepulchre' façade around their professional practice. Goffman (1959) named this 'impression management' where professionals develop techniques to create an impenetrable exterior that effectively shelters their leadership practice from the gaze and critique of peers. Thus principals do not usually discuss the leadership issues that awake them at 3 a.m. or, indeed, do not speak about any real leadership challenges that they are facing when they meet with their professional colleagues. The reciprocal dialogue and sharing through working in partnership builds relational trust to the point where partners will pierce the professional veneer and share beyond the façade and support each other in that process. Such relational trust is not only necessary for shared vulnerability but is built from such shared vulnerability (Bryk and Schneider, 2002; Robertson, 1998). Trust is an essential element in the learning process, at all levels, in a learning school culture. This is when new leadership learning and challenges to values, beliefs and assumptions about professional practice will occur.

New learning will often instigate an emotional engagement (Webber and Robertson, 1998). The support and challenge that a learning partnership can bring to professional practice can assist the leader through the emotional engagement necessary for new learning and hence new practice to occur. Experiencing professional learning through peer partnership relationships can help bring new ways-of-being naturally to their repertoire.

The aspiring principals described the very different and powerful, professional learning relationships they enjoyed with their mentors. This also led to the development of strong learning relationships with other leaders and the students within their schools.

Amy said:

It has been quite obvious that within my school there has been a mentorship happening with my teachers which has simply emerged from our daily work. I plan to make that a little more clear to the group and show them how that's working so that they can – in fact – they do that for one another ... it's building strong bonds [across disciplines] in supporting the whole process.

Thelma said:

I have noticed that the process of coaching has changed how I work with students and therefore their achievement. I work primarily with struggling and vulnerable learners and I think the attributes of the coaching relationship are the foundations of good relationships – and so working with students who are so often isolated and quiet, giving them their voice and giving them the chance to talk, the amount of think time they need to formulate their thoughts, and providing them with supportive questions, has helped them to become a little more independent in their learning.

As the partnership relationship developed, throughout the two days of intensive coaching and mentoring, and throughout the year following, the aspiring principals were surprised at the depth and breadth of what they were willing to share with their colleagues. They saw how powerful it was to approach this space of vulnerability in order to challenge one's own values, beliefs and paradigms about learning and teaching.

Amy said:

The three words I would use to describe the programme would be trust, respect and vulnerability. The partnership allowed both the learners to express their frustrations and difficulties that come with being in a school every day without that impacting negatively on the staff or the students in the situation.

Facilitating the ownership of change

The building of strong trusting relationships is the essence of social capital (Caldwell and Spinks, 2008) and the basis for trusting respectful learning cultures that are open to challenge and change. Educational leaders will be modelling educational leadership characterized as facilitative, collaborative, adaptive, informed, proactive and constructive – the features of the transformational leadership so necessary in a rapidly changing, postmodern educational context (Robertson and Webber, 2002). Effective educational leadership thus creates the conditions for successful learning and focuses on student outcomes (Robinson et al., 2009).

A coaching and mentoring culture of mutual influence embodies the conditions for successful learning and it is the leaders' work to create that coaching culture through their relationships with their colleagues as they facilitate the change process. As Gorrell and Hoover (2009: xii) point out 'the bottom line is this. You cannot coach a culture but you can coach individuals who create and sustain a culture. As a result, both individual and organization can and should win' and coaching becomes an organizational learning process for educational leadership. According to Hargreaves (2003) the building up of the school's social and intellectual capital, is a necessary prerequisite for innovation to occur. Goleman (2004: 3) also highlights 'proficiency in managing relationships and networks' as one of the five tenets of emotional intelligence. Cultures rich in social and emotional capital at all levels, provide rich learning environments for children and adults to thrive. Such cultures build the ownership of the change process and importantly, self-regulation and ownership of one's own learning processes in that change journey.

Portin et al. (2009: vii–viii) also found in their recent Wallace Foundation study 'Principals and other supervisory leaders ... need to create working partnerships with other staff around the building as part of collective leadership work, and they need to establish the "space" – that is, the conditions of trust, openness to critique, and focus on instruction – for learning-focused teacher leaders to do their work'. The support and challenge offered through peer-coaching partnerships provides opportunities to create new knowledge and the ownership of change.

The leaders all talked about how they became more facilitative in their leadership in their own schools, taking on the role of mentor or coach with their professional colleagues, as they worked throughout the year. One aspect of the coaching meta-cognition had highlighted the importance of developing the ownership of change through recognizing that leaders do have the answers to their challenges in their context, and, through the understanding of the powerful way this affected their own practice, these aspiring principals used the same philosophies and methodologies when leading their colleagues through the change process.

Amy describes it in this way:

Last year when I was the individual being coached we ran an inquiry for the first time in my school that involved the science teacher, an English teacher and myself. We wanted to help grade nine students improve their writing of reports using the performance standards. This year a different science teacher with a brand new curriculum has decided to involve herself in the project again and ... we have seen a shift in one year's time from four adults to nine adults, probably the best part of it being that the last person to come into the group was actually a very experienced senior science teacher who wanted to be sure that her students were having the same experiences as the others. My role has been that of adviser, keeping the project rolling, being a part of the adult feedback crew and helping to establish the structure and format for the inquiry so that everyone was freed up to do what they needed to do.

Strengthening the moral purpose of educational leadership

Research and development work over 18 years with leaders working in coaching relationships to improve and change their practice, has continually upheld the original findings (Robertson, 1997) that peer coaching can assist leaders to focus more fully on their educational leadership role. This entails a focus on the quality of education they are providing, their own professional learning and the improvement of student outcomes (Sutton, 2005). Coaching partnerships can reduce feelings of isolation and provide the support and affirmation necessary to maintain and build self-efficacy, thus rekindling leaders' moral authority and their belief that they can make a difference. Educators become more reflective, more willing to learn, more understanding of the complexities of their work, and consequently are reflecting in action and on action, for future action as posited by Argyris (1976) and Schön (1987) to be essential in professional learning. Key to this is a focus on the leaders' values, beliefs and assumptions about learning and leadership, and opportunities to critique their theories-in-action against espoused theories, through reciprocal coaching.

The aspiring principals became more agentic, strong in their moral conviction that changes in teacher practice were necessary and strong in their belief that they could initiate and facilitate the change that was necessary to achieve the outcomes they wanted to see. The curriculum of their academic course of study had focused on social justice and equity in leadership, and developed the necessary mindsets and dispositions for effecting change in the leadership of learning through the inquiry focus (Kaser and Halbert, 2009).

The mentors helped the aspiring principals to keep the focus firmly on their educational leadership role in leading their inquiry. Troy and Gary described the importance of this systematic focus, support and challenge from their mentor in the attainment of their outcomes.

Troy said:

The engagement that the students experienced because of this clarity of vision was paramount to their success in the literacy, in their own agency in terms of what they felt that they could accomplish and I directly attribute that to the clarity of vision that was provided for me, or fostered in me, by this mentorship process ... and with that intent you can really make some magical things happen.

Gary added:

I worked on a project on social responsibility and helping clarify some ideas both on what type of work to do and certain ways to approach it from the mentor helped make the project more specific and more concrete working with the students and ultimately I think did have an effect on what went on in the classroom and how the students learned.

Conclusion

Coaching leadership can provide the deep leadership learning in context that is necessary to facilitate the self-awareness essential to creating the disposition to change one's practice. Support and challenge are important elements of the process, provided in part through the vicarious learning of observation and reflection about somebody else's practice in a similar role. The co-learning that can be facilitated between peers, who have the skills for questioning and challenging, deep and meaningful reflection on practice, can lead to the development of shared meaning and an agency and capability to work systematically through the leadership of change and innovation. The outside perspectives of a coach can support the ongoing inquiry process essential in a school that is continually questioning and challenging the current paradigms and practices of the people in that community. Strong, trusting ongoing relationships built through reciprocity and respect, will lead to a willingness of participants to enter a place of vulnerability in order to challenge and then change assumptions and ways of being and thinking in education. Education and thus leadership and learning is relational and those educationists who can build formative trusting relationships will recognize that every interaction is an opportunity to build trust and every interaction is an opportunity to learn.

Reflective Questions

1 Do you use coaching in your leadership of learning? Why or why not?
2 In your work culture, how high would you rate trust in relationships? How do you and your colleagues seek feedback and outside perspectives on your practice in the continual search for improvement?

Further Reading

Kaser, L. and Halbert, J. (2009) *Leadership Mindsets. Innovation and Learning in the Transformation of Schools*. London: Routledge.

This book presents a different way of thinking about leadership. Developed over 10 years' working with hundreds of leaders throughout British Columbia, Canada, Kaser and Halbert found that persistent work, underpinned by six leadership mindsets, have benefited schools and the young people in them.

Earl, L. and Timperley, H. (eds) (2008) *Professional Learning Conversations: Challenges in Using Evidence for Improvement*. Dordrecht: Springer.

The authors in this edited book present chapters on the theory and practice of developing evidence-informed learning conversations between those in the school community. An inquiry habit of mind, relevant data and relationships of respect and challenge are essential to this process.

References

Argyris, C. (1976) *Increasing leadership effectiveness*. New York: John Wiley & Sons.

Ball, S.J. (2006) *Education Policy and Social Class. The Selected Works of Stephen J. Ball*. Oxford: Routledge.

Bishop, R. and Glynn, T. (1999) *Culture Counts: Changing Power Relations in Education*. Palmerston North: Dunmore Press.

Bryk, A.S. and Schneider, B.L. (2002) *Trust in Schools: A Core Resource for Improvement*. New York: Russell Sage Foundation Publications.

Butler, D.L. and Schnellert, L. (2008) Teaching for deep learning: making self-regulated learning a way of life, paper presented at the Leadership Learning Seminar of the Network of Performance Based Schools, Vancouver, BC, 29–30 April.

Caldwell, B.J. (2002) Autonomy and self-management: concepts and evidence, in T. Bush and L. Bell (eds), *The Principles and Practice of Educational Management*. London: Paul Chapman Publishing. pp. 24–40.

Caldwell, B.J. and Spinks, J.M. (1998) *Beyond the Self-managing School*. London: Falmer.

Caldwell, B.J. and Spinks, J.M. (2008) *Raising the Stakes: From Improvement to Transformation in the Reform of Schools*. Abingdon: Routledge.

Choy, C.K. and Fatt, L.W. (1998) Scenarios in school management in Singapore: trends from future studies, *International Studies in Educational Administration*, 26(1): 31–7.

Colvin, R.L. (2008) Why school and district leadership matters, in Hechinger Institute, *Leadership and Learning: A Hechinger Institute Primer for Journalists*. New York: Teachers College Columbia University, Hechinger Institute.

Earl, L. and Timperley, H. (eds) (2008) *Professional Learning Conversations: Challenges in Using Evidence for Improvement*. Dordrecht: Springer.

Goffman, E. (1959) *The Presentation of Self in Everyday life*. Reprinted 1982. New York: Anchor Books.

Goleman, D. (2004) What makes a leader?, *Harvard Business Review*. January. Available at: www.hbr.org/2004/01/what-makes-a-leader/ar/1 (accessed 3 September 2010).

Gorrell, P.J. and Hoover, J. (2009) *The Coaching Connection: A Manager's Guide to Developing Individual Potential in the Context of the Organization*. New York: Amacom.

Hallinger, P. (2003) Leading educational change: reflections on the practice of instructional and transformational leadership, *Cambridge Journal of Education*, 33(3): 329–51.

Hargreaves, A. (2003) *Teaching in the Knowledge Society: Education in the Age of Insecurity*. New York: Teachers College Press; Buckingham: Open University Press.

Kaser, L. and Halbert, J. (2009) *Leadership Mindsets. Innovation and Learning in the Transformation of Schools*. London: Routledge.

Kohn, A. (1993) Choices for children: why and how to let students decide, *Phi Delta Kappan*, 75(1): 8–20.

Lambert, L., Collay, M., Dietz, M., Kent, K. and Richert, A.E. (1996) *Who Will Save Our Schools? Teachers as Constructivist Leaders*. Thousand Oaks, CA: Corwin Press.

Leithwood, K. (1996) Introduction, in K. Leithwood, J. Chapman, D. Corson, P. Hallinger and A. Weaver-Hart (eds), *International Handbook of Educational Leadership and Administration*. New York: Kluwer.

Lim, L. and Renshaw, P. (2001) The relevance of sociocultural theory to culturally diverse partnerships and communities, *Journal of Child and Family Studies*, 10(1): 9–21.

Muijs, D. (2009) *Networking and Collaboration – What is the Evidence*, keynote address presented at the International Congress for School Effectiveness and Improvement, Vancouver, 5–8 January.

Noddings, N. (2005) Caring in education, *The Encyclopedia of Informal Education*. Available at: www.infed.org/biblio/noddings_caring_in_education.htm

Portin, B.S., Knapp, M.S., Dareff, S., Feldman, S., Russell, F.A., Samuelson, C. and Ling Leh, T. (2009) *Leadership for Learning Improvement in Urban Schools*. Seattle, WA: University of Washington, Centre for Study of Teaching and Policy.

Robertson, J. (2005) *Coaching Leadership: Building Educational Leadership Capacity Through Coaching Partnerships*. Wellington: NZCER.

Robertson, J. (2008) *Coaching Educational Leadership: Building Leadership Capacity Through Partnership*. London: Sage.

Robertson, J.M. (1997) A programme of professional partnerships for leadership development, *Waikato Journal of Education*, 3: 137–52.

Robertson, J.M. (1998) From managing impression to leadership perspectives, *International Journal of Educational Research*, 29(4): 359–70.

Robertson, J.M. and Webber, C.F. (2002) Boundary-breaking leadership: a must for tomorrow's learning communities, in K. Leithwood and P. Hallinger (eds), *Second International Handbook of Educational Leadership and Administration*. Dordrecht: Kluwer. pp. 519–53.

Robinson, V., Hohepa, M. and Lloyd, C. (2009) *School Leadership and Student Outcomes: Identifying What Works and Why*. Wellington: Ministry of Education.

Schön, D. (1987) *Educating the Reflective Practitioner.* San Francisco, CA: Jossey-Bass.

Sutton, M. (2005) Coaching for pedagogical change, *New Zealand Journal of Educational Leadership*, 20(2): 31–46.

Vygotsky, L. (1978) Interaction between learning and development, in L. Vygotsky, *Mind in Society.* Trans. M. Cole. Cambridge, MA: Harvard University Press. pp. 79–91.

Webber, C.F. and Robertson, J. (1998) Boundary breaking: an emergent model for leadership development, *Educational Policy Analysis Archives*, 6(21). Available at: www.olam.ed.asu.edu/epaa/v6n21.html

CHAPTER 17

Fusion and the Future of Leadership

Andy Hargreaves

Before Fusion

In the 1950s and 60s, when I was growing up in Northern England, there was only one kind of cooking: British food. It wasn't really a particular cuisine. It was all that there was. Stew, broth, minced beef, shepherd's pie, steak and kidney pudding, best end of neck, boiled cabbage, mashed carrots and Brussels sprouts – all cooked to oblivion until every last shred of taste had been boiled away: these were the culinary 'delights' of post-war Britain. Fish and chips in newspaper wrappings were a Friday night luxury. Pizza was an exotic curiosity. Burgers had only just made it across the Atlantic. You ate or you didn't. And there was only one kind of cooking. Eating British food was like cows eating grass. You weren't even aware there was anything else.

This is how management used to be. You were a manager or a worker. You managed well or badly. Aside from something called the Human Relations School of Management, advanced by American sociologist George Homans, there was no real theory of management at all (Homans, 1950). Management was something that happened to you when you got promoted and crossed the line from the factory floor to the office. Of course, you needed to have authority, be able to organize a budget, and ensure you got results. You might even have entertained private philosophies about how to get the best out of people. But management theorists like Herzberg, Mintzberg, Handy and Schein, along with self-styled corporate gurus like Tom Peters, Peter Block and Jack Welch had not yet entered the management arena. You either managed or you didn't. That's really all there was to it.

In the 1960s, an expanding economy brought waves of immigration into many parts of Britain to toil in its factories and work in its mills. When the Empire came home, it carried its different cuisines with it. After a few beers, young working-class men, like my eldest brother, learned to test their virility with an excoriating vindaloo at the town's only Indian restaurant, underneath the railway viaduct, on a Friday night. 'Instant' boxed meals, something of an innovation in themselves, began to offer exotic options like beef stroganoff and chicken chow mein. Increased immigration, the start of mass continental travel and the emergence of the first chefs (women known simply as 'cooks') on black and white television introduced 'foreign' food to the common English table. French meat dishes, Italian pastas and even Spanish paellas added themselves to the British diet. Chicken Kiev was a dining out indulgence. As the century progressed, and globalization advanced, Thai, Vietnamese, Lebanese and many other cuisines became part of British eating at home and also, with the growth of affluence, in restaurants. The British diet was now no longer a predictable functional necessity, but a pleasurable consumer choice.

The later decades of the twentieth century witnessed similar diversification in leadership theory and practice. Social psychologist, Kurt Lewin, who invented the idea of action research, had laid the foundations for a more diversified view of leadership as early as the 1940s when, with colleagues Lippitt and White, he tested children's mask-making capabilities under three different kinds of leadership (Lewin et al., 1939). Children working under *laissez-faire* leaders were the least productive; those working under authoritarian leadership produced the most masks; and those under democratic leadership made the best masks.

In the 1960s, Douglas McGregor contrasted the autocratic styles of Theory X leaders who believed that people could not be trusted and needed to be monitored and motivated by external rewards and punishments, with 'human relations' style Theory Y counterparts who believed in developing and supporting workers who were assumed to be honest, capable and industrious (McGregor, 1960). By and from the 1970s, many different kinds of leadership were being advanced and entertained: autocratic and democratic; transformational and transactional; charismatic and bureaucratic; heroic and distributed – to name just a few.[1] Leadership was now a matter of style and preference: a question of choice in how to lead and how to be.

The evolution of fusion

Over the past decade or so, the profusion of multi-ethnic dining choices has further inspired culinary innovators to create fresh fusions of eating styles. Fusion cuisine is a movement to combine and blend different ingredients, tastes and styles from different ethnic, national and regional eating traditions. In the world's most cosmopolitan cities, Pacific Rim and other innovative cuisines generate new dishes and menus from disparate sources and styles – finding new compatibilities among different flavours, and producing menus of unusual courses that follow on from and complement each other in unexpected ways.

Fusion cuisine is not a random conglomeration of oddly or accidentally assorted elements. The blend is deliberate, principled and practical. It is fusion, not confusion. Nor is fusion cuisine a smorgasbord of varied items where the only principle of integration is what is easily available, combined with the customer's personal preference. Fusion cuisine, rather, is a principled and practical quest to locate and create three kinds of integration:

- an inner and individual integration of culinary sensations in the diner's tastebuds, palate and aesthetic sensibility

- an outer and collective integration of different cultural styles and traditions of cooking into new culinary cultures and themes

- a temporal and sequential integration of innovative menus where exciting new dishes, resulting from the creative recombination of old, familiar, but previously unconnected ingredients, make coherent new meals and overall dining experiences.

In many respects, leadership theory and practice are also moving away from one way to lead, or even different definable styles of leadership, towards a fusion of leadership principles and practices that seem right for the leader and for the leadership challenges that he or she is facing in a particular time and place. However, what may look like fusion in theory, can be more like diffusion and dissipation in practice.

While, for some authors, leadership has largely become a matter of style or overall approach, for others, it is a set of practices: an aggregate of skills sets, standards, or competencies. Distributed leadership theory tends to look at how leadership is actually done – at the actions and interactions that weave it altogether in any place or time (Spillane, 2006). Situational leadership theory addresses how leadership varies according to the circumstance in which leadership is done (Gates et al., 1976). Evidence-based approaches to leadership itemize the measurable leadership effect sizes of different leadership practices and try to elicit those practices that have the highest yield (Robinson et al., 2008).

These understandings of leadership that are based in practice, in variable circumstances, and in measurable leadership effects move us beyond the arguments for and against particular leadership styles – what Mulford calls the 'adjectival' approach to leadership (Mulford, 2008). But in the worst and all too common scenarios, there has been a widespread tendency and movement to draw up detailed frameworks of leadership standards and competencies to pinpoint particular attributes and measurable outcomes that are seen as applying to leadership performance in all times and places. These 'laundry lists' (Fink, 2005) often overlook how effective leadership attributes can vary depending on the situation from one kind of school or institution to the next (Gates et al., 1976), on the context in which the schools find themselves (for example, Harris and Chapman, 2002), on the level of performance a school or institution has already reached (Hopkins, 2007), and on how they can and do evolve over time within and across individuals through the processes of leadership development and leadership succession (see Hargreaves and Fink, 2006).

In their book *Fusion Leadership* Daft and Lengel point to the dangers of what they call *leadership fission*, of splitting leadership and performance into discrete and unconnected elements (Daft and Lengel, 1998). Their advocacy of *fusion leadership* concentrates on the coming together of different inner qualities and capabilities within an organization or individual through a single story or narrative of leadership. Such fusion, they claim, 'unlocks powerful forces' that are to be found in the 'yearning for meaningful work', in the 'desire to contribute', in 'dreams', 'creative potential' and 'courage' (Daft and Lengel, 1998: 13). Leadership fusion, they say is about 'joining, coming together, creative connection and partnerships' (Daft and Lengel, 1998: 16).

Fusion leadership moves beyond multiple styles of leadership not just by drawing attention to situational differences, or to developmental evolutions of leadership over time, but by acknowledging people's higher-level capacities to integrate different characteristics, competencies and capabilities into a unified whole. Just as integration is one of the highest order characteristics of psychosocial development, (Erickson, 1963) personal and organizational integration in leadership constitutes a high level of development also – increasing people's capacity to exercise different skills and to express different leadership qualities as appropriate but within a unified whole that defines the core of the person expressing and exercising these things (Kets de Vries, 2006: 16).

With a transatlantic team of seven researchers, Alma Harris and I have come to understand and appreciate the significance of fusion leadership in our investigation of 18 organizations that perform above expectations in relation to peers' performance, prior performance and relatively modest levels of resources and support – in business, sport and education (Hargreaves and Harris, in press). This study draws on Daft and Lengel's conceptualization of leadership fusion, but takes their ideas further.

For the originators of the concept, leadership fusion is an inner integration of personal capabilities and dispositions comprising heart, integrity, vision, mindfulness, courage and communication (Daft and Lengel, 1998). It is a normative, narrative and almost spiritual quest. Fusion leadership is advocated as much as it is analysed. It is based on a survey of literature and on an exploration of stories and examples from personal experience and the world of leadership that are real but not rigorously evidence-based. By contrast, our own arrival at the idea of fusion leadership comes from our bottom-up analysis of 18 organizations in three sectors and five countries, that have performed above expectations. One of the cases that exemplifies the presence and the power of fusion leadership is a secondary school in the North of England – Grange Secondary – which I now explore to exemplify the nature of fusion leadership in action.

Fusion in action

The town of Oldham in Northern England is the site of some of Britain's worst ever race riots in 2001. On indicators of deprivation, some areas of the town are among the poorest 1 per cent in England. Grange Secondary School is right at the centre of one of them.[2] Graeme Hollinshead started his long career at Grange in 1971. It was the town's 'flagship' school when it was established, drawing in young people from across the community. But as Pakistani and Bangladeshi families came to work in the cotton mills and as the cotton industry then collapsed, bringing unemployment in its wake, the staff at Grange Secondary began to struggle and the school fell 'into the doldrums'.

By the late 1980s and into the 1990s, academic standards had fallen dramatically and pupil behaviour was poor. The Senior Leadership Team had isolated itself on 'the top corridor' where one of them 'even used to crochet most of the day'. The atmosphere 'felt lax'. One teacher recalled how senior leaders 'never set foot in my classroom'. Turnout at parents' evenings was very low and only 15 per cent of students were achieving the threshold standard of five grades A–C in their GCSE examinations. Parents 'didn't speak English. Some couldn't read English. A lot of them couldn't read their own language'. Yet the staff's response to these very real challenges was 'blaming the children, the community for being so poor and the fact that they were on free school dinners and that they don't speak English and that mobility is the problem'. 'The facilities looked grotty', one senior leader reflected. 'In the press, we were muck. The kids didn't have very high expectations of succeeding and we had quite a high staff turnover'.

A new deputy headteacher, Colin Bell, arrived in 1994 and went on to become the head in 1997. Graeme Hollinshead became his deputy in 1997 and succeeded Bell as the head in 2004. This was the perceptible start of a long turn-around in the fortunes of Grange Secondary. The leadership approach at Grange was at times courageous, creative, inspirational, distributed and sustainable. It was not one kind of leadership but many – a fusion and evolution of different styles and approaches across a community and also over time.

Courageous leadership

The low point for Grange Secondary was when it almost failed its external inspection in 1996. After the inspection, Graeme Hollinshead took sick leave for the first time in his career. Like a number of other dedicated colleagues at the school, he had worked at Grange all his professional life. But the inspection process was a wake-up call. He and the school, he felt, were utterly stuck. Frustrated and despondent, he went to discuss his troubling feelings with a hospital consultant. The consultant listened patiently, then delivered his expert medical advice. This was Northern England, not Southern California, so his feedback was bracing and brutally direct. 'He just advised me to get back in and sort it out,' said Graeme, 'which I did.'

Graeme moved up to being deputy. Bell arrived and was soon promoted to being the head. Together, they started to lead by example. They set down firm foundations for improvement by calming down student behaviour with a positive discipline strategy. 'Behaviour was poor, morale was poor, and attendance was 84 per cent. Everything needed improving.' At first, Bell and Hollinshead showed courage and fortitude by leading boldly and resolutely from the front. They took some of the worst-behaved students in the school into town and out to theme parks when they behaved well, even though their staff thought they were crazy. 'We used to do things like getting in our cars and rounding up the kids from the park. There was nothing we wouldn't do. We'd go knocking on doors, saying "Why aren't you in school?"' After leading by example, the staff were more ready to follow now they had respect for their leaders and realized that what they were modelling was actually achievable. The result was a new behaviour strategy that produced a climate characterized by 'calmness on the corridors', collective staff responsibility to care for children, willingness to listen to them and a capacity to understand the students and 'where they were coming from'.

Grange's leaders were courageous with their superiors as well as with their teachers and students. They knew how to 'manage up'. This was especially evident when the school's stellar performance record was suddenly placed in political doubt. The turn-around trajectory had, indeed, been remarkable – steady, sustainable improvement over time reflecting real changes in teaching and learning rather than creative accountancy of immediate achievement results. Just some of the evidence of performing beyond expectations is as follows:

- The proportion of students achieving 5+ GCSE grades A*– C increased from 15 per cent in 1999 to 71 per cent in 2008.
- Between 2000 and 2008, the proportion of students not going on to further education, training or employment (NEETs) fell from 12 per cent to 3 per cent, less than half the national average of 7 per cent.
- Over a decade, attendance improved from 84 per cent to 92.5 per cent, close to the national average of 92.7 per cent.
- In terms of the contribution the school makes to student progress between ages 11–16 (its contextual value added score), in 2008, Grange was positioned in the top 2 per cent of schools nationally and first among all 16 secondary schools in the local authority.
- Honours and awards include designation as a visual arts specialist school in 2002, becoming the highest performer of 30 such schools nationally in 2005 (and remaining in the top two today), and winning a number of significant visual arts prizes such as being the regional Arts and Minds winner in 2004.

Successive inspection reports by the Office for Standards in Education (Ofsted) support this overall trajectory of improvement far beyond expectations. Ofsted's 2002 report upgraded the school to the second highest category of 'good', which included 'areas of excellence' in the school's work. The report noted there had been 'very good' improvement since the 1996 inspection. 'There has been significant improvement in attendance and good improvement in the quality of the curriculum for Years 10 and 11. Teaching has significantly improved and standards are rising faster than nationally.' By the 2006 report, Grange was still a 'good school' at grade 2, but now with 'some outstanding features' particularly in terms of supporting and caring for learners and forming partnerships with others. Although GCSE examination results were still 'below average', they were 'much better than at the time of the previous inspection'. This is an impressive improvement record after years of underperformance in the face of profound local educational and social challenges and compared with schools in similar circumstances.

In May 2008, the Labour Government introduced a National Challenge initiative that set 'floor targets' for secondary schools where at least 30 per cent of students were expected to gain 5+ GCSE grades A*–C including mathematics and English (the target had not previously specified these two subjects as requirements). Schools listed as failing to meet these targets included 638 secondary schools and were notified that they would be subject to intervention and possible replacement by or redesignation as academies if they did not meet their targets within one year. Despite its 10-year improvement trajectory on previous measurable criteria, its increasingly favourable inspection reports and its collection of honours and awards, the Grange's positioning below these newly-defined floor targets placed it on the list of 638.

Graeme Hollinshead was headteacher of the Grange in 2008. His reputation had led him to be appointed as a consultant by the Specialist Schools and Academies Trust to advise other schools on how to improve, and to serve as a school improvement partner or mentor for other headteachers. He appeared in the national press, on public radio and on the BBC's *Panorama* because the Grange had the largest disparity in performance rankings of all schools in the country between previous examination results that excluded Mathematics and English and the National Challenge criteria that included these two subjects. The *Times Educational Supplement* described Hollinshead as 'indignant about a statistical exercise which led to hundreds of schools being branded as failing'. 'Is this a high-performing specialist school or a failing school? Make your judgement,' he says. 'Every head I know would say Grange is a high-performing school. Who has got it wrong?'.[3]

Hollinshead had publicly challenged the sudden shifts in performance criteria imposed by the government in the middle of the school year. His advocacy on behalf of the school, its teachers and students, was not undertaken alone. The headteacher in 2009/10, Gilly McMullen, also stood up to unfair inspections or against local authority (district) staff when they did not understand the school:

> We had so much documentation and we could challenge (the inspection team). We will challenge people outside the school like the local authority. We won't take on board certain strategies they might present and ask us to do. We will say, 'No, we're going to do it this way. We've thought about it and we don't want your expertise because we've got it in-house.' So we were very, very clued up.

Inspiring leadership

Most leaders who perform beyond expectations find ways to lift people's spirits and raise their hopes. Until the mid-1990s, Grange had been managed by 'nice' people but 'there was no initiative at all'. Then, 'all of sudden we got a deputy head in who's got vision, who's got experience of other things'. 'He had been a deputy head of a very challenging school in Manchester and was rather streetwise as well – very unlike the two heads that we had previously'. The new deputy was 'not tied to the social history of the school and was like a breath of fresh air'. When he became head, Bell met with the governing body responsible for the school and set out his vision:

> He had plans and he brought them to the governing body, and at a time when the percentage of A–C grades was minimal, he was able to look to the future and say, 'Well in two or three years' time, this is what I want and to get that vision across to everybody and working for it'.

Staff felt 'he was quite a visionary sort of leader. He was quite inspirational. Still is. He started to make people believe that this school could be successful'. Staff 'got the motivation speeches: "this is my vision, this is what we're going to do"'. At a time when the school building was very run down, the teachers were 'taken out and treated'. 'We all got taken off to the local hotel for inspirational presentations and to hear his vision for the future.'

Bell 'did wonders for this school in about 4 or 5 years – so much so that he moved on to bigger things'. He was 'extremely dynamic; very outward going'. 'He was young. He told you how it was.' One teacher felt the turning point was when Bell gave people the sense 'we were definitely going places' so they 'realized things could be done', 'wanted to be part of it' and knew they could do it themselves. Graeme Hollinshead generously recalls how his predecessor 'brought tremendous charisma. He was inspirational. He certainly got people doing things'. One of his strengths was that he was a 'very, very good people person'.

Bell was welcoming. He 'understood the children'. He took time to know his people, to learn about the staff, to make even the lowest status teachers and other staff feel wanted and valued. One teacher vividly remembers her very first contact with the school as a supply (substitute) teacher, when Bell was in charge of supply teacher appointments and coverage.

> He was asking me a lot of questions and explaining about this new senior leadership team and how they were trying to create a team of people who would come in on supply. He asked would I be willing to come in and do different subjects, etc, etc. I said that I would. But at the time I was thinking, 'Why are you asking me all this because I'm only coming in for one day?' Anyway, I did my day. And there was just something about the place that made you feel welcome. Maybe it was the fact that the guy took the time to sit down and have the conversation. Now people who come here on supply say there is definitely an ethos of being welcome in the school, which I think is about valuing people from a supply teacher coming in for one day, to the cleaning staff, the kitchen staff and the pupils. I think everybody feels that they belong to the school and that their contribution matters.

Performing beyond expectations involves more than raising people's hopes. Indeed, if hopes are not fulfilled or are actively dashed, then cynicism can sink to an even lower level. Eventually, the power of hope is when its promise shows evidence of fulfilment in action. When the promise of better times becomes evident even in small increments of concrete improvement, this can generate upward spirals of further hope and increased confidence that even greater improvements are possible (Kanter, 2006).

> You went from being a teacher at the school that was the worst-performing to someone who was working in a reasonable work environment with good facilities, with students who were improving and this was being recognized. I think all that has a very positive impact on you and encourages you to keep on going.

This spiral of confidence and ever-increasing achievement, worked across leaders, not just during the tenure of one of them. There was fusion over time. 'We've got very good leadership. Each one has improved so that the level that the school is at has improved dramatically: three different characters all bringing different skills and the school has benefited.'

Creative leadership

Leading beyond expectations often entails taking an unexpected, creative and counter-intuitive approach to a long-standing problem. In many underperforming schools, teachers are simply urged to work harder in tracking, monitoring and managing individual student progress so they perform more strongly at the existing curriculum. Colin Bell took a different approach. He put in many hours observing in classrooms and came to understand that the standard secondary school curriculum did not recognize how Grange's predominantly Bangladeshi students learned best. 'He said one of the ways we could make rapid progress is to allow the children to do more of what they're good at and more of what they enjoyed.' In Sir Ken Robinson's terms, he understood that children achieved most when they were 'in their element' – but Grange's traditional curriculum had been ensuring that, mostly, children in school were out of their element (Robinson, 2010).

The school tested students on their learning styles and found they were 'very visual, very kinaesthetic'. Grange school therefore made a bold move to get the curriculum to fit the child by moving it strongly towards visual arts. This meant introducing more vocational courses, and eventually becoming a Visual Arts College in 2002. This also brought in a boost of £5 million of new resources for buildings and new technology, as well as a number of visiting artists. Eventually, Grange school became one of the top two of 30 visual arts colleges in the country and received a range of national awards. With a wider variety of courses in art now on offer, students 'were leaving with a higher number of GCSE passes' and a stronger sense of pride in their accomplishments. Teachers started to feel that the curriculum really was 'designed for' and 'fits the needs of (the) pupils'. Between 2002 and 2004, results just 'zoomed' from 15 per cent GCSE 5 A–Cs in the 1990s, to over 70 per cent in 2008.

Distributed and inclusive leadership

Leadership at Grange is not just attributable to single individuals. For one thing, the head and deputies work as a team. When Graeme Hollinshead was Bell's deputy, he was seen as 'the practical one who made sure that things happened', while Bell was 'the visionary one' who 'had the dreams'. They 'complemented each other tremendously'. As a 'really good team', these two leaders 'started to bring in funding. The facilities started to improve. There was a big programme of rebuilding and improving the facilities including things like the staff rooms'. This was 'the start of Grange School being on its way up'.

Over time, it became clear that Graeme Hollinshead was not just the practical sidekick for his big-picture predecessor. Hollinshead came to be seen as a 'visionary too', with his own 'dreams', though in a different style than Bell.

Eventually, although not always instantly, Grange's most senior leaders encouraged and expected others to take responsibility for improvement too. Hollinshead tried 'all the time to distribute the leadership' and develop teamwork. The team comprised everyone – teachers, learning mentors, teaching assistants and support staff. Union representatives were always involved early when new directions were being taken. The business manager was complimentary about how everyone would 'rally round' when someone had a problem, and how Hollinshead knew how to delegate and how he 'lets you get on with it'.

Hollinshead's successor, Gilly McMullen, continued this approach in her support of involving everyone: 'It's very much a team effort. It's not just a team effort by teachers (but) by every member of staff right down to kitchen staff, cleaners. Everybody is helping one another to do even better.' A senior member of the governors who has spent his political life in this working-class town believed that 'you shouldn't put leadership on the pedestal'. At Grange, he says, 'Leadership is part of the team. They're all teachers. They all work together. There's none of this "I can't go straight to the head or I can't do this", because everybody's got a right to say what they want, when they want, and how they want it.'

After years of early struggle, of pushing hard from the front, and of facing scepticism and outright resistance from some staff members, the leaders at Grange eventually saw some teachers finally leave, especially at the end of the 1990s. Despite the turnover, a good number of long-serving and very committed staff also stayed – many of them moving into middle-level or senior leadership positions in the school. A hierarchical approach to pushing people forward through argument, example or inspiring persuasion, began to give way to a more team-based approach among well-known and trusted colleagues.

The leadership team does not see itself as omniscient or invulnerable. A teacher of English as a Second Language always felt his views were 'listened to' because 'the senior leadership team have had the sense to say that we haven't got all the answers; that people know more about issues or people know more about things than (them)'. Gilly McMullen acknowledged that 'if I make a mistake, I'm the one who's carrying the can, the one who's made the mistake, etc. and so I will put my hand up and admit that mistake'.

The composition of the senior leadership team at Grange was unlike that in many secondary schools: diverse, divergent, even quirky. In this Visual Arts College, many of the teachers who ascended into senior leadership positions were formerly teachers of design, technology, arts, music or physical education. In conventional secondary schools, their leadership opportunities would often have been crowded out by colleagues who came up through the ranks of higher status, mainstream subjects. The culture and curriculum orientation of Grange Secondary therefore brings forward leadership among many teachers who would be denied the opportunities and perhaps dismissed as being not interested elsewhere. Distributed leadership was, in this sense, also inclusive leadership – giving opportunities for leadership to those who were traditionally excluded by specialism or by ethnicity in the dominant cultures of more standardized systems (Ryan, 2005).

Former physical education teachers felt they had learned not only coaching skills but also the organizational capacity to put together team events. Many 'key members of staff' cut their teeth early in leading alternative assessment initiatives in the late 1980s. This connected them to the progress of individual students and how to track it. Senior leaders from art, design and technology backgrounds were equipped for 'creatively thinking about systems and procedures' and for making 'less formalized one-to-one relationships with the pupils'. As leaders, they could be on the dance floor and the balcony all at the same time.

Through building a culture of trust, warmth and loyalty, distributed leadership at Grange turned into collective responsibility. Hollinshead observed that 'the head can't do everything. He's got to have key people in key positions who are accountable no matter what they do'. With this collective, distributed and inclusive responsibility, the head did not always have to be in school, but could be outside advocating for it, and gathering other ideas and insights that could support it. This 'constant networking', even 'internationally' was essential. 'We're constantly looking for new things. Better things. We might go to different schools up and down the country if we're looking for specific things to improve.' So Hollinshead 'goes off all over the place'. Gilly McMullen, his successor, pointed out that 'he's out of school all the time' but 'it's just business as normal. When he's not here you would not notice'.

Finally, distributed and inclusive leadership in the school is not only an internal matter. It also involves the community. Indeed effective school leadership is effective community leadership – the school impacting on the culturally diverse and financially impoverished community that influences it; treating that community as an untapped asset rather than a pervasive liability.[4] Several staff at Grange had formerly been pupils at the school and now provided role models for current students. Learning mentors and teaching assistants were drawn from the local community.

> When I first came 16 years ago there were very few staff who came from the same cultural background as the pupils that we have now. But yet now we've got ex-pupils as teachers. We have classroom assistants. We have learning mentors. We have technicians, all sorts of people who come from the same community as the pupils. I think that is very, very important because they will bring an understanding and a knowledge to the school as a whole which will help all staff who maybe come from very different backgrounds culturally, religiously and in language terms. The institution is more reflective of the actual pupils in the school, which is a valuable thing.

Leadership stability and sustainability

Although the entire senior leadership team at Grange turned over after the barely acceptable inspection report of 1996, many members of the new team actually came from within the school itself. In 2010, the team included people who had been there for more than 20 or 30 years. The school had 'a very stable workforce. Many of the staff are still here. There are lots of people who have been here and nowhere else', one 30-year veteran said. 'We've all been here a long time and we've seen absolutely massive changes.'

> I've been a teacher here for 25 years. I think in some schools, you do get an attitude that 'I'm not going to change, I'm going to stick with what I know'.

Often, here, the older staff and the ones in the management positions are the most open to change. Obviously, that will drive through what happens with the younger staff.

Graeme Hollinshead worked at Grange for 37 years. He knew the staff, the students and the community inside out. 'The character and context in the school has changed. Staying in the same place has given me breadth of experience I never could have got by moving around the country.' Because he had 'seen several generations come through the school', it mattered a great deal that 'what we provide for the community, for the students is excellent'. Hollinshead was not alone in feeling that: 'Our kids like stability in staff. They want people who they can trust, they know. I was known in the community. In an all-Asian community that's sometimes difficult and we didn't want somebody new coming in with new ideas – because I had already started loads of new ideas.'

Graeme Hollinshead was not the only one to 'come up through the ranks'. Leader after leader had 'come up from being a probationary teacher here', 'came as an assistant head of department' 10 years back; 'started a career at this school and have never been anywhere else'; 'came as a second in department about 15 years ago' then went on to become department head. More and more teachers and middle-level leaders were former pupils of the school; coming from it and giving back to it. Orderly leadership succession and high leadership stability were vital to achieving persistent growth at feasible rates.

Conclusion

Grange Secondary School experienced a remarkable turn-around, and this was due to remarkable leadership. Courageous leadership of two headteachers with an ever-widening constituency of senior leaders, went into places that no one else was prepared to go in order to clean up the school and establish an orderly environment of calm discipline, a practical example of what was achievable, and a platform for further improvement. They modelled what was needed to their staff, and defended what was necessary against unwarranted bureaucratic intrusion. Their inspiration was matched in equal measure by perspiration and sometimes desperation as departments improved, results turned around and students and teachers developed strengthening loyalties to their school. They did not try to push their school further and further along the customary grain of conventional, tested achievement, but took creative and counterintuitive steps to match the curriculum to students' culture and learning styles.

Trust grew, responsibility spread and the leadership became increasingly inclusive and so effectively distributed across the school and the community that headteachers could be absent for a day or more without anyone feeling that they had been abandoned, worrying that the school would be in jeopardy or even noticing that the most senior leaders had left. All this occurred in an environment that welcomed and sometimes interjected elements of leadership change but also capitalized on and recombined the expertise of highly-experienced educators within the school that avoided volatile shifts of direction and supported leadership stability and sustainability instead.

Many kinds of leadership have been responsible for Grange's trajectory of improvement, not just one – courageous, instructional, creative, inspirational or transformational, distributed, inclusive and sustainable. These have interacted, evolved and fused together over time in a way that demonstrates how effective leadership encompasses more than one style, is not reducible to a single adjective, and takes an evolutionary path of development and change over time. Grange Secondary represents a narrative of improvement, and its leadership is more a narrative of progress over time than a set of timeless competencies that stand forever.

Fusion and the future

In the Beyond Expectations study, Grange Secondary is not alone. In our sport and our business organizations, apparently charismatic leaders ironically are also the leaders who are most able to 'let go' and cede distributed responsibility to others (see Kets de Vries, 2006; also Sennett, 2008). Unsung heroes who establish firm foundations often pave an essential path that their more inspirational successors are then able to follow. Innovative entrepreneurs learn that they need the prudent partnership of more linear-minded accountants, and vice versa. Insider leaders who have come up through the ranks work alongside outside appointments who inject new ideas, and with prodigal sons or daughters who had put down early roots in the organization and developed lasting loyalties to it, but then went away to gather outside experience that added other important insights and dimensions to their leadership when they eventually returned. It is how leadership fits together, in the right way, in the right sequence, at the right time, that matters most for effective performance and sustainable success.

Leadership, especially leadership beyond expectations, cannot be timelessly categorized in a single style, described by one adjective, or captured in a giant smorgasbord of leadership competencies. The essence of leadership beyond expectations, rather, is its capacity to shift and flex over time, as the organization evolves and the circumstances require. Leadership beyond expectations is a story narrated over time, rather than a single style or elaborate checklist. It is to be found in the capacity to fuse many leadership styles and components together into an integrated and self-assured whole that can lift people up, bring them together and connect them to something greater than themselves to serve a common good.

Fusion leadership is more than a repertoire or array of multiple skills. It is not confusion or diffusion. Instead, it is the psychological integration of a personality and a community combined with the knowledge, empathy and strategic capability to know what parts of one's own and one's colleagues' leadership are the right ones, for the right time and for the challenges at that moment. Leadership beyond expectations is not a fission of competencies but a fusion of qualities and characteristics within oneself, one's community and over time.

Leadership beyond expectations is a fusion of qualities, characteristics and behaviours – some of them apparent opposites. This fusion arises within individuals as a matter of personal integration and integrity, it emerges throughout communities as an achievement of collective capability, and it evolves over time as a means of securing progression and sustainability. Leadership beyond expectations is a combination of leadership that is charismatic and ordinary, autocratic and shared, top-down and distributed – defying the opposites and extremes that often define the field. It is the strongest leaders, most comfortable in their own skins, who are eventually most able to let go of power and decisions to others. They are more likely to distribute than merely to delegate and still less to micromanage others' every action so as to deliver someone else's agenda.

In the end, leaders who perform beyond expectations fit the courageous and creative characterization made by Leonardo Da Vinci that, 'People of accomplishment rarely sat back and let things happen to them. They went out and happened to things.' These kinds of leadership actions require not just flashes of inspiration but investments of tedious yet relentless perspiration. 'Without stones,' Marco Polo said, 'there is no arch.' This is perhaps why it is equally true that performing beyond expectations depends not on one leader, in one moment, with one style. Rather, leadership beyond expectations exhibits a fusion of many skills, styles and people. Nicolo Machievelli told us that, 'The first method for estimating the intelligence of a ruler is to look at the men he has around him.' Early childhood icon, Maria Montessori, also reminded us that a good leader is like a good teacher. The greatest sign of success for a teacher, she said, is to be able to say 'the children are now working as if I did not exist'.

In a complex and rapidly changing world, the future of leadership is all of these things: not a *fashion* or a style embodied in one approach to leadership, nor a *fission* of fractured competencies, prescribed practices and interminable checklists, but a *fusion* of inner personality, inclusive culture and organizational sustainability. Fusion leadership is like fusion cuisine in that it is an integrated, inclusive and innovative blend of elements that contribute to a coherent and newly created whole. But fusion leadership is also more than just a way of achieving a new kind of systemic coherence – in cooking, music, business or schools. It is also an inclusive strategy in its ends as well as it means – pursuing a compelling and inclusive moral cause that serves a common good over significant periods of time. It is greater inclusion and integration serving a greater good.

Reflective Questions ?

1 Think of the leadership practices that you have been involved in over the last week. Have they come together in principled and practical ways to create fusion or does it feel more like fission? If it feels like fission, how could you move towards fusion?
2 Review the case of Grange Secondary School. What are the features of this case that are particularly relevant to your context? Does it provide some pointers for where you could do something differently?

Further Reading 📖

Daft, R.L. and Lengel, R.H. (1998) *Fusion Leadership: Unlocking the Subtle Forces that Change People and Organisations*. San Francisco, CA: Berrett-Koehler.

Notes

1   For transformational leadership, read Burns (1978), Bass (1985) and Leithwood and Jantzi, (1999). For distributed leadership, see Leithwood et al. (2009), Harris (2008, 2009), Spillane (2006). Sustainable leadership is discussed in Hargreaves and Fink (2006). The idea of inclusive leadership as an end as well as a means was introduced by Ryan (2005). For other 'types' of leaderships, see, for example, Olivier (2002), Davies and Davies (2004), Starratt (2004), Sergiovanni (1992), Lambert et al. (2002), Ubben and Hughes (1987) and Blankstein (2004).

2   Case details for Grange Secondary School are drawn from extended interviews with leaders, teachers and learning mentors at the school – including headteacher at the time of data collection, Gilly McMullen, and former headteacher Graeme Hollinshead. For inspection data and evaluations, I have drawn on the 2002 and 2006 Ofsted Reports on the school produced by the Office for Standards in Education (Ofsted). Deprivation indices for Oldham in general and the area in which Grange school is located within the town can be consulted at www.oldham.gov.uk/indices-of-deprivation-2004.pdf. The public quote from Graeme Hollinshead regarding the National Challenge is reported in Judd (2008). This issue, as it affects Grange Secondary School, is also reported on the BBC website (BBC, 2007). An extended article about the wider social cohesion agenda and its relationship to the establishment of Academies in Oldham along with Graeme Hollinshead's critical remarks on its possible impact on Grange Secondary School's community can be found in Wilby (2007).

3   See note 2, report in Judd (2008).

4   The idea of school leadership as also involving community leadership is in Starratt (2004).

References

Bass, B. (1985) *Leadership and Performance beyond Expectations*. New York: Free Press.

BBC (2007) 'Falling down the new exam table', *BBC News*, 11 January Retrieved from http://news.bbc.co.uk/2/hi/uk_news/education/6251577.stm.

Blankstein, A.M. (2004) *Failure Is Not an Option: Courageous Leadership for School Success*. Thousand Oaks, CA: Corwin Press.

Burns, J.M. (1978) *Leadership*. New York: Harper and Row.

Daft, R.L. and Lengel, R.H. (1998) *Fusion Leadership: Unlocking the Subtle Forces that Change People and Organisations*. San Francisco, CA: Berrett-Koehler.

Davies, B.J. and Davies, B. (2004) 'Strategic leadership', *School Leadership and Management*, 24(1): 29–38.

Erickson, E.H. (1963) *Childhood and Society*. New York: W.W. Norton.

Fink, D. (2005) *Leadership for Mortals: Developing and Sustaining Leaders of Learning*. Thousand Oaks, CA: Sage.

Gates, P.E., Blanchard, K.H. and Hersey, P. (1976) 'Diagnosing educational leadership problems: a situational approach', *Educational Leadership*, 33(5): 348–54.

Hallinger, P. and Heck, R.A. (1998) 'Exploring the principal's contribution to school effectiveness: 1980–1995', *School Effectiveness and School Improvement*, 9(2): 157–91.

Hargreaves, A. and Fink, D. (2006) *Sustainable Leadership*. San Francisco, CA: Jossey-Bass.

Hargreaves, A. and Harris, A., with Boyle, A., Ghent, K., Goodall., Gurn., McEwen, L., Reich, M. and Johnson, C.S.J (in press) *Performing beyond Expectations*. Nottingham and London: National College for Schools and Children's Services, and the Specialist Schools and Academies Trust.

Harris, A. (2008) *Distributed School Leadership: Developing Tomorrow's Leaders*. London: Routledge.

Harris, A. (ed.) (2009) *Distributed Leadership: Different Perspectives*. Dordrecht: Springer Press.

Harris, A. and Chapman, C. (2002) *Effective Leadership in Schools Facing Challenging Circumstances*. Nottingham: National College for School Leadership.

Homans, G. (1950) *The Human Group*. New York: Harcourt Brace.

Hopkins, D. (2007) *Every School a Great School: Realizing the Potential of System Leadership*. London: Open University Press.

Judd, J. (2008) 'The issue: National Challenge – 'Is my school high-performing or failing . . . who has got it wrong?', *Times Educational Supplement*, 5 September. Retrieved from http://www.tes.co.uk/article.aspx?storycode=6002054.

Kanter, R.M. (2006) *Confidence: How Winning Streaks and Losing Streaks Begin and End*. New York: Crown Business.

Kets de Vries, M. (2006) *The Leader on the Couch: A Clinical Approach to Changing People and Organizations*. San Francisco, CA: Wiley.

Lambert, L., Walker, D., Zimmerman, D.P., Cooper, J.E., Lambert, M.D., Gardner, M.E. and Szabo, M. (2002) *The constructivist* leader. 2nd edn. New York: Teachers College Press.

Leithwood, K. and Jantzi, D. (1999) 'Transformational school leadership effects: a replication', *School Effectiveness and School Improvement*, 10(4): 451–79.

Leithwood, K., Mascall, B. and Strauss, T. (eds) (2009) *Distributed Leadership According to the Evidence*. New York: Routledge.

Lewin, K., Lippitt, R. and White, R. (1939) 'Patterns of aggressive behavior in experimentally designed social climates', *Journal of Social Psychology*, 10: 27–99.

McGregor, D. (1960) *The Human Side of Enterprise*. New York: McGraw-Hill.

Mulford, B. (2008) *The Leadership Challenge: Improving Learning in Schools*. Melbourne: ACER Press.

Olivier, R. (2002). *Inspirational Leadership: Henry V and the Muse of Fire – Timeless Insights from Shakespeare's Greatest Leader*. London: Spiro Press.

Robinson, K., (2010) *The Element, How Finding Your Passion Changes Everything*. London: Penguin.

Robinson, V.M.J., Lloyd, C.A. and Rowe, K.J. (2008) 'The impact of leadership on student outcomes: an analysis of the differential effects of leadership types', *Educational Administration Quarterly*, 44(5): 635–74.

Ryan, J. (2005) *Inclusive Leadership*. San Francisco, CA: Jossey Bass.

Sennett, R. (2008) *The Craftsman*. New Haven, CT: Yale University Press.

Sergiovanni, T.J. (1992) *Moral Leadership: Getting to the Heart of School Improvement*. San Francisco, CA: Jossey-Bass.

Spillane, J. (2006) *Distributed Leadership*. San Francisco, CA: Jossey-Bass.

Starratt, R.J. (2004) *Ethical Leadership*. San Francisco, CA: Jossey-Bass.

Ubben, G.C. and Hughes, L.W. (1987) *The Principal: Creative Leadership for Effective Schools*. Newton, MA: Allyn and Bacon.

Wilby, P. (2007) 'Multiple choice: Peter Wilby reports on a bold plan – based on an old idea – to unite communities that are currently segregated', *Guardian*, 20 November. Retrieved from http://www.guardian.co.uk/education/2007/nov/20/faithschools. schools.

Index

PROFESSIONALIZATION, LEADERSHIP AND MANAGEMENT IN THE EARLY YEARS

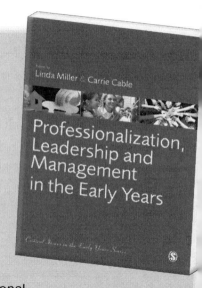

Edited by **Linda Miller** and **Carrie Cable** *both at The Open University*

With the rapid change experienced by the early years workforce over recent times, this book considers what constitutes professionalization in the sector, and what this means in practice. Bringing a critical perspective to the developing knowledge and understanding of early years practitioners at various stages of their professional development, it draws attention to key themes and issues. Chapters are written by leading authorities, and case studies, questions and discussion points are provided to facilitate critical thinking.

Topics covered include:

• constructions of professional identities

• men in the early years

• multidisciplinary working in the early years

• professionalization in the nursery

• early childhood leadership and policy.

Written in an accessible style and relevant to all levels of early years courses, the book is highly relevant to those studying at masters level, and has staggered levels of further reading that encourage reflection and progression.

CRITICAL ISSUES IN THE EARLY YEARS
November 2010 • 184 pages
Cloth (978-1-84920-553-5) • £65.00
Paper (978-1-84920-554-2) • £22.99

ALSO FROM SAGE

CHANGING BEHAVIOUR IN SCHOOLS

Promoting Positive Relationships and Wellbeing

Sue Roffey *University of Western Sydney and University College London*

Good teachers know that positive relationships with students and school connectedness lead to both improved learning and better behaviour for all students, and this is backed up by research. This book will show you how to promote positive behaviour and wellbeing in your setting.

Taking an holistic approach to working with students, the author provides examples of effective strategies for encouraging prosocial and collaborative behaviour in the classroom, the school and the wider community. Chapters look at the importance of the social and emotional aspects of learning, and ways to facilitate change.

Issues covered include:

- developing a sense of belonging in the classroom
- teaching approaches that maximize engagement and participation
- how to respond effectively to challenging situations
- ways to re-engage with students who have become marginalized.

Each chapter has case studies from primary and secondary schools, activities, checklists and suggestions for further reading.

READERSHIP
Trainee teachers and newly qualified teachers

November 2010 • 232 pages
Cloth (978-1-84920-077-6) • £65.00
Paper (978-1-84920-078-3) • £20.99

ALSO FROM SAGE

Printed in Great Britain
by Amazon